EDUCA
TOWARDS
FREEDOM

RUDOLF STEINER EDUCATION
A SURVEY OF THE WORK OF
WALDORF SCHOOLS THROUGHOUT
THE WORLD

Text: Frans Carlgren
Preface: R. Brien Masters
Picture Research: Arne Klingborg
English Edition: Joan and Siegfried Rudel

LANTHORN PRESS, PEREDUR
EAST GRINSTEAD, ENGLAND

First published in 1972
under the title «Erziehung zur Freiheit»
by Verlag Freies Geistesleben, Stuttgart

© 1976 LANTHORN PRESS
EAST GRINSTEAD

This Edition 1993 © LANTHORN PRESS
All Rights Reserved

ISBN 0–906155–32–0

Printed in Germany by Greiserdruck Rastatt

Table of Contents

pg 107. 54.
117 65
49. 120
51

Foreword

Since its first appearance in 1976 well over ten thousand copies of «Education Towards Freedom» have been sold in English-speaking countries, in addition to its wide-spread distribution in the original German and several other languages.

The remarkable increase in the number of Waldorf schools throughout the world must reflect in no small measure the interest engendered by this clear and artistic presentation of Waldorf education.

The recent political changes in Eastern Europe have brought in their wake an upsurge of interest in Steiner education. This new and slightly condensed soft-back edition of the book will give an ever-widening circle the opportunitiy to become acquainted with Rudolf Steiner's unique concept of the needs of the developing human being and its significance for the future.

Joan Rudel, Lanthorn Press 1992

Introduction

This remarkable book first appeared shortly after Rudolf Steiner (Waldorf) education had been practised for 50 years. There were then over 100 Waldorf schools throughout the world. Now, twenty years later, there are some 600 schools world-wide, plus many separate kindergartens and playgroups. This growth is reflected in the number of schools in the UK and Ireland (from 6 – 24) and in North America (from 12 – 96), with a challenging inflow of requests for new schools and training opportunities.

During this time, and even more important than the growth factor, the recognition of the value of Waldorf education has been evident in the widespread support received from many States, most notably perhaps from those in which Waldorf schools were closed during the Totalitarian regime of the early 40s.

How differently the scene looks today! There is the outstanding contribution of the Waldorf Movement to the educational provision in Germany, its establishment in cultures as different as Israel und Japan, and the recent eruption of the interest shown in it by Eastern European countries, simultaneously with the disappearance of the Berlin Wall. This interest has resulted in many initiatives, including the establishment of the first (State supported) school in Budapest and the Waldorf education seminar in Moscow.

Such developments may certainly be seen as symptomatic of the times in which we live. For, notwithstanding the setbacks that have arisen at certain points in the 20th century, the main hall-mark of culture in the present age has been the emergence of human 'freedom'. Waldorf education takes its stance firmly and centrally in this search and necessity for freedom. It comes to expression in several ways: in the autonomy of each school, despite the shared educational philosophy from which the movement springs; in the fashioning, development and delivery of its curriculum; and in the personal dedication and social striving of its teachers both in the classroom and through the fact that the organisation of each school takes place without a head teacher or heads of departments.

But all the above, however vital they are to Waldorf schools, are merely means to an end, this end being the education of the child in such a way that as an adult he or she may *experience an invigorating inner freedom,* together with the abilities and faculties needed to enable such freedom to be of service to the community as a whole – local, national and global – both in the shorter and longer terms. In very recent years, child-centred forms of education have been branded as too permissive to be productive. Waldorf education is probably best described as child*hood*-centred. At the same time, it is teacher-directed and orientated towards the free but cultivated, structured and discerning qualities of the individuality which can come into full expression in adulthood.

Flair, enterprise, initiative, creativity, ability to work in teams, integrated skills, thoroughness, drive, co-ordination, endurance under stress, and social sensitivity are among the faculties that are being demanded in society today, as a glance at any «Appointments» page will show. That the requisite qualifications are needed, goes without saying. With this in view, education must extend itself far beyond the 'piece of paper': *character* is what is needed. Although the Waldorf curriculum (as amply demonstrated in this book) is broad and amazingly rich, it can only be seen as secondary beside these educational, character-building aims, so vital in today's world.

In the face of these facts, one can understand whay many Governments are finding tangible means of making Waldorf education more and more available and why, to whatever degree this is the case, an increasing number of parents are exercising their basic human right of choosing this form of education for their children.

Brien Masters
Steiner Schools Fellowship
UK and Ireland

Rudolf Steiner and his Ideas on Education

Some Biographical Details

Rudolf Steiner was born in 1861 on the borders of Austria and Hungary, the son of a needy station official on the Austrian railways. After he had passed the final examinations at the Realschule, he went on to the Technical College at Vienna where he studied mathematics and science*. He also attended lectures at the University on Philosophy and Literature as well as Psychology and Medicine. During this time too he became familiar, both through experimental research and study, with Goethe's methods of scientific observation. At the age of twentyone he was asked by Professor Kürschner to edit and provide a Commentary on Goethe's natural scientific works, which were to form part of a comprehensive publication called 'The Literature of the German Nation'. Seven years later in 1889, he was invited to join the Goethe-Schiller Archives in Weimar, as editor of part of Goethe's scientific works for their first complete publication in the Sophien Edition. Alongside his work at the Archives, he was busy with his own philosophical writings and in 1891 submitted at Rostock University the thesis for his PhD., taking as his theme the theory of knowledge. Two years later appeared his most important book on philosophy 'The Philosophy

of Freedom', sometimes referred to in English as 'The Philosophy of Spiritual Activity'. After concluding his work on the Goethe edition, Steiner moved to Berlin, to become editor of the 'Journal for Literature'.

As well as pursuing his studies and research work, Steiner had been engaged for several years in educational activities of one kind or another. From the age of fourteen he had financed his school career and later his university studies by giving private lessons in various subjects. After leaving college, he became the tutor of a boy who was suffering from a hydrocephalic condition and had been considered ineducable by more than one specialist.

Through his special way of training and teaching this boy, he achieved such remarkable results that two years later the boy was admitted into a class of his own age-group at a normal school. Subsequently, this boy passed his school-leaving examination and successfully studied to become a medical doctor.

After moving to Berlin, he was from 1899 to 1904 a lecturer at the Workers' Institute of Further Education founded by Wilhelm Liebknecht Snr.** His contribution in this realm of

---

* college for modern sciences.
** 1826–1900. An active social reformer of his time.

adult educa ion has often been spoken of with great appreciation by his former students.

Already at the early age of seven, Rudolf Steiner had begun to have inner experiences of a nature that were later to determine his whole life. He began to experience a supersensible world as a concrete and ever-present reality. As his father was a free-thinker and no one in his environment would have had the least understanding for what would have been looked on as a figment of his imagination, he did not speak of these experiences. Although he was of a very sociable nature and came to have in the space of time a wide circle of friends, for many years he spoke to no one of this facet of his inner life. Side by side with his manifold outer activities, he pursued in inner quietness the systematic path of spiritual training, which he later described in his fundamental writings, especially in the book 'Knowledge of the Higher Worlds and its Attainment', and in many lectures.

Anthroposophical Activity

By about the turn of the century, Rudolf Steiner had achieved such a degree of conscious control over his faculty of supersensible perception that he was in a position to regard it as a real basis for spiritual-scientific research. He now took the decision, by no means an easy one, to speak of these things as opportunity offered to those people who were willing to listen. In the Autumn of the year 1900, he began to give lectures to small groups. On October 8, 1902, he lectured to the scientific Giordano Bruno Society, of which he was a well-known and well-respected member. In this lecture he spoke openly of his future life task—to find new ways of soul-spiritual research based on scientific methods. A week later, a discussion on this theme was introduced by the Deputy President of this Society and in summing up Steiner's lecture, he expressed his regret that the audience had numbered only some 250/300 hearers instead of "the 2000 or 3000 who are the representatives of the cultural life of Germany".

At the time that Steiner took this step which was to prove such a decisive one for his whole future, he was held in esteem in German scientific circles and was on friendly terms with such well-known and eminent personalities as Eduard von Hartmann and Ernst Haeckel. He had, however, no illusions as to what reception the ideas he was now presenting might have in the academic scientific milieu to which he had himself hitherto belonged, a world which assumed as its natural right the authoritative decision as to what was or was not true science.

The reaction was as he had expected it to be. From now on Steiner was regarded as a Theosophist. In actual fact it was indeed within the framework of the Theosophical Society that his main field of activity lay from October 1902 to January 1913, but at that time a parting of the ways came about. Within the official cultural life of Germany, however, he was for many years completely ignored.

From the year 1902 onwards, Steiner used on occasions for his researches a new term, which he was later to employ consistently. As this path of knowledge led to an understanding of the true nature of man, he named it Anthroposophy—from the Greek "Anthropos" (man) and "Sophia" (wisdom).

The fundamental results of his research were presented by Steiner to a small circle of enquirers, both in lectures and writings. Some of his most important and most widely read books belong to this period, 'Christianity as

Mystical Fact' in 1902; 'Theosophy'* and 'Knowledge of the Higher Worlds and its Attainment' in 1904; and 'An Outline of Occult Science' in 1909.

It was in answer to the request from the continually growing number of his collaborators and students that Steiner in the course of time initiated activities which had their origin in the impulse of Anthroposophy.

He wrote and produced four Mystery Dramas and created eurythmy—a new art of movement which aims at expressing in gesture and movement the living quality of the sounds of speech and music.

As a place where these various artistic activities could unfold more fully and, at the same time, as a focal point for the whole Anthroposophical Movement, Rudolf Steiner founded at Dornach, on the outskirts of Basle in Switzerland, a centre which was eventually called the "Goetheanum", in honour of Goethe the great German scientist and poet. Steiner, after his move to Dornach in 1914, made the designs for the new building there and supervised its erection. He himself took part in the actual work. For example, the paintings inside one of the two large cupolas were his own creation and large parts of the gigantic wooden structure were carved by hand by members of seventeen different nations in accordance with his instructions, actually throughout the years of the First World War.

During these years there had been no special interest in Anthroposophical circles for questions of social and educational importance, although Steiner had tried to draw attention to these spheres in various articles and lectures.

* With the Sub-Title "An Introduction to the Supersensible Knowledge of the World and the Destination of Man."

In his lecture of 1907, 'The Education of the Child in the Light of Anthroposophy', given in various places in Germany, almost the whole of his new ideas on education are expressed, as it were, in a germinal form. Contrary to his usual custom, he revised the shorthand report and had it published in book-form, adding a postscript which merits quoting. He stresses the point that the cultural isolation of the Anthroposophical movement can only be overcome when the spiritual impulses at its root can be consistently carried over into practical spheres of life, "otherwise people will continue to regard it as a variety of religious sectarianism for a few cranks and enthusiasts. If, however, it performs positive and useful spiritual work, the Anthroposophical Movement cannot in the long run be denied intelligent recognition."

Amid the enormous upheavals and catastrophes which the First World War brought in its train, new avenues of possibility were opening, new demands were coming to expression, and thus the appeal contained in the words quoted above could find a ready ear.

The Social Question

In the spring of 1919, Germany was threatened by civil war. The guns at the various fronts were silent but the Allied blockade continued. The economy was collapsing, epidemics were spreading, and starvation was rife. Unemployment, demonstrations and riots were the order of the day. Many people joined cultural and political movements which were radical in nature. But the more level-headed man whatever his tenets was often in despair; the Empire was about to collapse. How could class differences ever be bridged?

There was a confusion of voices expressing

opinions about the future of Germany and the world. It was then that Rudolf Steiner decided, at the request of some prominent people in the government, as well as industrialists and scientists acquainted with anthroposophical ideas, to present openly his concept of a new social order. With this he emerged from his former isolation and in March his statement: "To the German people and the Civilized World", signed by a large number of leaders in the cultural sphere, was made public. In April, he published his book 'The Threefold Commonwealth' (Die Kernpunkte der sozialen Frage), and started giving lectures and talks. He spoke to industrialists in small lecture halls, and to huge crowds of workers in factories and smoke-filled taverns.

Some of the examples which Rudolf Steiner used in his lectures and articles on social issues may now seem dated. But many of them are even more pertinent today than they were then. Some basic aspects will now be considered. Since sociological factors are nowadays part of the necessary background to education, it might not be amiss to look at this aspect of Rudolf Steiner's concept of education as an art which he tried to realise in the first Waldorf school. Education and training were considered by him to play important roles in the development of man and in the shaping of society. They must, therefore, be seen against this wider background.

The Concept of a Threefold Society

With the idea of a threefold structure of the social organism, Rudolf Steiner presented neither an abstract idea nor a political party programme. It was by taking into account the nature of man in conjunction with existing social conditions that he was able to set forth how a fundamentally new social order could come about and how current problems could be solved, both in society at large and in the individual human being. Three "spheres of life" may be distinguished, each of which has its own particular characteristics; the spiritual-cultural sphere; the economic sphere; and the legal-political sphere. Since about the fifteenth century, when the modern states began to evolve, we have gradually become used to a largely centralised management of these three spheres. It appears to us that the obvious form of social life is the "homogeneous state", in which the prince (or in more recent times a group of responsible politicians) has decision making powers not only in matters of foreign policy and the administration of justice but also in questions of the spiritual and economic life. In many states, this power extends to the minutest details. We shall subsequently turn to the problems and dangers which are brought about by this centralisation, not only in the totalitarian states but also in those which are considered democratic. But it should be mentioned here that Rudolf Steiner was in favour of a 'Threefold Social Order', which would regard and deal with the spheres of business, legal, and spiritual life as three co-existent spheres which are administered as independent entities. He was of the conviction (in conscious opposition to his as well as our contemporaries), that the situation of modern humanity demands such a decentralisation of social life.

Liberty, Equality, Fraternity

Human needs, which according to Steiner's view can only be satisfied by a threefold social order, can be simply summarised. It is no accident that the words "liberty, equality, fraternity" have been able continually to awaken enthusiasm in so many people not only during the time of the French Revolution but since that time as well. Upon closer examination, these three ideals are seen to correspond to deep instinctive feelings which we all bear within ourselves more or less consciously. As will be immediately made clear by a single example, each of these ideals can only be realised within a limited area of social life: before the law we can and must all be equal. However, to compel by law our spiritual and material needs to fit the demands of just such an equality would, as many examples from ancient and modern history substantiate, bring about a disastrous levelling. Rudolf Steiner strove for a clarification of the concept of equality in which he assigned these three ideals in a consistent way to specific functions of human society. The goals which form the basis of his work for the threefold social order can be expressed in three brief formulations: spiritual freedom in cultural life; democratic equality before the law; and social fraternity in economic life. The following examples illustrate this point of view and the fact that this is not mere theory but can be put into practice at almost any point of life:

Cultural Life

Freedom is a basic condition for the existence of a creative spiritual life. We live in an age in which the tendency to overall planning in industry, necessary in its own sphere, reaches ever more deeply into the structure of education and research and thus into the whole area of cultural life. To an ever greater degree schools, universities and scientific laboratories are regarded and treated as factors in an international economic-political competitive struggle; curricula, the form of instruction, decisions concerning examinations, research programmes and methods are consistently adapted to the needs of industry, government or even the military machine. It cannot be contested that through this process the freedom of cultural life is endangered in those nations which consider themselves "free".

A child's upbringing and education play a decisive role in this context. The future of the human race appears already in its children. In the final analysis, all innovations and creativity in the world go back to individual achievements and the extent to which they are adopted by society. But the chances of the individual to unlock his inner sources depend upon the attention he receives from his parents and teachers. The most important task of the educator is to encourage the talents of the individual and allow them to bear fruit in society, not to exploit the new generation for the benefit of the one-track continuation of pre-established technical-economic paths of development.

According to Steiner's view, the human being should grow up free from the demands of the state and economic life, until as an active citizen he can take part himself in the shaping of these branches of society. When the demands of the modern industrial state influence the pace of work and the examination requirements of the educational system to too great a degree, then the inevitable result is youth and student revolts. (See further the chapter on 'The Industrialised School'.)

The right of the coming generation to such a free education which allows their impulses and talents to unfold in a comprehensive way, so that they can someday reform the existing society, is probably the most important reason Rudolf Steiner gives for the establishment of free schools and free universities. These can be

11

financed by gifts and donations as well as by legally established grants from the economic sphere of society. Teachers in the schools and universities form free co-operatives which by working independently together with their students and others around them, care for the rising generation of teachers and which autonomously decide on all questions relating to curricula, methods of teaching and other aspects of their common work.

This same independence must also hold good in the field of science. The misuse of power practised by government and industry in many countries (especially by the great powers for their military ends) offers proof in many instances that influential circles of politicians, or businessmen, who have the financial means at their disposal, can (with respect to their special goals) "order" researchers, research programmes, and even the outcome of research. Today this is wide spread and can only be prevented in a radical way if the whole field of science governs itself independently and autonomously in a manner similar to that of education. It goes without saying that researchers who are so financed, and even if the grants which they receive have no specific conditions attached, remain dependent on their environment in many practical respects. But it must also be equally clear that the final decisions on the selection of projects and methods of investigation must be within the jurisdiction of the panel of researchers themselves.

One consequence of this independence would be that the institutions of education and research throughout the world would be free to interact and collaborate without regard for political boundaries.

These same possibilities for financial support, self-determination and international co-operation would appertain in a similar manner to all bodies of independent spiritual life (eg. religious communities, cultural institutions, media of information).

It is no doubt evident from the above what an important role an autonomous spiritual life could play in modern society. Institutions are necessary in the complicated network of modern existence whose acknowledged task it is to represent and defend in all situations that which lies within the "purely human" sphere, irrespective of economic or political interests. This task cannot be fulfilled without the official guarantee of autonomy.

Law and Government

Just as each person needs the institutions of a free spiritual life to fulfil certain purely individual needs, so also does he need the structure of the state to maintain due protection of those rights which must be held equal for all men. The authorities of the legal-political life, which are established through free democratic elections, face enormous challenges within a three-fold social order, challenges which are relatively new. One must, for example, also see to it that the financial grants and contributions given for the advancement of education, research, etc., do not involve conditions which might endanger the free spiritual life. Care must also be taken that independence in economic life, which we shall soon discuss, does not give rise to a concentration and increase in the means of power, which already lie in the hands of leading industrial circles (above all in the "capitalist" countries).

Whoever considers these tasks insoluble, should bear in mind that they mainly occur in those countries where the patterns of thinking, the formation of laws, and the exercise of government make possible, or even favour, a control or at least an influence on the common cultural life as well as on Parliament and the general administrations. Once the necessity of a threefold social order is realised, laws can no doubt be made which gradually lead to an effective distinction between the political, economic and spiritual-cultural functions. Up until now such a thing has never been carried out thoroughly. In those areas, where the decisions of democratically chosen government bodies (rather than economic interests) must be the last court of appeal, belong—according to Steiner's conception—those standards which are valid for work in general, for social welfare, and for the regulation of earnings. That the state makes it a principle to refrain from directly interfering in the matters of cultural life or of its undertakings, need not cause any weakening of the judicial functions to be fulfilled by the state. On the contrary, a government which is not involved through self-interest in other realms of the social structure, can arrive at objective, non-partisan directions and measures. Without any other means than those belonging to it as an administrator of justice, the state can offer decisive assistance in overcoming social conflicts and anomalies.

The Economic System

In order to satisfy his material requirements a person living in an industrialised region is completely dependent on the achievements of his fellow men. No matter how sure the individual may feel that he works merely to earn money, it is quite clear that within the modern economic system he serves other consumers through his activity. In such parts of the world the self-sufficient man is a thing of the past. Without assigning any moral connotation to the word, one can speak of a "Fraternity" that is the immediate consequence of modern processes of production.

Since we nowadays always want to buy a product where it can be produced most cheaply and easily, the economic system has the natural tendency to create a network of connections which in modern commerce embrace the entire world. At present this tendency is hindered by customs duty, embargoes, foreign currency regulations etc. However if this tendency were given the opportunity to develop freely, then, independent of all political boundaries, economic associations would be formed in which the participants themselves or their chosen representatives could consult with one another on production, distribution and consumption, as well as on the necessity and possibility of satisfying the existing demands. The associations can approach the given tasks according to circumstances, if in some cases they work more on a local basis and in others become world-wide. The essential point is that they develop out of purely economic considerations without being influenced by political demands. In this way possibilities will arise for completely new forms of economic relationships between the inhabitants of both industrialised and developing countries.

Whether the individual associations link up to form larger groups or not, all of them are active in a common field of work, which is one of the three independent spheres of the threefold social order. Their activities embrace the production and distribution of goods of all sorts, which serve to meet most diverse needs of society. Such a system cannot be carried out in nationalised industries. On the other hand government measures are necessary to guard against the difficulties which are associated with private enterprise in the traditional sense. Here Rudolf Steiner proposes a

13

solution to the problem of ownership which in certain ways represents a middle road between communism and capitalism. If one wants to avoid too strong an element of bureaucracy and bring into play the strength of individual initiative, then capable individuals must be given the opportunity freely to control capital and means of production during their most productive years. However, when they leave their posts the right to take over and administer the undertakings which they have built up and expanded is handed over to other capable persons or groups. This is done after an informed council of the free spiritual life has given its approval. Administration of law directed in this way renders it impossible for rich economic enterprises to be handed down through inheritance into unproductive hands.

Is the Concept of the Threefold Social Order Utopian?

The construction of a decentralised social order in which each person takes part in three independent spheres of life with their different institutions would, without doubt, cause profound changes in the social life of humanity. One especially significant result would be that the representatives of states and groups of states would not be able to count on the automatic support of world-wide internationally orientated institutions of the cultural and economic spheres for the realisation of their own political and military aims. It is obvious that the authorities of the state must have at their disposal all means of assistance which they need to be able to attend to social justice within their confines. The legal functions of the state would then become more important than ever. But beyond that the state would

have no further authorised power. Compulsory powers would be extremely limited.

Is it not then Utopian to believe that responsible politicians would ever co-operate in bringing about such an order of things?

Let us take a look at the present world situation. A number of centralised governments in industrialised states today, especially the "super powers", possess war machinery of almost inconceivable strength. How this machinery of destruction will ever be dismantled, no one knows. The mutual threat of states and allied states rests on a monstrous conglomeration of political, intellectual and economic might which in the "totalitarian" states is always concentrated in the hands of a few state functionaries. In the "democratic" states this is the case at least in times of unrest and war. This is one of the primary reasons why a large part of humanity is constantly in danger of war. The ever-increasing centralisation and the enormous expansion of the fields of operation which it creates—above all in the areas with economic poverty and unstable social conditions—often produce in politicians and military commanders the irresistible desire to seize power by force—total power which can be gained at a stroke.

Only when the functions of the intellectual life (upbringing, education, research, formation of public opinion) and the functions of economic life (industry, agriculture, finance) are removed from the direct sphere of state power, can these dangers be avoided. One of the most widely-spread Utopian ideas in our contemporary society is that the world-wide wish for peace and security can be satisfied *without* such extensive decentralisation.

If such a social change were ever to become reality, public opinion would have to be re-educated on an international scale, even in countries at present governed by a dictatorship. Much detailed information would have to be passed on, much time would have to be expended, and perhaps also much suffering endured.

In 1919 Rudolf Steiner hoped that the required social measures initiated through conscientious statesmen could be understood and then carried into effect peacefully and along democratic lines. But the hoped for reformation never materialised. And thus he predicted that the way of humanity would lead through violent take-overs, revolutions and wars, so long as the requirement for a social order in keeping with the times was not fulfilled.

His descriptions of conditions to which one can aspire on the path to a three-fold social order were quite down to earth. He constantly emphasised that individual measures could be formed quite differently from the way he himself outlined them. Contrary to many reformatory and revolutionary thinkers, he consciously emphasised that the life-form he wished to promote would not lead to a social paradise. He cherished no illusions about the moral capabilities of those with political and economic power or of people in general. The goal he worked for was no Utopia, but rather a system of society which recognises the social and anti-social impulses of the human being. In its realisation this society promotes just those social capabilities which, in spite of all weaknesses and egoisms, can come to life when healthy forms of social life are developed on the basis of true humanity and a feeling for the needs of the time. Whoever wishes to understand the Rudolf Steiner education in its full implications will have to come to terms with the ideas of the three-fold social order. Because one of the fundamental goals of his art of education is the endeavour to awaken and to cultivate these social capabilities already in childhood and youth.

The First Waldorf School – an Outcome of the Movement for a Threefold Social Order

Of the seeds sown by the "Movement for a Threefold Social Order" after the First World War, only one really took root. That one, however, proved to have strong life forces. It was the first Waldorf School.

It all began on April 23, 1919, in the tobacco storeroom of the Waldorf-Astoria Cigarette Factory in Stuttgart, Germany. The workers were crowded together on benches and on chairs. Some were sitting on large bags of tobacco lined up against the wall at the back of the hall. The head of the firm, Kommerzienrat Emil Molt, introduced Rudolf Steiner as a "social philosopher". How could someone coming from abroad, from neutral, well-fed Switzerland, understand the needs of the common people in the midst of post-war misery and famine? The listeners were markedly reserved until the speaker turned to problems of education: "All of you, as you sit here, from the sixteen-year-old girl apprentice to the workers in their sixties, suffer from the fact that your real personality has been buried because from a certain moment there was only the hard school of life for you, but no longer any real education." He began to speak of something that did not yet exist but was a need of the times, namely a comprehensive school of twelve classes (grades), comprising primary and secondary school (public and high school in North American terms), and available to everyone, regardless of social background. Now he had won the hearts of his listeners!

Herbert Hahn who was present at the time called this moment "the actual hour of the birth of the Waldorf School".* The wish of the workers for such a school, so clearly expressed, created the basis for its formation. On the following day, some of the workers came and asked whether their children could attend such a school as Steiner had described.

For some time Emil Molt had already nurtured thoughts about a school. Now he wanted to act upon them. His first step was to ask Rudolf Steiner to take over the direction of the educational side. His aim was to open the school in September 1919. He bought an empty building which was for sale overlooking Stuttgart, and which had previously been used as a restaurant. He had it renovated and acquired the necessary equipment.

Only two days after the lecture in the tobacco storeroom the first talk between Steiner, Molt and two future teachers took place. It was late at night. Steiner, as usual, had a day of intense work behind him. He came straight from a lecture to the workers at the Daimler works. "Rudolf Steiner quickly shook off the last traces of fatigue. What he had to say to us became ever more fresh, ever more invigorating." He made a number of suggestions for the initial preparations and commented in some detail on the timetable and curriculum he envisaged.

A Course on "Education for the People"

In the Course on "Education for the People", given in May and June 1919, Rudolf Steiner formulated his ideas on the art of education. This impulse of his for a new form of education for all classes of people had nothing in common with the social ambitions or denominational interests normally associated with the term "private school". It encompassed everyone, independent of his world-conception or position in society. The basic thoughts of the Course on "Education for the People" outlined the social intentions of the Waldorf School and proved to be all the more up-to-date in the light of present-day tendencies to do away with traditional forms of schooling. A few passages serve to illustrate this:

The school of the future must be based on a more fundamental knowledge of man. "If we start from this premise, nothing else can spring from it but a comprehensive school for everyone. For, of course, the laws of human development between about the seventh year and approximately the fourteenth to fifteenth are the same for all." Later, education has to be more specialised. "But above all . . . a certain part of education must be the same for people of all classes . . . Everyone must have the opportunity of the same *general* education, whether he is eventually going to do manual or professional work." Up to the age of twenty everyone should be allowed to go to such a differentiated school in order to develop his powers of responsible judgment. "When in the future the carpentry and engineering apprentices sit together in the same places of learning as those who may one day be teachers then the result will be an education that is at the same time specialised and 'comprehensive'."

In a lecture to teachers in January 1922, Rudolf Steiner enlarged on this idea when he proposed the inclusion of preparatory vocational training in conjunction with workshops in the schools for those young people inclined towards practical occupations. Teaching in such schools would include certain subjects common to all: "Nobody should pass through this part of his life without acquiring some

* 'Rudolf Steiner and his pupils', Golden Blade 1958.

16

notion of what happens in agriculture, trade, industry and the crafts. These must be treated as special subjects, they are much more important than a lot of stuff crammed into the teaching of adolescents." All the teaching, especially of history, geography and science, should be the same for all the students, "but in such a way as to be always related to man, so that man meets and recognises man as a being belonging to the universe."

There is only one goal for such a school: the education of man (Menschenbildung). The first condition of reaching this goal is a fundamental reform of teacher-training. "Today, when a candidate for the teaching profession is being examined, he is very often tested on his knowledge of facts which, with a little application, he can later pick up from an encyclopaedia or a textbook, should he not be familiar with them. This kind of test can be entirely omitted when examining teachers . . .

Conversely, present-day examinations should establish whether the person who is to teach and educate evolving human beings is able to form helpful relationships with the growing, developing pupils, and capable of appreciating their needs."

Preparations for the Opening of the School

The right of the independent school to choose its own teachers, Rudolf Steiner regarded as an essential condition for the independence of a free spiritual life. In the negotiations with the South German school authorities, as well as in his further activities on behalf of the school, he agreed to compromise regarding official curricula and regulations for examinations, but not with regard to the principle of the free selection of teachers. As soon as his plans concerning this point were accepted, he saw his way clear to start a school.

Now the foundation for the new education had to be laid. This was and still remains a knowledge of man approached from the three aspects of body, soul and spirit—a concept of man based on spiritual science, therefore scientific, yet awaking love for the human being.

On the morning of August 21, the teachers who had been asked by Rudolf Steiner to undertake the teaching came together. Most of them, but not all, had had some pedagogical experience. Today it is regarded as essential for a future Waldorf teacher to have attended a seminar on Waldorf pedagogy for a year, in addition to his other qualifications. In the place of such a seminar, Rudolf Steiner at that time gave a fifteen-day course, and followed this up by further lecture-courses during the school's early years.

Every morning from 9 to 11, he spoke on the "Study of Man": concentrated descriptions of the most important functions of the human soul in connection with physiological processes.

These lectures were taken down in shorthand and published, as were almost all of the lectures given by Rudolf Steiner. This course of lectures is not easy to comprehend but it is of particular depth and value. It is something to return to again and again, a scientific basis for meditational study from which the teacher can profit throughout his life. It contains the essence of Rudolf Steiner's pedagogical insight.

At 11 o'clock followed the hour-and-a-half long practical teaching course. In these sessions the curriculum from the first to the eighth class was presented in lively and comprehensive descriptions. Here one finds the fundamental outlines of Waldorf methods of teaching.

The many lecture courses which Rudolf Steiner gave later on educational subjects can be regarded as elaborations of what he described here for the first time. The 'Practical Course for Teachers', as it was called in the English edition, is an inexhaustible source of practical advice to which the teacher can refer time and again.

During the seminars in the afternoons, those attending the course did speech-training, made contributions themselves, and held discussions about the temperaments and other educational topics. During these seminars Rudolf Steiner made very detailed suggestions for handling human and practical problems in the classroom.

On September 6, a festival took place in which the first pupils of the school participated with their parents and met their future teachers.

Steiner's Activities in the New School

On September 7, Rudolf Steiner opened the school. In concentrated form he outlined the pedagogical aims he had in mind and, in conclusion, stressed that the Waldorf School was not going to be a school embracing any particular philosophy (Weltanschauungsschule) saying, "Anyone who says that anthroposophically orientated spiritual science is now founding the Waldorf School with the intention of establishing its outlook (Weltanschauung) in this school is not—and I say this on the opening day—speaking the truth. It is not our intention to teach the growing human being our principles, the contents of our world-conception. We are not aiming at education for the sake of any special dogma. Our aim is that what we have gained from

spiritual science shall become a living force in education."

When the school started it had eight classes and about 300 pupils. It carried the name of the factory with which most of the parents, at that time, were connected, "The Free Waldorf School". Although he lived in Dornach, Switzerland, and was constantly burdened with many other responsibilities, Rudolf Steiner was closely involved with the work of the school.

Caroline von Heydebrand, one of the first teachers at the school, has given vivid descriptions of those early days in her book, 'Rudolf Steiner in the Waldorf School': "At the beginning, teachers and children alike had many difficulties. The children were presented with something completely new. Right up to the top classes, children from all social strata were included in all classes. The Waldorf School was the first in Germany to carry this comprehensive principle right through the whole school. There were pupils from grammar, secondary and elementary schools (high schools, junior high schools and public schools) in the classes. Boys and girls were together. The children were not used to this, nor were the teachers. Learning to live together presented problems.

Naturally, there were difficulties over discipline. One day, Rudolf Steiner—who on his frequent visits to Stuttgart spent much of his time at the Waldorf School—came into a noisy and unruly class. He began to tell the whole class a story ... He knew a city and in that city a school, and in that school a class, and in that class there were children of such and such characters, and they did such and such things. The children began to nudge one another: "That's us ... he means us!" But they did not resent this, for he had not said anything critical. He went on to describe how the children's behaviour would affect the teacher's health. At the end he told them how that class had improved. At that, the children were deeply satisfied. One always had the feeling when Dr Steiner was taking a class that an immensely deep sense of satisfaction was present. Peace spread over the children. They were quite natural, quite lively, but not particularly quiet. They did not try to give the impression of being particularly well-behaved. However, one sensed a quiet satisfaction which permeated the class."

"When, in teachers' conferences, one spoke to Dr Steiner about one of the children in any of the classes, he would ask where the child sat in the classroom. He was able to recall everything about the child when he was told where he usually sat—near the window, or in the centre of the third bench, in a corner, or close to the door etc. That was the case when the Waldorf School was still small. Later, as the School grew, he would ask to see the children singly.

In one class there was a particularly difficult boy. During lessons the teacher often had to hold his hands as he stood by his side. From time to time, one had to take him for a walk outside for a while, and then he would calm down. Dr Steiner's advice about this boy was that he should make shoes. The teacher at the Waldorf School who knew how to make shoes let this boy do repair work. He improved greatly and could be kept at the School until almost the end of elementary school . . . Often the advice Dr Steiner gave for the treatment of difficult children was of this nature. Hundreds of examples could be given. Many children at this School were cured by him or set on a healing path."

Herbert Hahn describes a boy who had a kind-hearted mother but whose domestic circumstances were pitiful. He disturbed the lessons by his fidgeting and his almost pathological talkativeness. The class teacher was very worried about this child's development. Rudolf Steiner advised the teacher to put a question to the boy every day to be answered on the following day, and to continue this practice over several weeks. The teacher, following this suggestion, became aware of a look in the eyes of the boy when he gave his considered answer to the question put to him on the previous day. Gradually, there was something quiet, open and serious in the boy's gaze, something which was not there at other times. The whole face took on the same expression. This went on for some time. "And strangely enough, the fact that he was questioned day after day and allowed to give his answer the following day, had a healthy influence on the soul-life of this boy. Slowly, his self-confidence, hitherto weak, began to grow stronger." He changed—and the change was permanent. The observations and suggestions made by Rudolf Steiner arose quite naturally from the day-to-day work. At teachers' conferences he would report in detail, in an objective and factual manner what he had observed about the character of specific children, and how these observations had led him to his diagnosis and to the required therapeutic measures. Many examples could be given. To indicate the way in which Rudolf Steiner proceeded, here is just one case:

Dr Eugen Kolisko, the school doctor, described a seven-year-old boy who had just come to the school and was causing special difficulties. He could hardly keep still and had a strong impulse to be destructive. In sudden outbursts of temper he would hurl furniture and other objects about with abnormal physical energy. It required the strength of several people to control and calm him. "His walk was awkward, swaying without firm control. His face was pale and drawn with a drooping lower jaw, and a darkly scowling forehead. I do not believe that he had laughed much in his life. At the slightest provocation he would fly into a violent rage. His whole face was like a mask which the soul could not seem to penetrate." Unable to take part in regular class work, he went to a Special Class. To the surprise of the teachers and the doctor, Rudolf Steiner was confident of his recovery. He described how formative forces active in every living organism (observable to supersensible perception), were only partially able to penetrate this boy's head. Steiner suggested a number of medical and pedagogical measures. "After a few months, the boy was able to laugh, had developed a more human expression, began to wake up, stopped his tantrums, and finally proved to be a very lovable boy, something one would not have suspected possible before. After he had undergone treatment for three years, he fitted in quite well with the other children of his age. His parents were then transferred to another place. Today, at the age of about eleven, he is at another school with his own age group. I am convinced that without this treatment, it would never have been possible to include him in ordinary lessons. Rudolf Steiner saw him only once or twice, but what he observed on the first occasion and what he could say about him saved this child."*

The Waldorf School was founded definitely for healthy and "normal" children. This is still the case in Waldorf Schools today. There was no selection and no "confrontation" between teachers and pupils—discipline being created out of confidence and co-operation—in fact, independent children with initiative were particularly well-placed in this school.

* 'Rudolf Steiner in the Waldorf School.'

Pupils with special difficulties were transferred to a Special Class. This was directed by an extremely skilled teacher whose work Rudolf Steiner followed with special attention.

Teacher-child Relationship

For the times when the Waldorf School was founded, many aspects of its organisation were unusually permissive. Rudolf Steiner was not in favour of compulsory home-work in the lower classes. He recommended voluntary tasks, formulated in such a way as to stimulate interest. Not until grade six or seven did he regard compulsory work as being of any value. He rejected strict and enforced discipline. Occupation with paints and brushes, notebooks made by the children, reciting plays, songs and music made life in the classroom colourful and busy. Judged with an ordinary yardstick, the atmosphere in the school was rather easy-going. Especially in the higher classes, the pupils were free to a degree which was undreamt of by their contemporaries in state schools. Rudolf Grosse, who was later a Waldorf teacher for many years, joined the tenth class in 1922 at the age of seventeen. In his book, 'Pedagogy Experienced' ('Erlebte Pädagogik') he reports on his first impressions:

"For a pupil coming, like myself, from the usual grammar school, everything at the Waldorf School was astonishingly new. When I came into the class, with which I was to become very closely connected, I met a group of young people who were utterly frank, straightforward and with an air of freedom about them. I was speechless with admiration. For each seemed to set his own standard of behaviour."

In the lower grades there were, of course, some rules of discipline but they were as few as possible. On the whole, all the work in the school was held together by one force only, the direct relationship between the teachers and pupils. Where this contact was absent or had deteriorated, problems quickly arose, which called for renewed efforts on the teacher's part.

The Upper School (High School)

Rudolf Steiner had noticed a growing rift between the pupils in the senior class and some of the teachers. He said that lessons had become lectures, with too little discussion and human contact. Gradually, as Steiner predicted, trouble broke out. One of the girls wrote a letter to Rudolf Steiner who then invited the whole class to talk in the teacher's room. Rudolf Grosse reports:

"He sat behind a large desk, and we were standing around him in a semi-circle. At his invitation, one spoke—then another. Four or five of the pupils spoke and to each one Rudolf Steiner listened quietly and seriously. He himself did not say a word. What had been troubling them? Well, for example, one teacher was lacking in authority. During the lessons, he could very easily be diverted from his subject. This the class exploited—but consequently one did not learn enough. In another instance, the complaint was that the teachers only knew one in class, but not out of class etc. The talk lasted for less than half an hour and then we were dismissed in a friendly manner, without any discussion having taken place. When school began again after the holidays, we noted to our surprise that we had different teachers for two important subjects, and our lessons were as we had wanted

them to be for a long time." Perhaps it should be added that the changes were made by Rudolf Steiner in full agreement with the teachers concerned.

As the preparation for the lessons included considering every single pupil, allowing a picture of him to stand before the mind, the problem of over-taxing the teacher arose. How was he to find time for all his tasks?

As can be seen, the Waldorf teachers were involved with only part of the programme. Even so, their work and their daily routine were strenuous enough. However, Rudolf Steiner showed them by advice and example how one can prepare lessons and lectures carefully by strict self-discipline and well-balanced study, even under great pressure of work and time.

Culmination of Events

During the years 1922–1924, Rudolf Steiner's life culminated in a series of outstanding events. He accepted the pressing offer by a well-known lecture agency for two lecture tours through Germany's largest cities. During the first two weeks of his tour, he spoke in all to some 20,000 people. In the same measure as interest in Anthroposophy and Rudolf Steiner grew, opposition also increased. The second tour, in May 1922, put Steiner in some dangerous situations. In two cities, Munich and Elberfeld, agitators at the meetings endangered his life. The instigators, the kind of people who later adopted National-Socialist ideas, saw in Rudolf Steiner a decisive threat because of his cosmopolitan social ideas, and his attitude toward establishing the freedom of the spirit of man. On New Year's night 1922/23, the wooden structure of the "Goetheanum" was destroyed by arson.

Parallel with these events, the anthroposophical movement, which had begun to work in many social, scientific and artistic fields, out of the impulse for cultural renewal, passed through its own inner crisis. This was largely due to the fact that some of Rudolf Steiner's collaborators had taken responsibilities upon themselves which they could no longer cope with, either practically or spiritually. Finally, in the Christmas days of 1923, he decided to renew and reorganise the whole anthroposophical work, by founding the General Anthroposophical Society, of which he became President.

The Waldorf teachers felt much involved personally in these events—while work at the school had to continue undisturbed. They were capable of these superhuman efforts only because they were helped by working with Rudolf Steiner. The comment of Rudolf Grosse (as mentioned before, at that time in the upper school) is quite revealing: "Looking back on the achievements of those teachers, one can only describe them as outstanding. I have known no other body of teachers so unreservedly devoted to their educational tasks as that original College of Teachers of the first Waldorf School."

Between October 19 and November 13, 1925, the Württemberg school authorities carried out an offical inspection of the Waldorf School. Their extensive report recognised and praised the methods used in the school. Their comments on the teachers was that this "College of Teachers, intellectually and morally of so high a calibre bestows upon the Waldorf School its special character and its considerable level of achievement."

In all of these events, Rudolf Steiner himself presented the chief enigma. It was often noticeable that the treble pressure of a) the tremendous burden of work; b) harsh public attacks; and c) the inadequacies of those who collaborated with him, was hard for him to bear. However, he lost neither his creative powers to produce results, nor his self control. On the evening of Year's Day in 1923, only hours after the catastrophic fire had wiped out the "Goetheanum", and the ten years of his architectural and artistic effort, he entered the improvised lecture hall, commented briefly on the sad event, deeply moved but quiet and composed, and then proceeded to give the lecture on a scientific subject as previously announced for that evening.

During 1924, when he was already seriously ill, his work culminated in a continuous sequence of important lecture cycles, courses and discussions. Of the many and varied fields of practical social work for which he then laid the foundations, the bio-dynamic method of agriculture and the curative educational treatment for mentally retarded or disturbed children and young people soon became especially prominent. All who met Rudolf Steiner during that year agree that he radiated more than ever his infectious enjoyment of life and his spontaneous kindness.

Work with the College of Teachers

Rudolf Steiner let the teachers know that he thought each day of every pupil. When he was in Stuttgart, the College of Teachers felt the high degree of responsibility with which he regarded his work in the Waldorf School. The minutes of the teachers' meetings report the concentrated work done on the everyday problems of teaching—questions of time-table and curriculum, methods of teaching, always with the needs of the individual pupil in the foreground. Rudolf Steiner was extremely well informed in every detail relating to the current work being done in the school. During this phase of the foundation of a new pedagogy, the role of leader was rightly his. The quick grasp and detailed knowledge he brought to difficult queries on special subjects, such as history, literature, history of art, biology, physics, chemistry and mathematics was simply amazing. Yet he never let his superior ability overawe his colleagues. "Here one sensed no self-praise, no vanity, no satisfaction in impressing others with his superior knowledge. One experienced rather a man who in humility served the spiritual world which lay open to him. He respected and appreciated every single human being with whom he came into contact. Even when he spoke of the most sublime subjects, one could breathe absolutely freely in his presence. One felt addressed in one's own idiom and experienced the good fortune to meet him quite naturally, as man to man." (Herbert Hahn, 'Birth of the Waldorf School' in 'Recollections of Rudolf Steiner, Memories of his Students')

Under the leadership of Rudolf Steiner, the meetings of the College of Teachers became a continuous seminar. He trained the teachers especially to see a challenge in every single child, a divine mystery which the teacher had to penetrate through the art of education, permeated with love, until the point when the young person found his own self.

He was not concerned just with this mystery in the child as an individual. Time and again, and by no means in empty phrases, Rudolf Steiner in lectures and addresses expressed his thanks and that of the teachers, not only to the parents who had entrusted their children to the school, but also to the higher powers who had sent these children down to earth. To his way of thinking, every child is a gift to which one can lay no personal claim. For a few, brief years one is permitted to guide and to care for him until he goes out into the stern school of life with powers to choose his own path. The aim of all education must be self-education.

The Pupils

The objective love and interest which the pupils received they repaid with affection and love for their school. When Rudolf Steiner, speaking at school festivals, used to ask, "Are you fond of your teachers?", the answer was a thunderous "Yes". This was not the result of mass suggestion. The generous gratitude later shown by former pupils to their school and the teachers, proved clearly that their assent had come from genuine feeling.

During the last year of his life, Rudolf Steiner experienced how strong the link was with the pupils when the members of the first graduating class expressed heartfelt desire to keep in touch with him and with the teachers through personal conversations, by asking advice on studies and careers, at old scholars' meetings, and by personal visits. Experience showed that generally speaking the love of former pupils for their school continued, but that in their thinking the young people consistently went their own ways. "There was sufficient proof to show that the teachers had fulfilled their duties in a purely pedagogical sense through the fact that few former Waldorf students later found their way into anthroposophy."*

Rudolf Steiner once spoke in Oxford on August 19, 1922, in the lecture-course 'The Spiritual Ground of Education', of the 'three golden rules' which should form the funda- .

* Rudolf Grosse "Erlebte Pädagogik".

mental attitude of every educator. By his own example he showed that they could be put into practice. He said: "The three golden rules must be embraced by the teacher's whole being, not held merely as a theory. They might be summarised thus—to receive the child in gratitude from the world it comes from; to educate the child with love; to lead the child into the true freedom which belongs to man."

The Social Aims of Waldorf Education

As we have seen, the actual objective of the movement for the threefold social order was to call forth and foster specific human capabilities necessary for a relatively harmonious social life on earth. It is a matter of arriving at the social qualities which can be called the "inner organs" for freedom, equality and fraternity. Already after the First World War, when Rudolf Steiner was forced to give up the hope of realising a threefold social order corresponding to these qualities, the possibility arose of founding a way of education through which social capabilities could be fostered.

The following statements may seem arbitrary. However, they give in concentrated form what is to be taken up in detail in the rest of the book and originate from a genuine observation of real life. Rudolf Steiner was the first person who indicated in an all-embracing manner the fundamental laws underlying the life of the human soul, which is here the fundamental issue. But everyone who is willing to take the trouble can test and confirm the validity of these laws in his own environment as well as in social life in general.

The urge to imitate predominates in the preschool age. Not only the visible actions but also the thoughts and feelings of the people who constantly surround the child are transformed into a component of his own life and actions through his imitative faculties. The moral qualities which he absorbs in this way from his environment are decisive for his future existence. If a child at this age is neglected, above all by a lack of real inner contact with his parents, then he will always remain an imitator—an unstable, dissatisfied person, who not infrequently runs after the most primitive examples which he finds before him in life. In extreme cases—and these are apparently becoming more common in many industrialised nations—such an individual may become morally defective. Psychiatrists and criminologists can quote many cases of people who, through childhood neglect, are compulsively under the control of their more or less animal-like instincts. The consciousness of the uniqueness of each human individual and of the respect of his rights to personal integrity is based on one's capacity to hold back to a certain degree one's own lower impulses. Generally speaking this attitude is to be found only in adults whose own inner life and soul-qualities were cared for and fostered when they were children.

At about the age of seven a new tendency comes to the fore. The child wants to go to school, wants to learn—but actually only in a certain way: his inner wish is to follow his teacher, and to trust completely all he says and does. In other words, he needs what Rudolf Steiner calls "a figure of authority". A real authority is never gained by harshness or mere force. The only lasting respect is that which arises in the child through affection and inclination as if of its own accord. In the case of those children who found sufficient nourishment in their early years for their imitative impulses, this need for authority arises as a matter of course. If this need is not satisfied, then even here one can not make up for these deficiences in such people in later life. In the case of children who have been allowed to make all their own judgements and decisions at too early an age, a certain insecurity arises. Their mistrust and their constant desire to oppose do not reflect spiritual strength but rather inner weakness—such people remain unproductive. Because the need for dependence on someone else was not satisfied in early childhood, these people, especially in their teens, often seek out special "substitute authorities", such as pop-singers, Wild West heroes, or political dictators. The lack of stability which often prevails in their life of feeling, makes it very hard for them in later years to work with other people in a natural and harmonious way.

During the period of puberty a further need awakens: the urge to test and to learn to understand the external world as well as all aspects of man's existence. In other words, the young person has reached the age at which he is sufficiently mature to develop really profound interests. For this to happen he needs people who can give him help in an unauthoritative manner yet through warm spiritual contact. Such people can show him the way to knowledge and activity through which life can become meaningful even in the midst of the bleak and impersonal atmosphere which characterises so many areas of the modern work-a-day world. If he becomes bored with school or starts out in a profession which offers him no room for his thinking and his sense of taste he becomes vulnerable to many dangers—especially if he lives in a large city. For young people who have received a sufficient inner vitality and security through their education, the need in these years for a deepened knowledge of the world and people generally arises of itself. To sum-up, the social capabilities which can be fostered in the ways described above are as follows:

Through imitation in the pre-school years:
a feeling for the freedom and integrity of other people;

Through authority in the primary and middle school years:
a feeling of security in life and with that the ability to participate in democratic co-operation;

Through close, unauthorative human contact with instructors during the process of learning in the teenage years:
a deepened interest in the world and for the life-situations of other human beings.

In a lecture series which he held in Dornach in August 1919, 'Die Erziehungsfrage als soziale Frage' ('Education as a Social Question'), Rudolf Steiner points out the broad implications of what we are discussing. He describes how the foundations can be laid in early childhood for participation in a free cultural life, in the middle school years for respecting an egalitarian sense of justice and in the adolescent years for contributing to a really social economic life.

The arrangement of the present book has, therefore, arisen from a consideration of the needs and possibilities which arise at the three age levels briefly described here. The development of the growing human being is depicted in three main sections:

The Child During the Pre-School Years;
The First Eight Years of School;
The Last Four Years of School.

There are in addition chapters dealing with general educational principles and the modern world-situation.

The Child During the Pre-school Years

THE CHILD AS SENSE-ORGAN

When a new-born infant sucks its mother's breast, its whole body often quivers the moment milk flows into its mouth. It is not only the mouth that feels it; the child reacts as if its whole body were the organ of its sense of taste. During the first years of a small child's life, we observe the same phenomenon in other instances: the whole body moves whenever it suddenly sees or hears something. Even if nothing bad happens afterwards, the consequence of a strong impression can be overpowering and can precipitate a violent fit of crying. Even the most subtle feelings and gestures are perceived by the child. Many parents will have experienced how difficult it is to conceal their own fluctuating moods from their children. Even if one tries to conceal one's irritation it is noticed at once by the children, who suddenly behave more violently or obstinately than otherwise. For example, the following happened to one father:

After being drawn into an exceptionally irritating incident through the fault of others, he came home. He had to pass through a room in which his three-month-old daughter was lying. Usually she laughed when he leaned over her. This time when he opened the door he was still full of anger. He tried to conceal this and behave as usual. Nevertheless, as he bent down over his little daughter, she began to cry immediately.

Imitation

It is a well-known fact that children imitate their environment. No doubt every one has observed how little children imitate grown-ups—their gestures, the movement of their hands and feet, even how they clear their throats. At first, children imitate quite unconsciously and only gradually does imitation become a conscious process, coming to expression when children play at being such things as buses, or animals in the zoo, or mothers and fathers. The need to imitate is incredibly deep-seated. When it is inhibited by unsympathetic adults, the consequences can be dangerous. A typical example of this is cited by J. A. Hadfield in his 'Childhood and Adolescence':

"At present I am treating a fourteen-year-old boy with antisocial tendencies. When he is together with other children at school he becomes violent and often has sudden outbursts of crying. His behaviour pattern came about through his being continually prevented from doing what would have given him pleasure. In particular, he was always stopped from joining in with his parents' activities.

His mother was a bulldog-type, and the boy had a similar disposition. He was in a continuous state of war and rebellion because he would not easily give up what he had set his mind on. When his mother planted out flowers he was ordered from the garden. He resisted that and was beaten. He began to hate his mother and eventually everyone. How easily all this could have been avoided if his mother had only allowed him to partake in what she was doing, and if she had shown him how to dig without damaging the plants. After all, all he wanted to do was to imitate her."

Hadfield points out the significance of imitation when he says further:

"Abnormalities arise especially when children copy the bad example of their parents. Arrogant parents make arrogant children."

For children, imitation is as important as breathing, one might even say sense impressions are breathed in. Imitation could be regarded as the out-breathing process.

The Moral Effects of Impressions in Childhood

Rudolf Steiner calls the period from birth to the seventh year the "age of imitation". He emphasises the fact that the actual words spoken to a child in the way of exhortation or explanation are of little importance compared with what is happening in his physical surroundings. When a grown-up scolds him, the anger in the voice makes a much deeper impression than the actual words that are said. Steiner hardly ever expressed himself in such forceful terms as in a lecture of August 13, 1924, when he said: "What you say to a small child, what you teach him, does not make much impression on him. It is what you

are, whether you are good and manifest this goodness in your behaviour which is of vital importance, or whether you are irritable and subjects to outbursts of temper. In short, all that you yourself do reverberates within the child. One can say that he is a sense organ reacting to every impression to which he is subjected. It is therefore essential to realise that small children do not learn what is right or wrong through their intellects but through all that happens around them. This is transformed in his organism into body, soul and spirit. The child's future health even depends on the behaviour of those around him. The tendencies he develops later depend on the behaviour of those who influenced his earliest years."

Rudolf Steiner was certainly one of the first educationalists who portrayed the decisive significance of early childhood for the individual's later inner development. In more recent times, doctors, teachers and psychologists, and especially the protagonists of preschool education, have become aware of the enormous importance and possibilities existing in this field.

Some Results of Psychiatric Research

One of the pioneers in the field of child psychiatry, John Bowlby, was commissioned by the World Health Organisation to investigate the child in relation to his environment. An enlarged version of this report was published in 1951 under the title, 'Child Care and the Growth of Love'. Basing his remarks on numerous reports by British doctors, Bowlby declared that the most frequent reason for child neglect is not to be attributed to large families, bad housing, working mothers or other external factors, but has to do with the kind of attitude adopted towards the child. His description of the circumstances in which the children concerned in the study grew up was frequently shattering. Every teacher knows that very often it is just in the well-to-do home that the psychological neglect of children is evident.

Bowlby gives some instances of the drastic effects of psychological neglect:

"Psychological treatment was given over a period of some six years to eighty girls in a small home for delinquent girls between the ages of twelve and sixteen. Half were successes and half failures. Response to treatment was related neither to intelligence nor to heredity. Its relationship to the girls' early family experiences, however, was striking."

According to Bowlby, deprivation during the first years of life has just as devastating an effect on the child physically and biologically as the physical disease of rickets. On the basis of comprehensive observations for his studies, he points out the basic significance of the presence of the same mother figure being responsible for the child during the first years of its life. This mother-figure need not necessarily be identical with the natural mother. Bowlby asserts that mother love is decisive in the development of the child.

The American child psychiatrist, Professor Selma Fraiberg of the University of Michigan, has devoted a great part of her life to the study of diseases of non-attachment. In her moving and humorous book, 'The Magic Years', she has presented a wealth of observations on this subject. She sums up the result of her research about the development of the young child as follows:

"We have come to know that those psychological qualities which we would call characteristically human, are not part and parcel of the original make-up of the small child . . .

They are not instinctive reactions, nor are they acquired by way of natural development. Truly human love, for instance, which is more than self-love, arises as an outcome of human family-life and through the genuine bonds of feeling such as grow between members of a family. Human intelligence depends to a great extent on the ability to use meaningful symbols. Speech, in particular, is not simply the product of a superior human brain and speech-organ, but is acquired through early contacts based on real feeling. Self-consciousness, too, the concept 'I', that is an awareness of one's personal identity, arises through this early soul-contact between parents and children. Man's triumph over his instinctive nature, his readiness to restrain his own inner drives and to set them certain limits, or even to act against them when they conflict with higher aims and intentions, is something which has to be *learnt*, and which is only learnt through the unfolding of love in the early years of development. Even conscience—that highest achievement in the cultural evolution of humanity—is not just a part of our constitution, but a product of parental love and education."

Physiological Effects of Childhood Impressions

The effects of sense impressions in early childhood do not only work psychologically. They also have physical effects. Perhaps the most striking examples of this are children who have been brought up by animals. The 'wolf-children' of Midnapore, who were discovered in 1920 by the native protestant missionary J. A. L. Singh, were at that time approximately two and eight years old. They displayed a number of peculiar characteristics: "The incisors were longer and more pointed than is usually the case in human beings. The oral cavities were blood-red. The children could squat on the ground but were unable to stand. Their knee and hip joints had not adapted themselves to it ... The eyes were almost round. During the day they found it difficult to keep their eyes open, but at night, after twelve o'clock, they were opened wide and shone in the dark as do the eyes of cats and dogs. At night they were able to see considerably better. They showed no fear of the dark, but rather of light and fire." (J. A. L. Singh, 'Die Wolfskinder von Midnapore' /' The Wolf Children of Midnapore', Heidelberg 1964) The children were captured and taken along to the missionary station where they were looked after with meticulous loving care. The younger girl died one year after her discovery; the older child lived nine more years, learned about fifty words, and toward the end of its life showed clear signs of intelligence as well as spiritual growth.

This is a shattering example which shows the strength of the physical effect inherent in early childhood impressions. The physiological peculiarities which appear in children reared by human beings as a result of their early experiences— and not as a result of inherited tendencies—are naturally much less noticeable. But they are there. Rudolf Steiner emphasised that: "In the later periods also, growth takes place; but throughout the whole succeeding life, growth is based on the forms which were developed in this first life-period. If true forms were developed, true forms will grow; if misshapen forms were developed, misshapen forms will grow. We can never repair what we have neglected as educators in the first seven years. Just as Nature brings about the right environment for the physical human body before birth, so after birth the educator must provide for the right physical environment. It is the right physical environment alone, which works upon the child in such a way that the physical organs shape themselves aright ... What goes on in his physical environment, this the child imitates, and in the process of imitation his physical organs are cast into the forms which then become permanent. "Physical environment" must, however, be taken in the widest imaginable sense. It includes not only what goes on around the child in the material sense, but everything that takes place in the child's environment— everything that can be perceived by his senses, that can work from the surrounding physical space upon the inner powers of the child. This includes all the moral or immoral actions, all the wise or foolish actions, that the child sees ... The physical organs shape their forms through the influence of the physical environment. Good sight will be developed in the child if his environment has the right conditions of light and colour, while in the brain and blood-circulation the physical foundations will be laid for a healthy moral sense if the child sees moral actions in his environment. If before his seventh year the child sees only foolish actions in his surroundings, the brain will assume such forms as adapt it also to foolishness in later life." ('Die Erziehung des Kindes' / 'The Education of the Child', 1909) Coming at a time when the significance of the first childhood impressions were still not fully realised, such a statement as Rudolf Steiner's must have seemed completely incredible. The extraordinarily prolific material which has been gathered on this subject in the course of the last few decades by researchers and educators, however, thoroughly confirms his descriptions of the child as a sense-organ.

"When I cross the road." Self-portrait of a four-year-old girl.

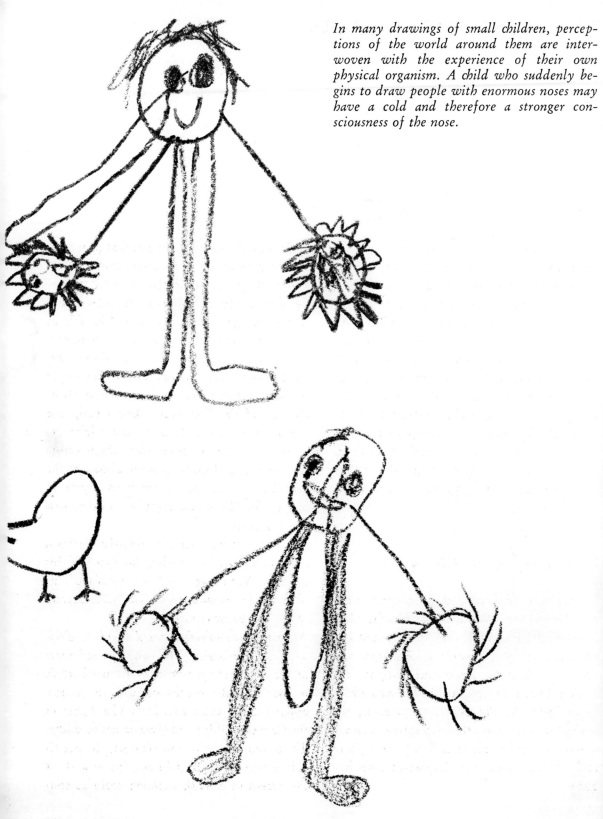

In many drawings of small children, perceptions of the world around them are interwoven with the experience of their own physical organism. A child who suddenly begins to draw people with enormous noses may have a cold and therefore a stronger consciousness of the nose.

THE FIRST THREE YEARS

The first three years have a special significance for one's whole life, not just for the years of childhood. That we do not remember these years consciously does not alter this fact at all. This epoch in our life, although hidden from memory, is alive in our human existence, in our whole life-course. At no other period were we so exposed to the impressions of our environment. Never again must we be so absorbed in our own bodily processes. Never again, through our own oft-repeated efforts of will, do we achieve such basic capabilities as these three: walking, speaking and thinking, which we shall then apply every day for the rest of our lives.

Walking, Speaking and Thinking

To learn to observe and understand what actually goes on when children practise these fundamental functions is one of the most important tasks of all people who educate and bring up children. From such insights the modern human being can gain the strength to bring forth the understanding patience, the tender warmth and the perceptive security which the child needs as a living atmosphere and which is even more important than hygiene.

Walking reminds us of the physical phenomenon of gravity: our long body-form with its centre of gravity near the top and the insignificant supporting area of the soles of our feet are no guarantee that we will be able to walk. Our vertical bearing is a constantly complicated balancing act. The children are greatly astonished as they become aware of this new capacity for the first time at about the end of the first year. Their triumphant attitude not only reflects the joy adults experience on this occasion. This delight comes from within and joyously bears witness to the fact that this is one of the great events in man's life. The whole organism is orientated anew in space.

The fact that we later can recognise a person immediately by his bearing, his gait and his gestures shows how much he reveals of his character in his movements. The hidden secret of the will becomes visible.

After a few months the next phase of development usually begins. The newly-gained view of the surroundings now allows a need which is found in the depths of man to become apparent. The child goes forth like Adam in the Garden of Eden and gives names to things. The sounds of desire and comfort, the inarticulate expressions of pain and joy as well as the repetitive childish babbling begin to converge into a meaningful unity. The child often learns several hundred words within as short a period as six months. Three and four-years-old children already command a number of complicated grammatical rules, whose logical significance they do not appreciate until much later. Through direct practice, they know perfectly well how to handle gender, number, case and tense, how to apply adjectives and how to use primary and secondary clauses. Never again in life can one enter into a new language so quickly and with so little effort.

Speaking reveals the relationship of man with things and with the nature of his environment—a relationship which is rooted in feeling. Thinking is awakened by language. When a two-year-old looks about at the dinner table and calls out: "Daddy spoon, Mummy spoon, Johnny spoon, Mary spoon—everybody spoon!" he has made a great discovery. All spoons have something in common which lies hidden in the name of the object, in the secret of the word. This is the concept. Learn-

ing to walk and speak are events which are played out in the physical world and which are characterised by a certain dramatic quality. The first attempts at thinking, on the other hand, show the first signs of the ability to detach oneself from the environment and to become quiet and contemplative.

The German child-psychologist, E. Köhler, has given a fine description of a two-and-a-half-year-old in the first moments of reflection: "When Anna doesn't completely understand something and thinks about it, she stands quietly and places her hands on her back. Her eyes grow large and she looks into the distance; her mouth tightens up a bit and she is silent. After this exertion a certain tiredness takes over. Her expression changes. Nature provides for relaxation." (Cited by K. König, 'Die Ersten Drei Jahre des Kindes' / 'The First Three Years of the Child') Thinking opens the door to all experiences of consciousness and self-consciousness; it is our most important means of orientating ourselves in the world and remaining awake.

The precise age at which children learn to walk, speak and think can vary a good deal. However parents need not let themselves become alarmed over this. One need only feel concern if the actual sequence is different. To understand this we may consider the following: what we want, we conceive of in a waking state; however if we indulge in feelings we are still in a dream-like state. Since the will develops entirely in a state of consciousness similar to that during sleep, children whose life of will is particularly strong seem to be half asleep and develop quite slowly in their early years. Later, sometimes not until they become adults, they show their true strength. Many children do not want to expose themselves either to criticism or ridicule. For this reason they can be reluctant to begin speaking.

One fine day they can suddenly express themselves almost flawlessly and with a remarkable vocabulary.

Walking, speaking and thinking follow one after the other. Gestures and movements are transferred to the speech centre of the brain and the entire physical organisation of the head. This relationship becomes obvious when we try to make left-handed people use their right hand. If a left-handed child is too forcefully trained to use his right hand, he will soon start to stutter. Life is first of all gesture and this carries over into the motor-apparatus of speech. For the educator there are three primary rules to bear in mind: when teaching a child to walk, accompany all offers of help with *love;* when teaching a child to speak, take pains to speak the *truth* yourself; do not confuse your child through haphazard commands, be *clear* in your own thinking! Because: "To produce confusion in the environment of the child through unclear thinking is the actual cause of nervousness in our modern society." (Rudolf Steiner, Lecture of 10/8/1923.)

Actually there is only one thing which can cause serious development disturbance in normal, healthy children; lack of contact with other people. If children grow up in institutions instead of in a family, most of them learn to sit, walk, speak and think later than others do. Through a lack of contact with others they can become hindered or confused in their entire development.

The assertion that the 'Walking Instinct' is innate is based upon the observation that a new-born child whose trunk is leaning forward a bit and whose feet are resting on a flat surface will attempt to take small steps. However, this reaction more or less disappears, during the first half year. First the child must struggle to acquire the ability to lift its head, to crawl, to sit and stand, before it once more can learn the art of moving its feet forward along the floor. Alfred Nitschke studied an almost three-year-old girl who had an unusual manner of walking, but in whom doctors were unable to detect any pathological abnormality. Upon closer investigation it was revealed that the little girl was imitating her father, who had one of his legs amputated and walked with the help of an artificial limb. At a children's home in Teheran with insufficient staff it was ascertained that 60 % of the one-year-olds could not sit and 80 % of the three-year-olds could not walk. One child, who had never had the opportunity to imitate people who walked upright, would probably never learn to raise itself, like the Wolf-Children.

Even if we know that imitation is of such salient importance for the development of small children, in practice we often lack the trust and courage to bring children up in accordance with this principle. We attempt instead to interfere with the development of the child by quite other means.

Unnecessary Interference

Small children are lovable. Many of the nice and pleasant things with which we busy them consciously or unconsciously result in influencing the learning process of young children in a definite direction. For example we stretch our fingers towards them and help them learn to sit and stand. But if we do this before their bones and muscles have developed sufficiently, damage to the bones and back may result. We may also notice that the same people who at one time buy a suitable picture book out of pedagogical enthusiasm in order to teach the child as many new concepts as possible in a short time, at another time speak to the child in babbling baby language because it sounds so charming. In this way, however, we actually retard the child's development. Small children want to develop and orientate themselves by the example of a real language. Often the children themselves are not particularly enthused at hearing infantile expressions. A well-meaning aunt described a dog to a three-year-old as a 'woof-woof'. After long, gloomy reflection the child said dryly, "It's called a dog".

On his own the child may for a while chatter away in his charming baby talk. Eventually, however, imitation leads the child along the right path. Still, an adult must never babble! He should keep his way of speaking free from sentimentality and pretence. Through imitating cultivated speech the child develops truthfulness, clarity, style, in speaking. As a result, both the inner life and the organs of speech develop harmoniously.

Can Prohibitions Be Avoided?

There are other ways in which adults may thoughtlessly interfere with the development of the small child.

Little children often cause enormous difficulties. Mothers are often exhausted and frequently have no help. Our complicated everyday life is full of things that are breakable or dangerous. How are we to prevent children from pulling down the tablecloth, taking books off the shelf, knocking pots off the window sill, lighting matches, chewing cigarette butts or starting the car when the key has been left in the ignition? Not only psychologists know that constant warnings and prohibitions can lead to dampening initiative in a child, and in extreme cases cripple it forever. Of course, one possibility is to cover the wall socket with safety plugs and to hide as many breakable and dangerous objects as possible. But there are always certain risks which cannot be avoided; furthermore, life in the living room would become empty and unnatural if we were to remove all objects not suitable for young children. Neither is it a good idea to allow children to handle the remaining objects in any way they please.

In his book on 'Punishment in Self-Education and in the Education of the Child' ('Die Strafe in der Selbsterziehung und in der Erziehung des Kindes') the Waldorf teacher Erich Gabert gives an example of how the stage of development of the small child can be dealt with. A child is to be warned against burning itself on the stove: "During the weeks before the stove was to be lit again, a little game was played with the child and repeated several times ... An adult placed his hand near the stove, withdrew it quickly without touching the stove, and then cried, 'Oh! That's hot! We don't touch that.' The child does the same again and again until the aversion for the stove is taken for granted."

Such preventative games can, of course, be devised ad infinitum. But do we have enough time?

The Individuality of the Small Child

When we consider how far we should go in our concern for the small child we are ultimately led to the greatest and most profound question: What demands do the individuality and nature of the small child make upon us? There are very few people who can remain aloof to the unusually deep effect children have on us during the first few years of their life. It is not simply a question of those characteristics which, according to biologists, arouse our protective and tender instincts: soft hair, round bodies, awkward movements, etc. All of these "charming" characteristics may be found in puppies and kittens as well. We can be moved by a sense of devotion when confronted with a very small child. We feel that we stand before something which surpasses our normal powers of comprehension.

The situation of the small child is actually a paradox. At an age when tasks such as dressing oneself, making a bed, eating with a knife and fork etc., present almost insuperable difficulties, these children effortlessly pick up impressions which place them in the position of learning two of man's most demanding accomplishments: speaking and thinking. There is no animal that can walk in a completely upright position, that is able to carry on a conversation about inner experiences, that can disassociate itself from the outside world in order to think about the world conceptually and formulate its conceptions in words. However, a child learns all this at an age when it is more helpless than any animal. After having studied the developmental phases of the growing human being for many years, the well-known American psychologist, Arnold Gesell, summarised his findings in words filled with a deep reverence for the underlying law of development he had discovered:

"Those parents and teachers who consider children to be so easily malleable that they can be moulded only through persistent external influences have not yet advanced to an understanding of the true nature of the psyche. The psyche can be compared to a plant, but not to a lump of clay. For clay cannot grow—it is shaped entirely from without. A plant, on the other hand, receives its form from within, more precisely from its inner forces of growth. It is these forces to which this book wishes to draw attention." (A. Gesell, 'The Child from Five to Ten'.)

Arnold Gesell might not associate himself with Steiner and his work—but it must be said that both describe the same forces; one describes their physical manifestation, and the other their supersensible phenomenon. Steiner portrays the child as standing in a different relationship to the spiritual worlds during the first three years of its life from that of its later years. Mighty, supersensible forces work upon the child which are no longer recognisable in the same way once the life of the soul becomes more conscious. "It is these forces that enable man to enter into a definite relationship with the force of gravity. It is also these forces that form the larynx, which in turn so moulds the brain as to make it a living instrument for thought, feeling and will." Of course, small children as a rule do not experience the supersensible directly and consciously. To be sure there are poets and philosophers who maintain with certainty that they had such experiences during their early childhood. But the intensive connection with the spiritual world need by no means be a conscious one. Steiner speaks in a drastic image of a vestigial "telephone" connection with the life in which the child found itself before birth. Later in his life the human being is never again so directly "subordinated to the direction of that spiritual world to which he belongs, as during his first three years". ('Die Geistige Führung des Menschen und der Menschheit'.)

But to this spiritual world also belong—from the child's point of view—his mother, father and the other people in his closest surroundings. That is the reason why their moods and thoughts so directly and so strongly influence the child. That is also the reason for the feeling of dependence, especially between the child and its mother to whom it is most profoundly bound and who has the most effect. That is also the reason why the child is so sensitive to impressions which come from strangers. If a person takes seriously this way of looking at the child he will hardly be able to avoid drawing several penetrating conclusions.

The circumstances through which the child learns everything basic present themselves to him as deep wisdom. One must not interfere with these processes. We should only be present so that he may imitate us. We must try to become human beings worthy of imitation.

In this way the picture is completed which Gesell painted of the soul of a child as of a plant; what the earth, the rain and sunshine are for plants, the child's surroundings and the adults within it should be for him.

Steiner's description of the first three years agrees with one of the most important discoveries of modern child psychiatry. When Bowlby and other researchers investigated the reaction of children to different forms of spiritual undernourishment, and the change from one "mother-figure" to another, they found, as already mentioned, that the sensibility of the child is decidedly greatest during the first three years and then later declines. They found that at this age the deepest of all the child's spiritual needs is to be cared for by one and the same mother.

Experiencing the Ego

Sometime during the third year the child's behavious often changes considerably. We all know that very small children like to speak of themselves in the third person: "Charles wants more jam", "Ann is sad". Gradually this changes and they begin to speak of themselves as "I". Selma Fraiberg points out that among American children this change takes place approximately at the age of two-and-a-half. The basic causes for this often truly mysterious transformation have often been described by Rudolf Steiner.

To experience oneself as an Ego, an individual, is something which many children recall as a dramatic event. A little three-year-old girl who had just made this discovery, called out, "I am I, I am I!" In all countries there are stories told by people who have had similar experiences in their own lives. Perhaps one of the loveliest is the one told by the poet Jean Paul: "One morning, as a young child, I stood by the door gazing at the wood pile on my left. All at once, like a flash of lightning from heaven, came the inner vision: 'I am I', and remained as a radiant experience. I had for the first time, and for all time, seen myself as an individuality. A trick of the memory here is hardly imaginable, since no outside account could have added additional elements to an event which happened in the hidden, sacred depths of the human being and whose newness gave eternal meaning to mundane, everyday circumstances." ('Account of My Life'.)

What happens is a kind of encapsulation. Part of the supersensible forces which formerly acted as a mediator between the child and supersensible worlds have separated themselves and become the child's "inner being" and facilitated his experience of the self. The often irritable and stubborn little fellow who now emerges, and with artfulness tries out the little word "no", frequently seems to be a totally new acquaintance to the parents. The age of defiance has begun.

To use an illustration from Genesis: For the first time man has eaten from the Tree of Knowledge and the portals of Paradise have closed behind him. But not completely; they are still ajar.

THE KINDERGARTEN-YEARS: LITTLE MATERIAL, MUCH FANTASY

Of the inner capabilities which are at the disposal of an adult, creative fantasy is one of the most important. It is no accident that large American industries have psychologists work out refined test methods in order to discover just this quality in prospective employees. Fantasy, however, is not only necessary if one is to advance in technology. We need it in our everyday life. The path of life of a person without fantasy is bound to a rut which others have drawn out; such a person cannot find his own way and is lacking in initiative and imagination. He is not free.

What actually is "creative fantasy"? Definitions are of little help in describing this quality which arises out of the most profound depths of the human being and brings him knowledge from the most distant heights. Fantasy gives him the strength to transcend everything that is and to relate himself to everything that is and—through his own activity—to relate to what is in the process of *becoming*. Fantasy points towards the future. It fits into existing reality but it also makes attempts to change what has come into being.

The foundation for this quality is established—or ruined—at an early age. Children are full of fantasy, and artists too. Any field of artistic endeavour has preserved much of the spontaneous productivity with which all healthy children are equipped. Only as adults do they lose this precious innate gift under the pressure of life's trivialities and of the eternal hankering after advantage and convenience—much to the damage of their enjoyment of work and enthusiasm for life.

Parents who wish to cultivate such qualities as fantasy and creativity in their children can do it in several ways. However, they can also unwittingly turn off the source.

What Parents Can Do

A nursing infant has no need to be "creative". New-born children have as yet no means of expressing themselves, but at the age of two to three the first attempts show themselves. Give the child some chalk or pencils and a piece of paper on the table or wrapping paper on the floor and he will set to work: expression of the will and the unbridled desire to make movements visible as a picture. The archetypal motif will never be absent: the swirl. It is like the beginning of the universe. When the child walks, runs, jumps, learns to hop, the first graceful pirouette appears spontaneously. The parents' ensuing delight carries the child into a richly developed production. The child is sitting in his bed, babbling and chattering. One morning he suddenly sings his first little melody, monotonous and almost undecided, almost always in the framework of the five-tone—pentatonic—scale. If the parents understand how important such expressions are, their joy and attention will encourage their children. If the parents themselves can play the recorder, the harp or perchance the piano, the children will dance to it. Anyone who has not experienced the passion with which small children can dance has no idea of the intensity of their feeling for rhythm. Instead of simply noisy toys, children should have a small wind instrument of clay (like the old-fashioned clay-cuckoos), and perhaps a xylophone (preferably with a soft "round" tone). At this stage they need lots of rhymes, songs, games and fairy tales.

A Minimum of Objects

One of the most important things is that children are not given too many objects, and above all, not only "finished" ones.
Why?
One could call the present age "The Age of Junk". It is the nature of the industrial process to produce many well-finished articles which can be used immediately for their special purpose and then thrown away. It is the nature of a child, however, to tire quickly of a specialised toy suited only to a specific purpose.
To present a practical example: three children, aged 7, 10, and 12, were by virtue of circumstances, placed into an environment in which for a long time there were few toys and playmates, but plenty of space outdoors. After using up the toys they had brought with them they started to build a grocery shop. An old toolshed became their shop. Two planks and

a table with a leg missing served as the counter. Large round stones were converted into loaves of bread, small ones into beans and lentils, tossed-away preserve jars with stuck-on labels were arranged as containers for their wares, various leaves were offered as lettuce and spinach, scraps of paper with writing on them were used as money. Another business, a ladies' hairdressers, was set up in an old glasshouse. In addition, a variety of different games followed: hide-and-seek, third-man-out, ball games. Even the adults were drawn in. The children refused to go on excursions because they wanted to stay at home and play. Undoubtedly, it was just this lack of toys which stimulated their gift for invention.

Even though it might strike a sore point in toy manufacturers, strictly speaking it would be better if children could grow up in an environment where there were no other toys than such things as boats made of bark, cows of pine-cones, and hand-made primitive dolls of wood or cloth. However, such a pedagogical principle seems Utopian in an industrialised country.

All parents who want to follow this principle will soon discover that their plans are systematically sabotaged by kind, well-meaning, grandparents, uncles, aunts, cousins and friends; because these people always bring along at least plastic toys when they visit and playmates with lots of toys like to show them off. Therefore, it is important that the parents also present carefully chosen toys which are durable and allow the fantasy as much free rein as possible.

What the Kindergarten Can Do

Here the kindergarten can be a great help. At most Waldorf schools there are kindergartens and hardly a school is founded on Steiner's educational ideas where a solid basis for parent contact has not been prepared.

Such a kindergarten contains as few finished things as possible. Naturally it must have pencils, chalk, paints, brushes, and modelling clay; and, of course, beautiful chairs and tables as well, and several simple but beautifully formed toys. Above all there are stones, sea shells, comically-shaped twigs and stumps. With such objects a child can do almost any number of things. Of course, "proper" things such as pictures, clay objects and decorative pieces of cloth, wool and yarn, paper and wood are very important, especially at or for festivals of the year (Easter rabbits and chickens, Advent calendars, Christmas elves, Christmas manger etc.). But the most important products are those created "just to pretend" during free play or in a group.

One can pick berries, make jams, juices and all sorts of dishes, as well as imitate all imaginable household and handcraft activities. One can build food-stands and grocery shops, little one-family houses and blocks of flats. From chairs, benches and tables one can make ships and trains, cars and planes, and be carried off to unknown lands where there are crocodiles. lions and elephants. The departure from the train station or airport with baggage, customs control and waving goodbye is all like the real thing. One can also fly on magic carpets to Never Never Land to fight giants and dragons.

A kindergarten teacher built an unusual telephone which for all practical purposes resembled a real telephone. A few boys laid out a wire for the "telephone" made of pine cones and other objects and explained excitedly, "That's the cable!" Short, simple songs can be improvised: "We'll bake a cake tonight—for everyone's delight." The melodies made up lie within the pentatonic scale. Each new day brings a new song.

A kindergarten teacher delighted Rudolf Steiner with the following story. She had little more than wooden boxes and some cloth of different colours. Out of these she and the children built a group of houses on a village street. She now came wandering through the village as a hungry wayfarer. The children invited her to a table of bread and food contrived out of mere air. She praised tho food and thanked them wholeheartedly. This game was especially popular and had to be repeated several times.

A Few Practical Examples

When Susan was in the kindergarten she sat still with her fingers in her mouth most of the time. But she was a good observer. One day Agnes began an exciting tale. Two years ago she had taken part in a game in which a goat in the meadow was caught in a snowstorm and had to find his way home. He hit his head against the low stall door and suffered many other misfortunes. This time Agnes made up her own game: a flock of sheep has become lost and can't find its shepherd. The sheep sing sadly, "The sheep have lost their way. Who will show them the way home? Who?" Suddenly Susan wanted to join in—her fingers flew out of her mouth! She wanted to be the one to lead them home.

One day Peter brought along several pieces of paper that he had painted in magnificent colours. The kindergarten teacher asked him what he had. "Fireworks!" Then he climbed up onto the table and tossed the pieces of paper all over the room. The others looked on and shouted with joy. Now they, too, wanted to make coloured pieces of paper. For a while everyone was immersed in this activity. As soon as the first children were finished, they climbed up onto the table, one after the other, and set off their fireworks. Quite peacefully they pick-

No steady Earth, no horizon, only a hovering man: drawn by a child of two-and-a-half.

ed up the pieces of paper and took turns scattering them about the entire room. But the pieces of paper did not have the same meaning for each child; for one child they were a rainbow, for another a cluster of shooting stars. Up the table and down again, up and down; the children never tired of their game.

Are these merely childish games? No, they are at one and the same time real life and imagery, fantasy and reality. In games the kindergarten teacher and the children find their element, their language and even the living pedagogical situations in which the adult can, when necessary, amicably intervene, arrange things, stimulate and appease.

Children and Television

Children who eagerly watch television at home often have trouble getting involved in the activity of games.

Thomas had always been allowed to watch TV-films indiscriminately and without restriction. His father has a gunshop. Of course, Thomas wants to do the same someday, but

43

his mother is against it. Thomas complains: "I'm not allowed to shoot anywhere, not at home, not in the yard, not in kindergarten—where *can* I shoot then?" His self-confidence is weak. As is often the case, a good deal of insecurity is hidden behind his aggressiveness. He is afraid to jump down from the big stones in front of the kindergarten. The first time Thomas was productively occupied in the kindergarten was when he was given beeswax to use. At first the wax was very hard, then it became soft in his warm hand, after he had worked it awhile. Then he started to knead a basket and other "friendly" objects.

It seems that Steven is an exception. He frequently watches television programmes, but is also frequently aroused through direct human contact. His father is an artisan and they often do things together. He teaches him skating and skiing and lets him look on when he's working. Steven is quite inventive and can get other children excited about his games, be it Donald Duck or Wild West. He's come to know both from television and they occupy all his thoughts. After one year in the kindergarten other things occur to him; in his paintings different fairy tale motifs appear. Even his parents become more approachable—television loses its importance.

Small children who seldom or never have access to television maintain their fantasy more easily and can create an inimitable childish compensation. They *make* their own "television set" with a frame of cardboard and moveable figures which they push back and forth, and they are happy with it.

What becomes of children who attend such a kindergarten? A certain sequence of events often occurs. After a child has attended kindergarten for a while, a satisfied mother phones and relates that her child has begun to play quite differently from before—not at all

insignificant at a time when the problem of engaging children in meaningful activity has become more and more difficult.

Parents tell each other about such experiences at the kindergarten's Parents' Evening. Perhaps the celebrating of festivals is one of the most important elements which are gradually carried over from the kindergarten into the home—birthdays, the festivals of the seasons, Christian festivals, and the saying of grace before meals. Life-habits are developed which unite the children with the good and the beautiful elements of our culture in an obvious and cheerful manner.

The Perception of the Bodily Organs and the Drawings of Small Children

One of the most important suggestions that Rudolf Steiner has made in the field of educating young children deals with their way of drawing.

We all know that when children draw or paint a human being they often put together the parts of the body in the most grotesque proportions; big noses, giant hands, and so on. In a course of lectures on education which Rudolf Steiner gave in 1920 in Basel, he showed what we can learn from such pictures.

"If you take a number of drawings by children and try to see how they have drawn the arms

A child's experience of the hand is often expressed in drawings in which the hands are disproportionately large, or have a great many fingers. In drawing a house too the child's own inner experience plays a part—such a drawing shows the extent to which he feels at home or otherwise in his own body.

and legs, then you will see that it comes from inner feeling, and what they draw in outline comes from observation. Their drawings derive from two sources of experience. Small children do not intellectualise—they draw experience, primitive observation, mixed with primitive feelings of their own organs. I believe one can always tell if the child has drawn from observation or from inner feeling: the outline of the mouth, for example, has been observed, *looked at,* by the child, whereas the teeth are, one can say, shaped by the inner feeling of the child's organs." (Basel, 28. 4. 1920.)

Rudolf Steiner now describes how small children have a capacity for feeling or perceiving their organs that in ancient times was quite common and that in Greek sculpture, for example, was still strongly cultivated. Their works did not grow essentially from the study of models, but simply out of the inner perception of their own bodies. Children who first begin to paint at the age of nine or ten do not develop their pictures of fantasy from direct experiences, but rather from something which they have thought out: reason has begun to enter the picture. It is important that children be allowed to busy themselves with chalk and crayons at an early age, so that the specific soul-quality of fantasy-filled experience is cultivated before it is dampened by the maturing of the intellect. To allow children to live out their organ-sensitivity in this way, results in a harmonious interplay of soul-experience and physical activity which is important for their whole life.

One can interest children in such painting through fairy-tales, in which they bring out the humorous, sad, calm or exciting mood of the tale in simple colour harmonies. A good example, which relates directly to the sensitivity of the organs, is the Swedish tale of 'The Three Grannies' with the drastic and touching de-scription of the three curious, but skilful, women who help the princess in distress ("Mother Bigthumb", with her strong thumbs, "Mother Bigfoot", with her powerful foot, and "Mother Fanny", with her mighty buttocks).

Eurythmy for Small Children

Of all the means of expression which can satisfy the child's need to give form to his fantasy, rhythmical movement is one of the most natural and archetypal.

Free play can develop into formed movements. To give an example: The children hear the Norwegian fairy-tale about the 'Three Billy Goats Gruff' who together managed to lead the big dangerous troll by the nose. The kindergarten teacher sits in the centre and is the troll. Around her stand the children, who have been divided up into three groups. The smallest children are the smallest goat who trips along so handsomely and lightly. The children who are a bit bigger are the middle-sized goat who walks with a steady gait and considerably more self-assurance. The oldest children are the big goat who stomps with heavy, forceful steps. Now all have to walk over the bridge under which the troll is hiding. With or without musical accompaniment each group must walk in its own way and with its own special rhythm. After the troll has been fooled by the first two groups, the big goat must give him a blow with its horns, so that he rolls away like a ball and never again in his life wants to see another goat. The children shout with glee.

It is important that not only the legs but also the arms are engaged in various rhythms. If the teacher wishes, she can let the children imitate a few simple eurythmical movements.

completely without correction or artistic pretentions, perhaps a protective "B" when the goats become anxious upon seeing their adversary, or an angry "F" when the large goats chase away the troll, a relieved "A" when they all finally come to the large and wonderful pasture in the mountain. (Eurythmy is described in detail in a later chapter.) To "play out a fairy-tale" in this way is an activity which quite obviously captivates children.

One kindergarten teacher, who herself was a trained eurythmist, tells of her own experience:

"It sometimes happens that some of the smallest children find it difficult to join in such a game and watch from a safe corner. But when they come home—as their mothers tell us—they often carry out the game on their own; they had simply been shy. The somewhat older children are without exception swept along by the game. It was especially interesting to observe their reaction when they were watching a eurythmy performance. We performed some fairy tales, among others the humorous Russian fairy-tale "The Cock and the Mouse". Even the children who watched a lot of television and often had difficulty in concentrating, sat completely still and watched for about twenty minutes! The mother of one such child told us later: "To our surprise we noticed that during the first few hours after the performance the children sat quietly and peacefully, as though they had eaten a good meal and were digesting it. Then the mood passed and they were once again full of life." A while later we repeated the first performance and we could see that the children still hadn't had enough of it. At the third performance some children cane especially well-dressed. They explained to us that they had made themselves "especially pretty" so that the cock and the mouse would come yet again to visit them.

On one parents' evening we took up the problem of television. During the course of the conversation we emphasised that small children are especially inclined to imitation and, therefore, always wanted to do whatever the parents did. All the parents listened with interest and showed a good deal of understanding. Now when the question of television came up, one mother suddenly realised that to some extent even the picture on the screen incited the child to imitation. She herself enjoyed sitting in front of the television and said with a sigh, "Is the meaning behind all this really that we should sacrifice our own way of life for the children"?

Does Fantasy Sever Us From The Real World?

If small children are constantly encouraged to live in the world of fantasy, are they not in danger of becoming cut off from the real world?

As we have just seen, a child picks up everything which is in his environment and which is expressed in the form of external gesture. If the people in his environment are ignorant of the world, then the risk of "inner infection" is great. If they stand with both feet on the ground and have a good sense for the practical side of life, then this attitude toward life will correspondingly "rub off" on the child. Here, as otherwise, parents as a rule naturally play a central role. Through her whole attitude to life, the kindergarten teacher can make an important contribution as well.

How does it happen that a child draws a man like this? To depict the trunk as a big wheel gives us a glimpse of the imaginative way in which this four-year-old girl experiences the human body.

48

Some Basic Features of Method

THE RHYTHM OF THE DAY

All children experience the rhythmic alternation of waking and sleeping and of active and passive states during the waking life. If this daily round as well as the greater rhythms of the source of the year are taken into account in making a time-table and the general curriculum, then the whole education will be characterised by certain features, such as:

—A well-ordered daily programme

—Block period lessons which strengthen the powers of concentration

—Artistic activities for developing the will-forces

—The living world as a means of deepening the life of feeling

Let us begin with a comparison. Suppose an employee in a large store had to carry out such a daily routine as the following:

9.00— 9.50	Manning the telephone switchboard
10.00—10.50	Selling in the perfumery department
11.00—11.50	Invoicing
11.50—12.30	Lunch
12.30—13.20	Negotiating for a bank loan
13.30—14.20	Tidying up
14.30—15.20	Window-dressing
15.30—16.20	Programming the store's computer

Nobody would dream of making such a schedule for an adult's working day. And yet in schools, we make timetables very like this for our children.

Rudolf Steiner describes in the lecture course, 'Education as a Social Question', how destructively this kind of timetable works on the child's faculty of concentration. Waldorf schools try to make each day an organic whole. It is easiest to think and concentrate during the early part of the day and so the morning starts with subjects that need knowledge and understanding and, therefore, call on the children's thinking powers. Each subject in turn is treated as a continuous theme for a number of weeks at the same time in the morning— the so-called "main lesson" period. Then follow those subjects which require regular rhythmic repetition in shorter lessons, such as foreign languages, eurythmy, gymnastics, music and religion.

The later morning or the afternoon is a suitable time for subjects which mainly require manual dexterity and artistic practice, such as handwork, woodwork, gardening or scientific experimental work. Homework too should be aimed at increasing various skills through practice.

Thus each school day has a broad rhythm of inner absorbtion and outer activity, breathing in and breathing out.

However, smaller and quicker rhythms have to be woven into this broad and slow "breathing" process. If memory and reflection are called on for too long a time, the children begin to look pale and tired. The circulation is stimulated and the child is refreshed when its feelings are aroused and its will is engaged again in some more active or artistic pursuit.

Especially in the younger classes, the teacher has to be aware of the effect he has through his way of teaching on the health of the growing child.

The act of forgetting is an important factor both in harmonising the actual teaching and in making the subject one's own. Rudolf Steiner repeatedly drew the teachers' attention to this fact. There is an eloquent expression in the Spanish language, "I will consult my pillow".

It is a general human experience that all that has happened to us during the day does not just disappear into nothingness when we fall asleep but undergoes a transformation. For children and teacher alike, the way in which things that have been learnt or experienced on the previous day rise up again into consciousness on the next is of great significance. This process of forgetting is important in education. It is especially obvious in manual activities, where having once learnt to do something we must forget the process of learning. If we had to direct with full consciousness every movement we make in using a tool, we should never achieve real skill. In order to write fluently too, we have to forget how we learnt the single letters.

There are the two extremes; what we call "fixed ideas" or obsessions are experiences that have not been sufficiently absorbed, they continually rise again to the surface of consciousness. On the other hand, there is the inability to remember, and this shows either that the impressions have sunk down too deeply or else that sufficient interest has not been aroused in the child to make a real impression. Memory and learning depend equally on the right measure of forgetting and remembering. This is particularly noticeable in the younger classes. At the beginning of the day, the children wake up best if a few minutes can be spent reciting a poem, singing, playing recorders or doing some eurythmy movements. Then they will listen and take part as the teacher recalls the subject-matter from the day before and leads it a stage further. Then they can become active again themselves, writing or drawing in their copy books, modelling or painting. Sometimes the teacher may end the lesson by telling the class something from the story-material suitable for that age group.

BLOCK PERIOD LESSONS

Roughly the first two hours of each school day are spent in one long "main lesson". While in the first class the subjects are less separated, later on three to four weeks are given up to a single subject such as arithmetic, grammar, geography, history, biology, chemistry, physics, or whatever else is indicated in the curriculum. Writing and reading are practised in connection with the subject of the lesson at various levels.

Since six months or more can pass before a particular main lesson subject is taken up again, the pupils have plenty of time in which to forget. The period between is as important as the night's sleep between one day and the next. It is interesting how easily the "dormant" knowledge can usually be reawakened when the subject is taken up once more, particularly if the children were keen and enthusiastic about their original contact with it. In fact it is often to be observed that a certain maturing has occurred during the intervening time and the child's abilities have developed further.

No other way of working is so suitable for awakening the pupils' interest and enabling them to concentrate their thoughts and attention on a particular subject. In addition, it means that each section of the curriculum can be coherent and complete because the teacher can present both the general view and the details of a subject within an overseeable period of time.

Other subjects besides those given in the main lessons can also be treated in block periods. In some Waldorf schools this is done with most of the afternoon activities, such as handicrafts and technological subjects, particularly in the older classes. Without experiencing it personally one can hardly imagine how beneficial is this way of working especially in our fragmented civilization with its jumble of changing impressions that make concentrated thinking and working ever more difficult. It is quite definite too that far less would be learnt in the main lesson subjects given the same number of hours, if these were to be spread over a longer period of time in twice or thrice weekly sessions interspersed with other lessons.

ARTISTIC ACTIVITIES

A sight met with particularly often in Waldorf schools is that of children drawing, painting, modelling, carving, doing handwork, making music, reciting, and rehearsing plays. Especially in the lower classes these artistic activities are woven into the lessons on every subject. One might think that the purpose was to train them all to be accomplished artists, or at least to encourage "children's art" as something in itself.

However, the real purpose of these manifold activities is quite different. To express the typical movements of an animal in wood or clay, to create form out of pure colour in painting, to let light arise through the interplay of black and grey shades of charcoal on a white background, these activities are experienced as a challenge both to one's courage and one's patience. To work out the lyrical nuances in a choral or orchestral work demands enormous perseverance on the part of both teacher and pupils. The rehearsal of a play can be fraught with crises and catastrophes. Their overcoming through common determination often results in a renewed feeling of class-community. The feeling of satisfaction thus engendered is all the greater if the ultimate performance is a success.

All these are exercises for the will. There is no better way of training the will than to practise again and again something one finds difficult. Adults, if they really wish to, can always find a way of doing this. But children need tasks which give them pleasure and enjoyment as well. Art is an area of life in which repetition is not monotonous. If the teacher is able to deepen and renew the common work through the impulses he gives, it need never lose its initial freshness.

THE SPOKEN WORD

There is a very realistic rule to which there are virtually no exceptions. How often are children heard to attribute their proficiency, or lack of proficiency, to the excellence, or otherwise, of the textbook on which the lessons have been based? Almost never! It is nearly always the teacher's ability, or failure, to enthuse which is seen in direct relation to what the child feels he has learnt or failed to learn. This rule applies to all types of school. However refined and excellent the textbooks and technical aids may be, they are quite outweighed by a far more significant factor, the individual ability or lack of ability of the teacher.

This reality is taken very seriously in Waldorf schools. The spoken and living word of the teacher is the real basis for all school work. The thread of continuity which runs through a main lesson block period cannot be found in any book. It is worked out by the teacher himself, who draws his material from many different sources and because of this can achieve an objective presentation. Readers in the mother tongue and foreign languages are of course unavoidable but printed textbooks are used only as incidental reading matter running alongside the content of the main lesson, and that only in the upper classes.

This method of working requires thorough preparation by the teacher but gives him much more freedom to go more deeply into questions and problems which arise and may be important to the class as a whole for one reason or another. The teacher's lively use of the spoken word enables pupils with very different degrees of ability to participate actively in work on one and the same subject.

The teacher may be tired and depressed when he is preparing his lesson or before he enters the classroom. But the living confrontation with the subject and with the children causes his "private self" with all its troubles and worries to step aside, allowing inspiration to enter from sources outside his own being. He gains the strength to give his lessons the necessary variations in mood, the alternation between seriousness and humour, between inner tension and relaxation.

As modern human beings we are often slightly suspicious when feelings or emotions are discussed. What Steiner sees as true feeling is the ability to leave the sphere of one's own emotions and "feel one's way" at least for a while into something which is quite outside one's own self. If the teacher is able to do this, of course without actually pointing it out, he carries the children along with him. Thus he helps to develop what for lack of a better word we must call the feeling life of the children. This is the most important aspect of all teaching; for the ability to "feel one's way" into the souls of others, to sympathise with their troubles and their joys, is the basis on which people can build their lives together. The best way of helping this to develop, especially in this age of tele-communication and the teaching machine, it to use the living word which goes direct from person to person.

THE USE OF TEXTBOOKS

It could be asked whether the children and young people might not become too dependent on the authority of the teacher if they have to depend only on what he has to offer them. The contrary is usually the case. The children are so stimulated by the living presentation that they turn to books of their own accord for further study of a subject. From quite a young age (V or VI class), they can be encouraged to give short talks which they work out on their own. The literature they use for this becomes an interesting and indispensable source of knowledge in quite a different way from an obligatory series of textbooks out of which they would be given set tasks.

Instead of being dependent on printed textbooks, the children learn to make their own copy-books as they go along. All the illustrations are done without help except perhaps in the form of a rough sketch made by the teacher on the blackboard. In the early classes, the text is usually dictated by the teacher after thorough discussion of the subject-matter with the class. Then the children start writing their own accounts later on and finally even bind the books themselves. Naturally not all of them find it easy to compose a clear and comprehensible text. But those who have difficulties quite often develop out of them a conspicuous ability to complement their own descriptions with quotations from their readers and other books. Early essay writing too lays the basis for the independent taking of notes during class in the upper school.

THE ROLE OF ART

To practise an art, we have to face problems which approach us from outside in the form of the material to be worked on: coloured paints, modelling clay, a movement diagram, a poetic work. We cannot solve the problems unless we enter fully into the material. This process of entering into the material often leads to a whole range of feelings in the soul: expectation, disappointment, anger, resignation, thoughtfulness, surprise, new hope, new efforts of will, intense joy at being creative. But it is not only in the soul that this entering into the material is felt. It goes right into the physical body, into finger tips and toes. Practising an art is particularly important in life today. In this technical age, life is full of physical actions which are carried out more or less automatically: switching on the light, turning up the heating, starting the washing-up machine, taking a seat in the underground, and so on.

Some activities also require alertness and attention. You cannot relax for a moment while driving a car, working a crane, or drilling somebody's tooth. But the concentration you need is cool and requires attentiveness, consideration and reflection. Only one or two of your senses and very few of the great range of skills requiring physical dexterity are called on.

An artistic activity places you in quite a different situation. Nothing is based here entirely on routine. Full concentration is certainly necessary but it encompasses a wide range. Learning to drive a car may be very exciting but it cannot lead to such manifold and deep inner experiences nor anything like the experience of pure bodily participation which occurs through modelling a form in clay, practising a piece of music on an instrument, or creating a part in a play.

In life today, there is an infinite paucity of physical activities which require the full participation of body and soul.

Children and Art

The intensive bond between body and soul is one of the characteristic qualities of childhood. Adults are at pains to conceal their feelings and emotions, though they may not always succeed. But children do just the opposite. Instinctively they stamp their feet when they are angry or jump up and down when they are happy, and so on.

By allowing children to express the feelings in their souls through artistic activities, we give free rein to their deepest needs; but not just any free rein. Sometimes the inner involvement of children in creative, artistic activities is looked upon as letting them get something out of their system. If this were the case, we might just as well let them bang on an empty tin can, run round the house a few times, or go and smash some china in the park. But art is formative, both in the material world and in the world of the soul. Some artistic tasks might require a different inner attitude to the one we instinctively adopt. In this way a cautious child can be persuaded to be more daring, an exuberant child more circumspect, a weak-willed child more persevering, an obstinate child more adaptable, and so on.

The educational effects of artistic activities on children have frequently been observed and stressed. But it is not always realized how far-reaching and lasting these effects can prove to be.

The most deeply rooted habits and patterns of behaviour are those which form when a child is at the copying stage of his development. Some of these change more or less naturally over the years in accordance with changes in the environment and in attitude to life. But others remain, and these are hidden beneath the threshold of consciousness and cannot be budged. One of these is a basic positive or negative attitude towards the environment and other people.

As teachers, we could help to make permanent in children another deep-seated instinct: to participate in everything they meet in the outside world, to occupy themselves with it and to try and give it form. There is no other form of activity which is more suitable for cultivating this instinct, even in early childhood, than artistic activity. Through this activity a person learns to enter with all the qualities of his soul and with every fibre of his body into the battle with a problem which is important not because its solution will bring any material gain but simply because it is humanly interesting. Thus the basis is laid in the child for the capacity of taking a real interest in the world around him in later life.

A Problem of Civilization

"To take an interest": this does not seem particularly remarkable. And yet the question of how we can pass on to children and young people the habits and occupations which can make their lives rich and purposeful is indeed one of the greatest problems of civilization. For a teenager entering a stage of life when everything seems uncertain, it can be decisive for the whole of his future if he has a real interest to which he can cling.

In the industrialised countries of the world the problem of what to do with increasing leisure time is gradually becoming more acute. Furthermore, average life-expectancy is increasing and in some countries at the same time the age for retirement is being lowered.

People who have an intense interest in the problems of the world at large and also for people and events in their immediate environment and who are thus able to remain lively and adaptable even at a ripe old age, such people usually have a number of common traits as well as their many individual characteristics: they have an artistic disposition and a certain naive openness. Old people of this kind can be found everywhere, for instance Leonardo da Vinci and Goethe in the "halls of fame" and, on the other hand, many a "robust" old person known to most of us amongst our friends and acquaintances.

It is by no means always the case that these people are professionally active in the field of art. But even their way of describing events and occurrences often has an element of keen artistry, particularly if they are country people. Their robustness is not always the result of good health. Their vitality may simply reflect their capacity to be interested in the out-

A miner at work. From the Local Geography period in Class 4.

side world, or maybe just their ability to conceal their aches and pains from those around them.

How is it that an artistic disposition brings with it the ability to produce and preserve vitality? Rudolf Steiner has pointed out an answer to this question. He described how artistic activities, in opening out a wide range of soul experiences and also an intimate interplay between physical and psychic activities, gradually bring about a change in the body. It becomes more approachable and receptive towards impulses which come out of man's inner life. It becomes a pliable and harmonious organ on which the individuality can play with the help of the soul forces.

The earlier this process can begin, the better it is.

DRAWING FORMS

Right from the beginning of Class 1 the children draw basic form-patterns.

Carvings on a rune-stone as an example of form-drawing, next page.

Exercises in symmetry, page 61.

The Problem of the Outline

No doubt we can all remember some of our earliest attempts to draw, let us say, a horse. Starting with the head we could draw a nice black line down the neck, down and up the front legs, along the belly, down and up the back legs, round the tail, and along the back to the tips of the ears where we started. But however nice the black line might have been, the result was not like a horse. So we would set to with the rubber, trying again and again and making more and more of a mess until finally the mass of ghostly horse outlines and the greyish smudgy paper would cause us to give up in despair. Even if we did still press on to colouring-in the horse, we would do so without any pleasure.

That sharp black outline killed something, not only in the picture but also in ourselves.

Of course, it is possible to learn to draw in this way. Thousands of artists the world over have done so and have produced superb works of art with the help of the outline. The most accomplished can simply dash off a few lines with amazing skill and produce a miraculous likeness.

But the fact remains that when we meet people in their houses or in the street we do not see them surrounded by a thick (or a thin!) black line from head to foot and back from foot to head. In reality there are no outlines, only colours which meet.

The Real Language of Forms

We cannot learn to understand the real language of forms if we only look at the lines which arise as the result of a meeting of colours.

Wherever we look in the world we find geometrical forms: the pattern of a snowflake, the hexagonal honeycomb, the many-sided crystal, the parabola of a trajectory, the spiral of a snail's shell, the regular pattern of leaves on many plants, the proportions of the golden mean as applied to the human body, the ellipses described by the earth and other planets. And there have been artists who have surpassed all others in discovering the secrets of geometric relationships, weaving them into their paintings like an invisible skeleton, an imperceptible pattern which gives their work a stamp of supreme harmony: Leonardo da Vinci, Raphael, Cézanne, and many others.

To discover the geometric laws in the universe and in art can be a deeply joyful experience. The two different languages of art and of science can merge into one at such moments.

So that the older pupils of a Waldorf school can experience these moments in all their intensity, not only in mathematics but also perhaps in geology, physics, botany, physiology, astronomy and history of art, they have to have undergone thorough preparation.

The rediscovery of geometry in the outside world makes the greatest impression on those who have first become acquainted with its laws quite independently of any external experience. It is possible to construct the whole of Euclid's geometry without a single thought to its application in reality. Its laws live within the human being.

Drawing Forms —
from the Very First Day at School

Rudolf Steiner recommends that children should start to occupy themselves with geometry long before they are able to handle compasses and rulers. He even pointed out that they could start on their very first day at school.

Having talked to the children for a while about their hands and how people use their hands for working, the teacher can then call each child in turn to the blackboard to draw, quite simply, a straight line. Then he can show them a semi-circle and again let each child in turn draw one on the board. Thus the children have accomplished their very first geometrical construction, and the teacher has learned much about them by observing the way each one walks to the board, looks at it and draws on it.

But geometry need not remain confined to the hands. The children can be taken out to the playground where there is room to do geometry with their feet, walking and running in circles and spirals. Then they can return to the class-room and draw the same forms in their books.

In a eurythmy lesson in class II the whole class can form a moving figure eight, crossing over at the central point by passing each other alternately. This calls for self-discipline, and indeed geometry can have the underlying element of creating order. It is good if the teacher, instead of telling a small boy where to stand, can say: "Andrew, you are making a dent in our nice circle."

Gradually the forms to be walked, stamped

Eva Kl 2a

or run in eurythmy grow more and more complicated. In class VI, when geometry is one of the important subjects, the eurythmy lessons can supplement the geometry lessons with "moving geometry". While moving in forms is important, the drawing of forms has value on its own account. For instance, the children can be asked to finish incomplete forms: make your own inner or outer form; find the missing symmetrical form; make a mirror picture. The forms illustrated are based on suggestions made by Rudolf Steiner in various lectures (14/8/1923, 15/8/1924).

Living Forms

In drawing forms in this way the lines made are not hard outlines depicting the more or less intellectually constructed "edge" of something seen with the eyes. They are the expression of an inner play of forces and therefore instead of destroying the reality they stimulate life.

An imaginative teacher can make unlimited suggestions and find endless variations, and drawing forms can become a favourite occupation with the children.

Is any other kind of drawing done in the lower classes of a Waldorf school? Not really.

Everything else is done with painting: colour exercises, illustrating stories, even the first learning of letters and numbers. In the IV class the children are led to perceive the forms they have been freely producing themselves in objects in the surrounding world, for instance the angles of a chair, or the curves of a vase.

The naturalistic copying of phenomena and scenes in nature and life is not encouraged before class VII or VIII. By then the children will have practised the basic techniques of artistic black-and-white drawing and a more thorough study of the physical surrounding with its perspectives and its light and shade will be justified.

FINDING A
RELATIONSHIP
WITH COLOURS

A simple colour harmony from Class 1 and a colour exercise from Class 3, facing page.

Asked why an absolute amateur might want to draw or paint, many people might easily answer: "To express one's feelings."

Expressing Oneself in Colours

It is quite true that through colours we can give our most excited moods a peaceful and harmonious expression. Somebody furiously angry might gain more satisfaction from splashing red paint all over a canvas than from smashing a window.

So for young children whose emotional life is as yet uncontrolled, the use of paints and chalks should be an ideal way of letting off steam. Rudolf Steiner did not ignore this aspect and contributed ways and means of putting it into practice.

"An excitable child should be surrounded and even dressed in red and orange colours and in contrast a placid child should be given blues and greenish blues." (Steiner here seems to mean the contrast between sanguine and choleric children on the one hand and melancholic and phlegmatic children on the other.) "What is important is the opposite colour reproduced inwardly. For instance, with red it is green, or with blue it is an orange yellow. This can easily be seen if one looks for a while at a suitably coloured surface and then moves one's eyes quickly to a white surface.

The opposite colour is produced by the physical organs of the child and brings about a suitable organ structure necessary for the child. If an excitable child has red colours in his environment, then he will inwardly produce the opposite greens. And the activity of producing greens has a calming effect, the organs take into themselves a calming tendency." (Rudolf Steiner, 'The Education of the Child from the Standpoint of Anthroposophy'.)

However, if one wants to make use of all the therapeutic possibilities of colours, it is not enough in the early school years simply to let the children express themselves and their experiences in colour.

Indeed, if in practice children today are allowed to draw and paint freely according to their temperament, it can often happen that in fact they become more and more involved in themselves and their emotions instead of beeing able to free themselves. Thus unruly choleric children might steep themselves in repeatedly painting burning cities, or melancholic children become more and more gloomy painting morbid things like gallows scenes.

At best, if the teacher or another adult is able to guide the children to painting more healthy and happy scenes, the function of "letting off steam" can only be limited to reducing tension. But in the depths of the soul not a great deal is affected.

Feeling what the Colours Express

If one uses colours only for self-expression, one never steps outside the magic circle of one's own inner life. But if one tries to enter selflessly into the language of colour, new and unlimited horizons open up. One's inner life is changed and enriched.

In learning to know colours, there is no point in beginning by trying to study and copy an external scene. If we do this, form takes precedent over colour. The better course is to start with the colours themselves by doing colour exercises. It is this kind of painting which is regarded as the most important for the younger children in Waldorf schools.

Chalks are not very suitable for colour exercises, since one cannot really mix them or make subtle nuances. But water-colours used on damp paper are relatively easy to use and the child has a feeling of space and flowing movement.

A painting lesson requires considerable order and discipline since all those wet paints and glasses of water for rinsing the brushes can be sorely tempting for a seven-year-old. But once he has stood in an orderly queue to collect his board, paper and brush, it can be a great experience for him to paint, under the guidance of the teacher, for instance a yellow patch surrounded by blue followed by a blue patch surrounded by yellow.

When the paintings have dried, they are hung round the room or propped against the walls and carefully examined. Gradually the children begin to realise that there are colours which obtrude, for instance all nuances of red and yellow, and colours which recede, for example, blues and violets. Green is more neutral.

Slowly the children attribute a kind of personality to each colour, as though it were a being with quite specific gestures and characteristics. "You can speak to the children in the language of colours. Just think how inspiring it is if you give the children to understand: this is a coquettish mauve, and there is a cheeky little bit of red looking over her shoulder; and both of them are standing on a humble blue. You must describe it quite graphically; it is formative for the soul . . . What is thus perceived as arising out of the colours can be put on paper in fifty different ways." (From a teachers' conference with Rudolf Steiner on 15. 11. 1920.)

The teacher can do these exercises with the children over a long period, always trying to give them a feeling for the hues, tones, perspectives and spaces of colours. When they have learnt to allow the forms to arise out of the gestures of the colours, it will be quite natural for them when illustrating a fairy tale or legend to choose scenes in which people and things can grow out of the harmony of colours. (See for instance the picture of St. Christopher, p. 94.)

In helping children to come to terms with their temperaments, painting can be an invaluable help. Speaking in a very generalized way, one could say that if cholerics were allowed to choose their own colour exercises they would spread dramatic shades of red all over the paper at the expense of the other colours. In the same situation, melancholics would paint something small and dark right at the top in one of the corners. Sanguines would hastily paint something small and bright and joyful somewhere on the paper and then start clamouring for a new sheet. And phlegmatics would spread something large and rather boring over the whole page.

Colour-exercise in red from Class 3.

It is more therapeutic to learn to use the whole sheet of paper in a balanced and economic manner and to do what the colours want and not what one's mood demands.

People visiting a Waldorf school or an exhibition of its work often ask: "Why are all the paintings so similar? Why aren't the children allowed to paint what they like?"

The answer has partly been given above. Naturally, as in all teaching institutions, there might be a danger in one or two cases of slipping into a routine. But it should be stressed that most of what seems so similar in the way teachers approach and solve artistic problems comes about because in Waldorf schools, painting follows a path of exercises dictated not by the individual teacher but quite simply by the nature of colour and by the necessity of taking the children's needs into account.

It is difficult to express in words what it can mean for people later in life if they have an early intense experience of colour. We are dealing here with inner riches which cannot be grasped with physical hands and with qualities and nuances which are too subtle to be described. It is quite definite that the whole world is different for someone who has begun to understand the quiet, entirely unintellectual and deeply penetrating language of colour.

Above right: In the handwork lessons of Class 6, pupils may be asked to make a doll for a younger child. They are shown how the smallest alteration can change the doll's whole expression and character.

Centre and bottom right: The typical gestures of different animals can well be introduced in the handwork class as a supplement to Zoology lessons.

HANDWORK

The visitor to the handwork classes in a Waldorf school will observe that boys and girls are mostly engaged in the same activities. He may also gather how important a part this subject plays in the general curriculum.

It is not only a matter of preparing young people for situations in later life where they will need this or that practical skill. The aim of the craft lesson goes far beyond this. It is concerned with fundamental human attributes, and was indicated by Rudolf Steiner as follows:

"When one knows that our intellect is not developed by the direct approach, that is by cultivation of intellectual pursuits themselves, but one knows rather that a person who is unskilled in the movement of his fingers will also be unskilful in his intellect, having less mobile ideas or thoughts, and that he who has acquired dexterity in the movements of his fingers has also mobile thoughts and ideas and can penetrate into the essence of things, one will not undervalue what is meant by developing the outer human being, with the aims that out of the whole treatment of the outer man the intellect shall arise as one part of the human being." (26. 4. 1920.)

In the first class the children begin to knit and in the second class to crochet. Gradually they become able to make garments for themselves or others until by class VII or VIII they can make a shirt, a dress, a pair of trousers etc., with the help of a sewing machine. The boys, as they approach adolescence, can also work in tougher material, such as leather and cane.

The attempt to create artistic form, even on a

primitive level, runs like a red thread through the whole subject, and comes to expression particularly in the making of toys from about the V class onwards. What the children have absorbed in their studies of Man and Animal in classes IV and V appears in the way they make animals and dolls and, too, through the medium of clay-modelling and wood-carving.

Modelling brings its own peculiar artistic problems. Details can be most vividly brought out. Nevertheless, they must remain subordinate to the whole conception, for the nature of the particular animal must be represented as a unified whole. When modelling with clay, more material can always be added, and thus convex forms arise more naturally.

Wood-carving goes in the opposite direction. Material is constantly being removed, and the concave form is more strongly experienced. Here will activity is manifest. Much concentrated energy is released when, for example, a twelve-year-old starts work with mallet and chisel on a big block of wood. Wood-carving is usually started in class VI.

Each material has its own special characteristics which come to meet the pupil and he experiences the nature of the different woods as he works with them. If the pupil, however, were to get used to throwing aside unfinished every article where he makes a mistake, he would never develop his real skill. It is an important step when with the guidance of the teacher he learns to correct his mistakes and bring his piece of work to some kind of conclusion, even if—as in the picture—the end result may be a spoon with a very small bowl on a disproportionately long, strong handle.

Above right: Clay-modelling is a voyage of discovery in the realm of three-dimensional form.

Below right: Animals-forms arise out of imaginative creations (Class 8).

Free Artistic Creation

The element of free artistic creativity developing more and more from the 4th and 5th school-years, was considered by Rudolf Steiner to be of great significance:

"The child should work out of its own will-forces, not according to anything prescribed to him from outside ... You can experience the fact that the children really bring things forth from within themselves if the teaching is alive." (23. 8. 1922.)

Naturally, the teacher must be present to organise things. If the lessons, however, proceed in a healthy manner, the teacher's role is fundamentally to help his pupils to fulfil their own intentions.

Art in a Technical Age

Living as we do in a technical age, we tend to make a sharp division between artistic creations and those that serve practical life. The former are usually hand-made and are expected to be "beautiful", the latter are factory-produced and their sole purpose is to be "useful".

Artists and technicians, who are concerned with the design of practical articles, often attempt to bridge this gulf. These problems come to expression especially strongly in the realm of architecture.

In other spheres, too, we are faced with this fundamental question. Can we afford to design our surroundings in such a way that they are not only technically practicable but also suit and serve the human needs of those who live and work in them?

To achieve something in this field there is a need not only for efficient experts, there must also be a sufficient number of "ordinary"

people who take such an interest in these problems, that they are prepared to accept the added financial implications. Through an artistically orientated education in handicrafts, schools can make an important contribution in this direction.

From about the age of twelve, children show an increasing grasp of the fundamentals of mechanics. The boy or girl who is making a toy such as the dwarf with the axe, cannot help bringing together artistic and technical considerations.

In the later school years, more complex tasks of a similar nature can be set. There are no end of possibilities in this sphere of work.

The wood itself asks for a certain treatment.

Above: Stages in carving darning-eggs. Class 6.

Centre: Not all spoons turn out as planned!

Below: The form is suited to the material in these individually-carved articles.

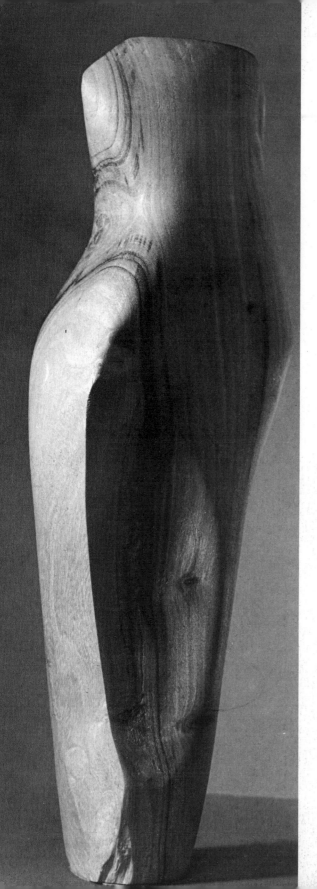

If a young person shows the ability to work with a very hard material, it is important that he familiarises himself not only with textiles, clay and wood, but also with metal. The creative possibilities which arise here can be interesting and stimulating to both boys and girls.

The pictures reproduced on the right show a silver bowl and an excerpt from a notebook, which describes how to finish metal objects of this type. Both the bowl and the notebook were made by two eighteen-year-old girls, partly during class time and partly as voluntary extra work.

In the hand-written text of the notebook it says, among other things: " . . . as an underlay one uses a piece of wood with a sawed indentation; then one pounds folds so that the bowl looks like a cake form; then one rotates the underlay slightly and the folds are smoothed out with the hammer. Now the object is heated until it is glowing hot. If one is working with silver, it must be heated until it becomes a glowing white. The next time folds are hammered out, it is best if they aren't placed in their former position. In this way one can produce a bowl quite quickly."

Left: An exercise in free form.

För sammandrivning behövs som underlag ett trästycke med nedsågad skåra, däri slås platen mer i veck tills skålen ser ut som en kakform. Man byter då till ett slätt underlag och vecken slås ut. Efter varje sådan omgång glödgas föremålet och vitkokas om det är silver. Nästa gång vecken hamras mer ska de helst inte hamna på samma ställe. På detta sätt går det ganska fort att få upp en skålformad form.

Planerhammare.

PHYSICAL EDUCATION

Facing page: Apart from physical exercise, Bothmer gymnastics has as its aim deepened experience of space and a strengthening of the will-forces.

A Civilisation of Sitters

The "futurologists" promise us a world in which an ever greater number of human activities can be carried out while sitting. Machines will take over most of our physical tasks. Essentially our participation in reality will lie only in observing and controlling with the intellect.

To compensate for this we need movement. How should this movement be stimulated? What form should it take? Should we, young and old, spend part of our free time in exercise or bathing suits, in the parks, on the sport fields, in the gymnasium and the swimming pool? Many people see no other way to maintain their physical health at all. By continuously being directed to forms of movement, which correspond neither to a social need (as does a normal physical task) nor to an impulse for a significant artistic activity, but only satisfy our own physical needs, we arrive at a problem, the extent of which cannot easily be encompassed. Our activity becomes somewhat "soulless", What then happens can be quite clearly observed in those kinds of sports in which "tackling", "scrumming", or other forms of physical brutality are an essential part (ice hockey, soccer, Rugby, boxing, etc.). A level of animalisation is reached, which can become crass, especially in the case of young people.

It will later be described how Rudolf Steiner wished to counteract this tendency through the artistic movements of eurythmy. In addition to eurythmy, there is also the special form of gymnastics as it is practised in most Waldorf schools.

Fritz Graf von Bothmer (1883—1941), gymnastics instructor in the first Waldorf school, worked out, at Rudolf Steiner's request, a system of gymnastics which has as its goal an in-depth experience of space and a cultivation of strength of will.

A Graded System of Exercises

After the rhythmical games and dances which have been practised in the first two classes, the actual gymnastic instruction begins in the third school-year. In keeping with the natural tendencies of the young child, it consists in the first three years in the free and joyous playing on apparatus, in gymnastic dances, and exercises in skill. The gymnastics teacher strives to stimulate the child so that he can combine feeling and fantasy with the exercises so that these never become simply bodily activities or competitive and "show-off" sports. Thus craftman's activities or characteristic animal-like movements are turned into rhythmical games. Climbing und jumping over the gymnastic apparatus becomes the acting out of stories in which adventures arise and in which helpful actions are performed. Ease and joy of movement stimulate the blood circulation and muscular activity. The child is refreshed and develops courage.

From the VI class on, the struggle with the forces of gravity as they affect the physical body is taken up ever more consciously. The mechanics of the bones and tendons must be activated and mastered. Strength and decisiveness must be concentrated in passing through hazards and tests. With increasing awareness the will is engaged in springing and swinging, in order to experience the dynamics of space and the sense of balance.

All exercises involving athletics, ball or running games as well as practice on the apparatus in the advanced classes, are arranged with the thought of gradually achieving a conscious harmony between the light and the heavy, between self-imposed goals and the demands of group exercises. It is important, especially in view of the fact that boys and girls are taught together in many Waldorf schools, that the teacher can allow for individual differences of approach. At the same time, attention to each other and a concern for weaknesses and helplessness is emphasised as a social element in such a form of gymnastic instruction. If one is successful in guiding the young people in such a way that they do not neccessarily strive for the victory of accomplishment in competition but are led to the joy in performance, which is attainable for each individual, then an essential goal of the gymnastic lesson is reached: self-assurance in moving through space, healthy strengthening of will and power of decision; social fairness and awareness.

A former student of Bothmer has vividly described how one can experience these exercises. "In the upper classes one sensed the relationship of this subject to geometry. One felt the powers of the surrounding space working upon oneself, and one responded with the will through one's own movement. Another experience was the perception of gravity in the body. Hardly had one become conscious of this gravity through the exercise 'fall into the point', when—through a rocking motion in which the counter pull arose and through a powerful upswing—it was overcome. All of this affected one as a strengthened and healthy awakening.

After the class one had not become merely fresher and warmer, as is usual after physical activity, but the greatest gain was this awakening of one's inner self through the resistance of the body. What can now be put into words was then present as an inner feeling after such gymnastic exercises. Thus Graf Bothmer succeeded in making gymnastics into a true pedagogical method: the building of the body and the awakening of conciousness were united in the exercises." (Rudolf Braumiller)

EURYTHMY

What is eurythmy? We will approach this question by quoting a few passages from well-known poems:

> Horchet! Horcht dem Sturm der Horen!
> Tönend wird für Geistesohren
> Schon der neue Tag geboren.
> Felsentore knarren rasselnd,
> Phöbus' Räder rollen prasselnd
> Welch Getöse bringt das Licht!

(Goethe, Faust Part II, Act I, Ariel-Scene)

> The fair breeze blew, the white foam
> The furrow followed free.   [flew,
> We were the first that ever burst
> Into that silent sea.

(Coleridge, The Rime of the Ancient Mariner)

> Säv, säv, susa
> Våg, våg, slå
> I sägen mig, var Ingalill,
> den unga, månde, gå.

(Fröding, the great Swedish lyrical poet)

For every listener such verses are an expression of a phenomenon that characterises all forms of poetry to a greater or lesser degree. The single sounds and words possess a value of their own well beyond their intellectual content, and appeal to a hidden realm of our inner being which lies below the threshold of consciousness.

We are not unfamiliar with the expression in movement of the contents of a poem, for example, in drama, mime, or various forms of choreography. Eurythmy, however, takes its start from the actual sounds of the language, namely vowels and consonants.

Pure vowels are often the expression of inner feeling, Ah!, Oh!, Ow!, etc. Words with strongly-accented consonants imitate happenings in the world outside, for example, rumble, clatter, whistle, rustle. In descriptive passages consonants tend to dominate, as is illustrated in the passages just quoted. But if one investigates the matter more slowly, one realises that the vowel-sounds produce a certain atmosphere in the poem. In the scene from Faust it is especially the A and O sounds, in Coleridge the Ö as in were, in Fröding Ä and O.

When we speak a sound it is accompanied by a kind of invisible gesture within us. It is this gesture which finds visible expression in the movements of eurythmy. Each vowel and consonant has its characteristic gesture. When we sing, too, similar unseen inner gestures accompany and correspond to the different tones. These also can be made visible as movement.

Eurythmy is, thus, "visible speech" and "visible song"—an art-form which did not previously exist and for which Rudolf Steiner laid the foundations. It is performed to the accompaniment of either recitation or music.

But how can one be sure that these eurythmic movements are not just arbitrary, but really do correspond to definite musical tones and sounds of speech? A merely theoretical approach will not lead far, and assurance can only be reached by one's own experience in watching a performance, or, better still, by doing eurythmy oneself.

At Dornach in Switzerland and in many other countries there are schools of eurythmy, whose trained eurythmists take part in public performances, or give eurythmy classes in Waldorf schools, or for the general public.

The Value of Eurythmy

What then is the value of eurythmy? This activity, this union of the inner experience of sound with bodily movements, leads as can no other subject to one of the chief aims of a Waldorf education; bodily movement penetrated by the forces of the inner life. In the lecture-course entitled "A social Basis for Primary and Secondary Education" (Stuttgart 11. 5.—1. 6. 1919), Rudolf Steiner stresses the educational value of eurythmy by saying, "Eurythmy can create forces of the will that remain throughout life, whereas a characteristic of other forms of education of the will is that the will weakens again later on."

Eurythmy In The Waldorf Schools

The eurythmy curriculum in the Waldorf school is wide and comprehensive. Beginning with simple rhythms and rod-exercises in the early years, it proceeds through more complicated rhythmical exercises and the simple beginnings of speech and tone eurythmy to elaborately worked-out representations of poetry, drama and music. In the regular school assemblies for children and parents, whole classes will often perform what they have learnt in class.

One of the important elements in learning eurythmy is its social aspect; each member of the class has to be aware not only of his own movements, but of that of his classmates, especially when different groups of the same class have to perform different movements simultaneously, which must flow together in a harmonious whole. This aspect stands in striking contrast to the competitive and often aggressive movement patterns which are associated with team-games of the usual kind. It is no exaggeration to say that eurythmy exerts an ennobling and socially educative influence which has valuable results in later life.

MONTHLY ASSEMBLIES

Monthly—or termly—assemblies, occupy a central place in the life of a Waldorf school. The children show each other and their parents what they have learnt in class in the way of poems, songs, plays, music etc. This may sound simple but it is quite demanding in many respects. It is not only a question of choosing a suitable item and working at it with the class as a whole, but also of taking a real interest in what other classes are presenting.

Older pupils feel amused when in the presentations of the lower classes they recognise those themes with which they themselves once worked. The younger pupils feel respect for the things which are presented by the upper classes, and they often think: "We'll be doing these things, too, one day!" For the eighteen and nineteen-year-olds the monthly festival is above all a review, and for the very young children a preview. For the pupils in the intermediate classes it is both.

When the pupils discuss their daily experiences with one another during classes and even during breaks, the most recent monthly festival is often an important topic of conversation. The feeling for what is genuine and original, which is always present in unspoilt children,

can gradually transform itself into a true and mature power of judgement. The sensitive person can learn a great deal from watching the various classes as they appear upon the stage.

Today people often speak of more general information about the background of their work as an indispensable instrument in making working life more democratic. Within the school there is probably no better means of informing the parents and the teachers about the daily life in the different classes than by these monthly assemblies.

These four pictures are taken from monthly assemblies in various schools.

THE WORLD OF LANGUAGE

Foreign languages already in the first school-year, even in the kindergarten! Is this not too early! Is it even practicable? With writing and reading the Waldorf schools, as is well-known, make a slow start. In arithmetic the methods of teaching make greater demands than usual on the child. Why, then, two foreign languages as soon as the child starts school?

Should language-teaching be conducted by a direct method based on imitation, or be based on translation, sentence-analysis and grammar? Arguments on this theme still go to and fro. Long before these discussions began, Rudolf Steiner developed a plan of language-teaching. His suggestions throw light on this problem and point the way to a solution.

Early Language Teaching in the Waldorf School

The fact that the child is still closely connected with the environment during the first three school-years (6 to 9 years) and imitation is still one of his strongest faculties, makes it obvious that only the "direct method" should be used at this stage. After the fundamental psychological changes at about the age of nine, however, language is part of the new experience of the world outside the child.

In recent years, as many readers will know, attempts are being made to introduce at least one foreign language in English schools at the primary level. At this point a consciousness for grammatical form can be awakened out of the child's experience of speaking the language. Two further observations speak in favour of an early start. The powers of thought that have begun to awaken as the result of the spoken word, become still more enlivened through the new experiences of the foreign tongue. The speech-organs, still so pliable, take on a more differentiated form than they otherwise would. Both these aspects enrich the child's soul-life.

In language lessons in the first class, little games can be played. For instance, each child can be given the name of an animal and have to perform an action when that animal's name is called. Or original singing games in the foreign tongue can be practised. The teacher can lead little conversations or tell a short story, using words the child has already learnt. In the third class, grammar too can be enlivened by rhythmical games.

The Significance of Grammar

The verb is the class of word which carries within it the greatest activity, so the learning of grammar should take its start with the simple verbs. The fourth and fifth classes should go on to the tenses and more complicated forms of the verb, as well as nouns, adjectives, exclamations, prepositions, pronouns etc. The principle is always to use many varied examples which need not be remembered and afterwards to write down and learn by heart the grammatical rules themselves. Every opportunity is taken to prevent boredom by bringing humour into the lessons. The learning of grammar should take up only a part of the lesson and, of course, should not take its examples from poetry, which should be experienced as an artistic whole.

Is it really necessary to treat grammar as something in itself? Rudolf Steiner calls it 'an inner skeleton'. It does build up a firm support in the child's inner being, just at this stage of development where consciousness needs to pass over into a stable self-consciousness. If this awakening process does not come about, not only does the pupil's own faculty of speech suffer, but his whole personality.

The Living Word

Although the learning of grammar is, therefore, important, it is not the heart of a language. The living word must always be the main thing, whether in conversation, description, recitation, the writing of essays and letters.

Every language has certain words which cannot be exactly translated, for example the German word 'Gemüt'. These words or turns of phrase with their special nuances call for careful attention on the part of the teacher. Yet although on such occasions explanation is needed, the aim should always be to use, as far as possible, the foreign language throughout the lesson. Especially in the lower classes it is not good to translate word for word. It is better for the teacher to tell a story in the foreign language first, and then let the children give a resumé in their mother-tongue or vice versa, rather than make an exact translation. When the children are older and approach the stage of taking examinations then, of course. they must learn to make detailed translations.

The language-teacher must always take pains to find little stories and jokes in the foreign language which illustrate the national characteristic in speech and behaviour alike.

For instance, an anecdote which well illustrates the difference between the Austrian and Prussian attitude to life is the following:

A little group of Viennese road-workers are trying to lift a drain-cover but after a few half-hearted attempts give it up, sit down and start chatting. A Berliner who has been watching them comes up, rolls up his sleeves and energetically proceeds to lift it. "There you are" ("Da habt Ihr's") he says proudly. Not at all impressed the Viennese gaze at him. "Well, of course, if you use brute force..." ("Ja, mit Gewalt").

Similar examples for other languages can easily be found, and one should prepare the children's understanding beforehand so that direct translation is not necessary.

Lessons in the Mother-Tongue

It is a great cultural achievement that so many children nowadays learn foreign languages. Yet it is often noticed that a real feeling for speech is gradually declining in adults as well as children and is especially noticeable in the use of the mother-tongue. In ancient Greece the practising of speech-choirs in preparation for religious festivals made a significant contribution towards a rich and wide use of words. In medieval times the traditional art of rhetoric and the study of Latin in the centres of learning exercised a strong influence on the use of language among all cultured people. We live today in the modern culture of the West, and the terse and unadorned statements of the sciences, technology and sport influence our use of speech. The decline in the ability to express oneself in words, whether in foreign languages or in one's own mother-tongue and the well-known decrease in vocabulary is well illustrated by the following incident. A Finnish traveller in a Swedish train was listening to a boy of fifteen or sixteen trying to describe to his friends a film he had seen. It was clear that the film had been about the adventures of the Scarlet Pimpernel at the time of the French Revolution. But he just could not manage to tell its contents to his friends, not even the simplest incidents. It was impossible to tell from his attempts at description whether it had been a farce, a comedy, or a serious film, let alone whether it had a "happy ending". There sat the boy, obviously full of the experience of the film but unable to express it in words. His cocksure manner gave way to obvious embarassment as he failed to make himself clear.

It is not only most important for the child's own later life but also for the continuance of human culture in general, that we strive as teachers to give the child a feeling for the subleties of speech and thereby enhance his inner life. This is a realm where the foreign language teacher co-operates with the teacher of the native language. It is important that the children learn to express themselves in properly constructed sentences, and not only in single words or ejaculations. Working at the cultivation of speech is one of the most worthwhile tasks of the teacher.

THE TEMPERAMENTS

Knowledge of the temperaments is rooted in antiquity. In recent times it has been presented anew by Immanuel Kant and Wilhelm Wundt, among others. Although many modern psychologists have considered it outdated, in recent years it has gained renewed attention through extensive research. This research has shown that the polarities choleric-phlegmatic and sanguine-melancholic correspond exceptionally well to certain basic one-sided forces of the human soul-life (cf. 'Facts and Fiction in Psychology' by the well-known English psychologist, H. J. Eysenck).

Rudolf Steiner has thrown new light on the concept of temperaments through his study of the human being. He considers learning to know the temperaments of his pupils as one of the teacher's most important tasks. Let us, therefore, go on to consider examples of the four temperaments in characteristic scenes from school life. Some of the manifestations of temperament are easy to recognise:

Some Characteristic Examples

As a rule, choleric children revel in danger. In a eurythmy lesson in Class 1 the children were asked to join hands and quietly form a completely round circle. Inside the circle, said the teacher, the sun was shining but outside there were great dark clouds which they were going to chase away with their movements. But the children were not quiet and the circle was not round. So the teacher began to describe imaginatively how thunder and lightning would soon start to come out of the thick, dark clouds outside the circle. After an expectant pause, a choleric child said delightedly, "Go on then. Do it!"

Phlegmatics usually take things calmly, even when by normal standards anger would be justified. During a drawing lesson in one of the younger classes, a child snatched away a box of chalks belonging to a phlegmatic boy.

The lad went on drawing and commented slowly and gently: "Oh, blast!" Rather shocked, the teacher asked: "What did you say just then?" Slowly and amiably the answer came: "I said oh blast, because David's pinched my chalks."

Melancholic children are sensitive but egocentric. Of all types, they find it most difficult to forgive if the teacher in their opinion does something unjust. The children of class III were lining up outside their classroom ready to go in. There was a disturbance in the queue and the teacher, thinking it was caused by a

rather highly-strung melancholic boy, told him to wait outside until asked to come in. Having started off the lesson, she opened the door to call him but found that he had disappeared. A few hours later a note was found at the main entrance to the school. It was obviously from the little truant and said: "There is a teacher called . . . (her name was given a comic twist) and she says a person is talking when he is not."

Sanguine children usually take life very lightly. Walking along a passage, a teacher came across two giggling little girls hiding in a corner. When asked what they were doing there in the middle of lesson time they said that they had been sent out of their class. "But why were you sent out?" "Oh, our teacher wasn't feeling very well this morning so he sent us out at the beginning of the lesson." On being told to go back to their classroom they

commented with further giggles: "He probably isn't feeling *that* much better yet!"

It is not always very easy to distinguish sanguine children from the rest, since virtually all children have a certain amount of sanguinity in their make-up. With their urge to pass abruptly from one impression to the next, children are born impressionists. It is this characteristic which lends such irresistible charm to their letters and essays. Here is just one example from an essay written in class VII: "Martin Luther had many children. He said: 'Here I stand, I can do no other!'"

The four temperaments are no theory. The teacher can experience anew every day how they come to expression in the child. In many cases it is the temperament that is the key for the understanding and treatment of a child's most striking characteristics.

Colour exercises typical of the four tempera-
ments: Page 88 — Choleric, Page 89 — Phleg-
matic, Page 90 — Melancholic, Page 91 — San-
guine.
The temperament is revealed not only through
the choice and composition of colours, but in the
way of painting and the final forms.

The temperaments also have their serious side and they can be the cause of quite serious problems at puberty if the tendency towards one of the four is too marked. A brief description of four young people will help to make this clear.

Penny is a sanguine. At fifteen she is a slender, wellgrown girl with a round childish face, fair hair, and brown eyes which flit from object to object in search of something that can hold her attention. She was already falling violently in and out of love at the age of eleven, usually with boys considerably older than herself. At fifteen, she stays out late with her current boyfriend, who is a member of a jazz band. Her parents, who are nice, respectable people, have insufficient contact with Penny. They once tried to persuade her not to go to the band's evening rehearsal, but the scene she made was such that they are not likely to try this again. During lessons she alternates between great enthusiasm manifested in questions and exclamations, and complete apathy. She keeps pace well with the rest of her class, thanks to her intelligence and a considerable portion of impudence.

When she has not done her homework her excuses are usually quite convincing but often turn out to be untrue. When confronted with this, she is briefly ashamed but recovers quickly. She loves water, swims like a fish, and in many ways reminds one of a water sprite, unapproachable and unpredictable. But she also has quite other, deeper traits. She has considerable character. When difficult decisions have to be made at home, it is quite often Penny who speaks the final word, with great prudence and good sense. If there are no external disturbances she can work very energetically. Which will prove stronger—Penny's temperament, irresponsible and unpredictable, or her true nature hiding underneath?

Samuel's temperament is melancholic. He is tall and thin and has a dreamy expression. His mother died when he was five and his father started occupying him with mechanical gadgets when he was very young. As a small child he frequently choked while asleep and awoke almost suffocated. His digestive system was weak and he suffered from stomach cramp.

When he joined the third class of a Waldorf school at the age of nine, he was a small, almost wizened little book-worm. During his first interview, a bulb went in one of the lamps. This precocious little professor said: "I expect there's something wrong with the wiring. If you show me the circuit diagram I'll soon put it right." He loved his new school and had a particularly good relationship with his teacher. He usually sat quite still during lessons, listening intently, though his bodily ailments sometimes distracted his attention. The most noticeable change in him was the development of quite exceptional imaginative powers. He was capable of entirely losing himself in the descriptive parts of his essays, often forgetting what he was really supposed to be writing about. Now that he is seventeen, he is a tall, slim boy with a dreamy expression. His artistic abilities have grown, his drawing is evocative and his love of music absorbing.

He enters deeply into all the artistic activities of the school. This provides a healthy balance for his ineradicable "professorial" tendencies.

His favourite subjects in school are chemistry and biology. He does a lot of studying on his own, makes his own experiments and is capable of giving lengthy lectures stuffed with figures and formula. Apart from the things he learns, his favourite subject in life is—himself. He is introverted and egocentric in a quite naive way. And yet on the other hand he has a very deep sympathy with all those who are weak and oppressed. Which of his traits will become dominant as he grows older—his egocentricity and introversion, or his interest in the world and his sympathy for those who suffer?

Emma is phlegmatic. As a child her greatest delight was derived from food and babies. She loved to visit families with smaller children, with whom she played for hours. Once she joined some children of her own age in giving a puppet performance. Her puppet was a princess who was supposed to be anxiously awaiting the outcome of a battle between a dragon and an elephant. Instead the little princess bored her audience to tears with a lengthy lecture on recipes and cooking. When aged about eleven, she was with a group of youngsters who were discussing what they would do if they were allowed to spend ten minutes in a toy shop, choosing as many things as they liked. Emma sat still while the others revelled in descriptions of all the toys they would quickly take. At length she said longingly: "If only I could stay in the shop a bit longer!" Going for walks with other children she would dreamily bring up the rear. Her performance in school was average and she was conscientious about homework. But her ability to express herself was poor and her understanding often unclear. At fourteen for a short time she was transformed. Her eyes became vivacious and her glance filled with sudden desires. Her dress was provocative. But soon she returned to her placid ways. Now, at the age of seventeen, she has a kind of voluptuous beauty that reminds one of Italy or Spain.

Only the temperament does not fit the picture. Had Emma not been sent to a Waldorf school, she would probably not have been able to cope adequately with secondary education. But it is just the studies of the older classes and also the artistic activities which she needs in order to be jolted again and again out of her inner lethargy. What does the future hold for her? If she develops into an active human being she will be able to do so much good with her harmonious and easy-going nature. But with her tendency towards the comfortable and the trivial there is a danger that she might sink into passivity.

Eric is choleric. At the early age of eight he looked his mother in a cupboard when she attempted to forbid something. Much of his upbringing lay in the hands of his two elder brothers, also cholerics, who were constantly fighting each other. Their favourite occupation together is sailing, and Eric has come near to drowning several times. But he loves danger. At home he was unmanageable and no school would keep him for long. He had an unfailing eye for the weaknesses, embarrasments and uncertainties of adults and made merciless use of his observations. In the end he was sent to a Waldorf school abroad. Fortunately he found himself in the hands of a teacher for whom he developed a genuine respect. The goodness of his nature began to emerge more strongly. He was fair and helpful to other children as long as they respected his superiority. But he could not bear to fit in with a group for long and hated school excursions and other collective activities. From time to time he became deeply depressed. On entering the upper school he was at first interested in all the subjects offered and took pleasure in co-operating and working. But gradually his unruliness broke through again to such an extent that his exploits included throwing a book at one teacher, hitting another, and demanding the right to choose the subjects he wished to study. This latter was even supported by his older brothers who claimed that he was 'so mature'. Only his final year at school passed without any violent incidents. He is now seventeen, is very strong, has red hair and looks thickset and uncouth. His protruding eyes almost give the impression of being in some way an additional pair of limbs. What will happen to Eric now that he has left school? Will he remain the eternal rebel, ever dissatisfied? Or will he be able to tame his temperament and put his intelligence and his ability in leadership to fruitful use?

Using our Knowledge of the Temperaments

What possibilities have we of helping children through education to cope with the one-sidedness and excesses sometimes caused by the temperaments?

First of all it must be emphasised that it would be in vain to try and suppress the manifestations of a child's temperament or persuade the child to "pull himself together". These are forces which must find an outlet and be lived to the full. This may sound almost Freudian but the therapy indicated by Rudolf Steiner has entirely individual nuances.

For instance, he recommends that the teacher should arrange his class in four groups, each of one temperament (of course, without the knowledge of the children). It is not difficult to understand why the melancholic children like sitting next to one another: they are not likely to be annoyed or perhaps even punched by their neighbours. But what of the others?

According to Steiner, the sanguines and cholerics rub off their liveliness on one another

and calm down after a while, whereas the phlegmatics grow bored with each other and try to become more lively.

The following once occurred in the middle of a lesson: after sitting for months quietly and peacefully besides a little soul-companion, a phlegmatic boy jumped up in exasperation crying, "Oh, it's so boring sitting next to Jane, please let me sit somewhere else!"

Steiner made many other suggestions. Without any theoretical psychological knowledge, children can be helped to look at themselves.

In a lecture given on August 22, 1919, Steiner says: "Let us suppose you are telling your class about the horse. You notice that a sanguine child in the group is thinking about something quite different. You try to make the child aware of this by asking him a question which proves that his thoughts are elsewhere. Then you find and show to the class that one of the melancholic children is still thinking about the cupboard you were talking of at the beginning of the lesson. So you say to the sanguine child: "You see! You have already forgotten all about the horse while your friend is still thinking about the cupboard!"

If the teacher wishes to devote a few minutes to the phlegmatic group, he can startle them into attention and make them receptive for what he has to say by making a sudden noise, perhaps clattering with a bunch of keys, and then keep them on their toes by asking them questions.

And in order to forestall an outburst of temper, a choleric can be sent out to climb a tree for a few minutes. One teacher had two cholerics in his class who needed to work off some of their boisterous energy. He made a secret arrangement with them so that the rest of the class should not wish to participate in the little plan. When he made a certain sign, the two boys were allowed to leave the room and run once round the school house. The system functioned perfectly and the two boys were much more attentive in the lesson.

Among the varied indications for educational treatment Rudolf Steiner also mentions diet. In the case of phlegmatics who are inclined to eat too much and too often, it is a good thing to avoid eggs and egg dishes. Cholerics who are themselves of a fiery nature should be given no strong spices. It is good for sanguine children who love sweet things not to have too many sweets; whereas on the other hand many a melancholic child will benefit from an extra allowance. If a class-teacher can establish the right kind of contact with the childrens' parents, they will usually be grateful for such suggestions.

Some Problems

The picture which emerges from a brief description of this kind is of necessity sketchy and simplified. Obviously examples as "pure" as those described above are relatively rare. Most children and adults have a mixture of temperaments. One must regard the melancholic disposition as the opposite of the sanguine temperament, and phlegmatic and choleric as another opposite pair.

We would assume that, for instance, a choleric or phlegmatic person would also have sanguine and/or melancholic traits respectively but that it would be unusual if marked phlegmatic and choleric traits were to be found in one and the same person, or if a sanguine person also turned out to be melancholic. That this is indeed the case in general has been confirmed both by Steiner and by Eysenck on the basis of entirely different approaches. Nevertheless, as a teacher one does come across exceptions: seemingly phlegmatic children who turn out to be extremely boisterous and irritable, or children who belie their melancholic expression, retiring nature and slender build with excessively restless and fidgety behaviour. In such cases it can be virtually impossible to distinguish between the traits which could be called the child's "own" and those which have been brought about by the environment.

A teacher who had studied Rudolf Steiner's educational ideas was to teach a young class in a school situated in a rural area. In order to gain a picture of her new pupils, she let them all paint on the first day of school. Afterwards she sorted the paintings into four groups, those with a lot of red, those with a lot of yellow, those with a lot of blue, and finally a group with blurred mixtures of colours. She assumed that this was an expression of the four temperaments and seated the children accordingly next day. Then she gave each child a roll of household paper with which he was to line his desk. The "red" children immediately began a fight with their rolls, the "yellow" eagerly set to and busied themselves with the job in hand, and the "blues" and the "blurred mixtures" just sat and waited for help. The teacher's assumption that the "reds" were cholerics, the "yellows" sanguines, the "blues" melancholics and the "mixtures" phlegmatics was borne out in an almost comical manner.

However, when the same teacher moved to a Waldorf school in a large town the same experiment did not lead to such clear results. And by direct observation it was equally difficult to "sort" the children into groups. They were too "nervy" and though most of them did grow calmer as time went on, it remained difficult to discern a dominant temperament in most cases. This is a common experience of many Waldorf school teachers.

What is Temperament?

Now that we have considered a number of concrete examples we can discuss the most basic question: What actually is temperament? In order to get at this problem we shall proceed from two basic facts.

On the one hand temperament is very deeply rooted in the human being. Deliberately to change his temperament is one of the most difficult inner tasks a person can undertake. From the examples we have shown it is obvious that the spiritual manifestation of the temperament can break forth in an intense and clear-cut way, and that a particular inner predisposition can even be bound up with a special physiological characteristic (especially clear in the cases of Samuel and Eric). We have probably all observed that many cholerics show a thick-set build. The intimate connection between a harmoniously rounded stature and the phlegmatic temperament, and between a lanky, thin figure and the melancholic temperament has often been observed and has been confirmed through the well-known investigations of Ernst Kretschmer.

On the other hand it is worthy of note that a person's temperament often changes a good deal during the course of his life quite without his own doing. In general one can say that each period of life exhibits its own characteristic temperament. Just as a tendency to be sanguine is usually inherent in every healthy child, so in every young person one finds outbursts of a choleric nature, in the adult a touch of serious melancholy, and in the elderly a mood of phlegmatic reflection.

Thus deeply rooted in human nature, and yet subject to change, the temperament is a complicated and mysterious phenomenon. Whence does it originate? Rudolf Steiner describes how the four members of the human being here become manifest. According to the way the requirements of the child's physical body, of his life-forces, of his soul life, or his ego, the actual spiritual individuality, predominate, so the temperament appears to us as phlegmatic, sanguine, choleric, melancholic. In a grown-up, in whom the interaction of body, soul and spirit takes place in a different way, the manifestations of the temperament also change. The often very striking variations in temperament, which occur before or during puberty, are related to the inner readjustments we are talking about. A more detailed description of the laws underlying this particular process of development would lead us too far at the moment (cf. Discussions with Teachers, Rudolf Steiner, 21. 8. 1924).

The Relationship between the Temperament and the Life-Forces

If the human being as a whole is involved in the creation of the manifestations of his temperament, there is nevertheless one part of his being which is marked by his personal temperament in a special way and which is especially noticeable. It concerns that level in which the etheric powers are to be sought, those powers which keep the physical body alive and give it its form. The memory and habits of a human being are, as Steiner has often described, woven into this field of power (cf. 'The Education of the Child', 1909). From this perspective we can see that the effects of the temperament are very influential and often reveal themselves in a very elemental way. The temperament itself is related to powerful supersensible structural forces. Whoever realises this can also understand that the climate, the earth, the customs, the language and the spiritual-intellectual atmosphere of a region or a country can so strongly influence the inner bearing of the person concerned (especially if he has grown up there) that one may speak of a characteristic "folk temperament" of the inhabitants of a specific region, although there may, of course, be marked exceptions.

Observed in this way the difficulty of finding a dominant temperament among nervously disposed children points to a really serious symptom of our times. That such children are fidgety is no indication of inner strength, liveliness is not the same as nervousness. On the contrary, Rudolf Steiner has described in a lecture of January 11, 1912, how aimless involuntary movements of the physical body indicate a weakness in the active "etheric field of energy"; meaningful movements indicate that this "field" is influencing and controlling the physical body in a healthy way. Teaching methods which tediously cram dead facts into the pupil's head result in an intensification of this tendency—simply because the feeling human soul is not connected to the outer activity in such a case. A weakness of this kind can be found in many children today.

In the light of this uncertainty it is becoming increasingly clearer that it is not simply a question of directing the children to somehow "control" their temperaments. The point is rather for the teacher first of all to approach the different temperaments vigorously and with full consciousness as he stands before the children in the classroom. In the chapters "Teaching Arithmetic", "Finding a Relationship with Colours", and "Study of the Animal Kingdom", examples are given of how the teacher can address himself to the individual temperaments in the most diverse subjects. Nowadays it appears more important than ever that the teacher should stimulate the vitality of his pupils through really lively teaching. When this happens, experience has shown that the predominant temperament suddenly reveals itself and often from a quite unexpected direction.

One simple example will serve as an illustration. A fifteen-year-old boy entered Class Nine of a Waldorf school. He had not got on very well with his classmates in the previous school. At the beginning he was shy and uncommunicative and sat almost benumbed in his seat. If anything disturbed his brooding, he often became frightened and shook uncontrollably. It seemed that he was of a melancholic temperament. After a while, however, he became talkative and turned out to be a happy sanguine person, who more and more through his droll jokes got the class to laugh. His vitality increased and his improvement lasted.

The Temperament of the Teacher

Though it is not always easy to apply Rudolf Steiner's observations about diagnosing and dealing with the temperaments in practice, there is no doubt that his descriptions are both valid and useful. The teacher who wishes to help his pupils to cope with their temperaments must learn to control his own as far as possible. He must keep his own fully developed one-sidedness within bounds and awaken those qualities which have hitherto been dormant in him.

The demands made on him in his dealings with the various temperaments will include among others the following:

Whenever possible he will have to ask questions and speak about his subject

— so rapidly that the sanguines will have to make an effort to keep up;
— with such human fascination that the melancholics will forget themselves;

— so dramatically that the cholerics are really interested and the phlegmatics shaken out of their apathy.

The point is not to work *against* the temperament but with it, to go along with it a certain way, but then gently to harmonise and change it.

Furthermore, he should be able to develop the following moods and feelings in himself:

— the phlegmatics should be aware of his genuine human interest in them, however uninterested he may appear to be outwardly;
— the sanguines should perceive as well as his ability to flit from one impression to another his seriousness and his perseverance in observing the world;
— the melancholics must observe his ability to overcome the difficulties of life with the help of good humour;
— the cholerics must experience his cool self-control, even when they have an outburst of temper.

The Teacher's Education of Himself

No human being can educate himself to perfection. But to attempt to do so and to think about it consciously can be a great help, and once in a while something can be achieved.

Most of us are in the habit of behaving largely according to what we think is our own nature or the mood we happen to be in. "I am what I am, I can't go beyond my own limits" or "I can't help it, I'm in a bad mood today." But this is not enough if we wish to educate ourselves even a little. If he wishes to react in a way which is necessary for the good of his pupils, the teacher must have the *will* at least sometimes to raise himself above his temperament or his momentary mood.

One of the most useful shocks a teacher can give his pupils is to react in an unexpected manner. It can be a tremendous effort for a choleric teacher to remain absolutely calm if one of the children persistently disturbs the lesson, a situation that might formerly have moved him to anger. And yet this reaction, so different from the expected outburst to which the children are perhaps all too accustomed, can open the way for a quite new and fruitful relationship between teacher and pupils.

A really thunderous "reading of the riot act" by a teacher who is normally calm or passive can be equally effective and fruitful. What matters is that he has to *force* himself to behave in the way he does.

The case of a melancholic teacher in one of the higher classes can give us another illustration. Being melancholic, his desire for clarity and order meant the pace of his lessons was too slow and the children spent a good deal of time chatting and making unnecessary remarks. And in spite of the slow pace, the lack of concentration meant that some children complained of not being able to keep up. This situation came to a head one day when a girl announced that she was not learning enough and had decided to leave school, a step which several of her classmates were also considering.

The teacher decided to try and give his lessons a more "sanguine" character, more speed, more facts, more colour, and more unexpected aside remarks. As a result the children became more alert, nobody mentioned leaving school any more, and despite the greater speed no one complained of being unable to keep pace.

Parents can also help their children if they learn to control themselves and do not fall into the trap of reacting to the child's temperament. A very choleric girl once made a tremendous scene and then slammed the door as she left the room. Her father calmly called her back and asked her to close the door quietly. She walked out and slammed the door again, and the whole scene was repeated once more. But her father still remained calm, called her back yet again and then gently lifted the door off its hinges and propped it against the wall. The girl was speechless, calmed down at once, and the normally good relationship between father and daughter was able to run its course once more.

DIFFERENTIATED RELIGIOUS INSTRUCTION

Nowadays many people are of the opinion that in their early years children should be spared any religious instruction and that, in any case, they ought to have a strongly "objective" religious education in the schools. At some future time they should be able to decide whether or not they wish to follow a religion.

An Experiment in Thought

We should like to conduct a thought experiment. Suppose that Mr and Mrs Smith have arrived at the view that their children should decide for themselves whether or not they want to become interested in music. The think a musical education would intrude upon their children's freedom. Thus it is denied them. The parents carry out their idea to all its practical consequences: the gramophone, the piano and grandfather's violin are sold. The mouth organ lands in the dustbin. Father stops singing in the bath. The children go to a school whose teachers maintain a similar standpoint, according to the direction of the highest educational administrative authority. The pupils must read and listen to numerous facts about musical styles, epochs and the great masters of music. In addition they must learn something about elementary music theory. But some things they must never do. They must not sing, play an instrument or listen to music.

The Smith children reach the age of puberty and begin to select their own interests. Through their own free time and association with friends they cannot avoid coming into contact with various sorts of pop music, which they perhaps enjoy. However, the music instruction in the school was, for them, dreary and boring.

Their path to the great musical tradition of the West is irrevocably closed. If, during a visit they should by chance hear a movement from Beethoven's "Missa Solemnis" or a piano sonata by Mozart, then it is only a sequence of meaningless sounds to their ears.

The Smith parents had an admirable motive; to give their children freedom. The measures taken, however, produced precisely the opposite effect. Their freedom was curtailed. The children will never blame their parents for this. They have no idea of what they have been deprived. Should someone be so tactless as to ask them their opinion of a composer or a musical genre, they would generally answer with a shrug of the shoulder, "I'm not musically inclined".

Should the ideas of Mr and Mrs Smith be practised by a great many families and at the same time be introduced into the central school system, then the consequences for the musical life of the country would become obvious in two generations; the concert halls would be virtually empty; the music shops would have to close; and most musicians would have to pursue another profession. The lives of many people would be profoundly influenced in a culture which had made a clean sweep of its musical life which had taken centuries to develop. In short, in the field of music we should find ourselves in a situation which in certain respects is reminiscent of the one we have at present in the field of religion.

Religious Predisposition

Of course the throught experiment is absurd, however it hits the heart of the problem. We know very well that the innate talents of children need care and attention if they are to develop into useful abilities. This point has been especially well established in the field of intellectual development. There is good evidence that parents can strongly influence the development of their children's intelligence in a positive manner by playing with, and above all speaking to, them during their first years of life. It would never occur to a psychologist to recommend to parents that they refrain from playing and speaking with their children in hopes of thereby enabling their children at a mature age to decide for themselves whether or not they wish to develop intellectually.

How many people today are complacent about religion: "I'm not concerned about whether or not there is a God", or discontented: "I should very much like to pray to a higher power but it's impossible for me." This is not because of any innate absence of religious interest but rather because their education was lacking in this respect.

No one would maintain that letting children sing and play the recorder during the early years of their lives is incompatible with their future choice of interests. If it is pursued completely as a matter of course, then early training in music is actually the best way to secure their freedom of choice. Only when they have acquired the ability of perception and skills through practice can the children later develop into musicians or music-loving amateurs. Not until they are fully acquainted with music are they also free to arrive at an opinion regarding listening to concerts or making music themselves.

There is no reason to believe that the same problem is essentially any different in the field of religion. Nevertheless, as the course of history shows, one's religious experience has a greater significance for one's life-style than one's musical experience. Keeping a child away from religion is, therefore, a greater deprivation than excluding it from the reality of music.

Religious Freedom

Religious freedom is not complete if it does not include the possibility of becoming religious.

Here is a topical problem, which can be expressed a bit crassly in the following way: are there reasons for atheistic parents to allow their children to take part in religious experiences, even at kindergarten age, in order to assure their future freedom of choice—by, for example, compelling themselves to pray with them?

The formulation of this question is hypothetical. Such a mode of acting would be deeply dishonest. Of all the insincere situations into which one could place a child, this would be one of the worst.

To anyone who penetrates and accepts the anthroposophical concept of man, it becomes increasingly self-evident that one should respect elementary facts of life. For him the interaction between the milieu of the home and the children appears as a significant configuration, which cannot be judged from the standpoint of personal wishes. No one has the right of interference in this sphere.

Anyone who has experienced atheistic families in which a good and deep-seated contact exists between the parents and the children and, on the other hand, religious homes in which human relationships are warped or neglected, will refrain from making generalised judgements.

The Practice in Waldorf Schools

The views which teachers in the Waldorf schools are accustomed to take in the field of religious instruction becomes clear when one sees them against the background of such considerations.

When the first Waldorf school was founded in 1919, it was the original idea of Rudolf Steiner to allocate the special religious instruction to representatives of the Catholic and Evangelical-Protestant churches, according to the wish and denomination of the parents. But at the same time, he was anxious to respond to the requests which were put to him by those parents without denominational affiliations: to create another form of religious instruction aimed at meeting the special needs of each age-group. Thus the "free Christian religious instruction" was established.

With due regard for local cultural conditions this practice was applied, with certain variations, in different countries. Every religious community should have the possibility, within the framework of the school schedule or at other times, to give religious instruction if the parents so desire. It is warmly recommended that parents allow their children to take part in some form of religious instruction.

The representatives of the different religious bodies arrange their instruction with complete freedom. A certain degree of collaboration with the other teachers on the question of handling the children is, of course, desirable. Many of the visiting religious teachers make a close contact with the school, since the religious element in the children is cultivated in a non-denominational manner within the framework of the curriculum as a whole. Others prefer to come and go unobtrusively. The irreplaceable pedagogical value of truly religious instruction can only be touched on here. It lies in the fact that a striving for depth, for transformation, and for inner growth is called on. Self-development of the young person and a reverence before a higher world are both elements that exert a positive influence.

The Free Christian Religious Instruction

The independent Christian religious instruction is given by Waldorf school teachers. As with the denominational instruction, it stands outside the general curriculum of the Waldorf school and is given so to speak as private instruction within the school.

It is primarily Christian, without being bound to any denomination. From puberty onwards into their later life, the pupils should be enabled by their earlier religious teaching to take a mature and perceptive stand on religious questions. In classes I to IV, the instruction is based on stories which instil respect for God and the divine in nature and which give strong impulses for developing human qualities such as gratitude, love of the truth, devotion and a willingness to help others. In classes V to VIII, stories are given from the Gospels and biographical descriptions of historical personalities who have come from very different cultural and religious milieus and who have also solved their life problems in an exemplary fashion. In classes IX to XII, descriptions of the history of religion and the church are given, including the presentation of non-Christian religions. The above-mentioned age-groupings need not always be strictly adhered to. Biographical portrayals can be given as early as class IV, if the teacher finds it suitable for the particular class.

For those children who take part in the independent religious instruction, a religious service instituted by Steiner is held once a week. Participation in the 'Sunday service' for children up to class VIII; "Youth service" for classes IX and X; and the "Festival of Offering" for older students is, of course, voluntary. Parents of the children are also welcome on these occasions.

The Principle of Tolerance

Occasionally the question is asked whether there is not the risk that a differentiated religious instruction of the type given in the Waldorf school can lead to unhealthy group feelings or even to intolerance.

Anyone who has worked for a few years in such a school has often had experiences that disprove such fears. It is a question of a basic principle. Tolerance, the spiritual attitude of respect and understanding for other people and their philosophy of life, runs as a strong and deep current throughout the biography of Rudolf Steiner and belongs to the strongest impulses which he has left behind as a heritage to his students. In his most important philosophical works, 'The Philosophy of Freedom', one of the most crucial passages runs as follows: "To live in love of the action and to let live with an understanding for the will-impulses of others is the principal maxim of the free human being." (Chapter IX, 'Die Idee der Freiheit', p. 171).

The same motive runs like an unbroken thread through the whole Waldorf pedagogy. It is expressed especially well in a course which Rudolf Steiner held for teachers in Czechoslovakia and Germany in April 1923. In one of these lectures he summarises the aims of the Waldorf pedagogy with regard to the education for social living in a few short words: "Just think what flows from these two things, loving devotion in one's own actions, an understanding interest in the actions of others. It then follows that human beings can work together socially. This you can pass on from generation to generation. In no other way will you bring it forth; you must fetch it from the very depths of human nature." (23. 3. 1923)

When the religious groups, organised according to the wishes of the parents, disappear into different class-rooms, the Waldorf school then realises a principle of tolerance and thereby helps to produce such an attitude in the pupils. Such a procedure can be felt as being quite in keeping with the spirit of the times. The widely divergent ways in which human beings think are after all a fact. It is of no use to try to wipe out certain views or to pretend that they do not exist. The only thing that we can do is to learn to recognise in full consciousness our fundamental inner differences and for that very reason to learn to live in full mutual understanding for one another.

CONCERNING
THE IDEA
OF FREEDOM

Realising that Waldorf pedagogy aims at developing moral impulses, the question might arise whether or not the students will become "stamped" with preconceived views. The answer to this question must be a definite "no", but it is well worth while to make sufficiently clear, how much must be done and borne in mind by the teacher, if young people are to be led towards a true individual freedom.

It must be kept in mind that each child, during his period of education, undergoes, as a natural necessity of his development, great transformations of his bodily constitution, of his perceptive faculties and experiences, and of his thought structure or state of consciousness. The child must find himself and his own view of the world through experiences in life and through social interaction and then through self-discovery he must learn to find his destined human environment and his task in the world.

If the teacher has his own decisive view of the world, then does he not, to a certain extent, impose his own views on the child during this changeable and impressionable period of life?

The Role of Anthroposophy

If one knew nothing about Rudolf Steiner and Anthroposophy, one might be inclined to think that the Waldorf teachers, with their anthroposophically-orientated view of the world, would carry out their daily work out of an impulse to make converts to their own point of view. This conception is based on a misunderstanding of what Anthroposophy is actually about. Anthroposophy is not a form of religion. Neither is it a final system of dogmatic ideas. It is instead a *path* for attaining a knowledge of the world and mankind. Whoever sufficiently pursues this path of inner development, with its exercises for developing the life of the intellect, the will and the feeling, can, through direct experience, become certain that our physical existence is permeated by a "supersensible" world and that man's inner being stems from this sphere, although people today are generally not aware of this. For children and young people up to about eighteen, it is generally uninteresting and, in any case, unsuitable in principle, for them to engage in the study of Anthroposophy and the inner exercises which are connected with such a path of development.

The teacher does not need Anthroposophy, in order to present it directly in his class, but rather for his own development. Rudolf Steiner emphasised often and quite forcibly, that a teacher, through such inner training, could fundamentally improve his pedagogical skill and his ability to perceive the stages of development of the child.

The Task of Waldorf Education

The task of the teacher is not to infringe on the pupil's self, or "I", but rather to help the instrument, the body and soul, to develop in such a way that the individuality, the spirit, can eventually live freely within it.

But how can one carry through such subtle differences in actual practice?

Since Waldorf pedagogy was founded by Rudolf Steiner, one might ask how he himself would answer such a basic question: "The task of the teacher is the greatest self-denial; in the presence of the child he must so live, that the child's spirit can develop its own life in sympathy with the life of his teacher. One must never wish to make the children into a mirror image of oneself. That which was in the teacher himself should not live on in the pupils in compulsion and tyranny, after they have grown up and left school. One must bring children up in such a way that one eliminates the physical and spiritual hindrances to make way for that which, in each generation, enters the world anew from a divine world order through the children. For each pupil one must also create an atmosphere, through which his spirit can enter life in full freedom." (19. 8. 1922)

Whoever cannot imagine that there is a supersensible world in which the human being originates, may find such a passage incomprehensible or peculiar. Whoever sees the possibility of living within the new perspectives which the anthroposophical conception of the human being offers, will learn much from these words. What is meant by the "self-denial" of the teacher one can experience concretely in any relation with children, and by this means find his own way to "serve" the child's individuality instead of "forming" it. But there are yet deeper reasons why any wish to convert others to his own world-view must remain foreign to the Waldorf teacher.

The Concept of Reincarnation

The task of the teacher consists in shaping his teaching material, in cultivating the general habits of life of his pupils, and regulating the activities of the class as a whole. In no way, however, does it consist in shaping the innermost being of the child. The child's ego, or "I", his individuality, comes from supersensible worlds. When it enters physical existence through birth, it carries with it definite capacities and intentions which cannot be derived from heredity or environment, and which, as a rule, cannot come to full expression until adulthood. Through observing external symptoms the teacher ought to try to form for himself a picture of these future possibilities hidden in the innermost being of the child. Sometimes the teacher can get the impression that in his class individualities manifest themselves which are strikingly "old" and "wise". In addition to the characteristics which are clearly determined by age, environment and inheritance, they possess something of an inner maturity in gesture and intonation of speaking which otherwise is only found in people experienced in life. Without giving way to superficial speculation, in such situations one can have the immediate and strong feeling of confronting manifestations of individuality which come from an earlier life on earth. In meeting with such an individuality the teacher can often feel "younger" or even inferior. To say this directly to the pupil in question would, of course, be completely inadvisable. The inner respect must express itself in quite a different form.

Through Anthroposophy one gains a respect for the human individuality. This respect allows Anthroposophy—in contrast to usual world-conceptions—to become an actual help for the instructor who wishes to avoid impressing an unjustified "stamp" on his pupils.

As a Waldorf teacher, one can only advise those doubters, to whom these ideas are presented and who still cannot rid themselves of the suspicion of more or less hidden missionary efforts, to test the facts themselves or to speak to former pupils.

It must be emphasised that the things which are discussed here are seldom or never experienced as problematic in the daily work of the school. Sooner or later, the pupils discover that their teachers are "Anthroposophists", or that they, in any case, have a special kind of worldview. If they make jokes about it, then the teacher tries to answer with a joke. Any deeper interest on the part of the pupils is not the rule, as long as they are still in school. Should questions arise in the upper classes, naturally the teacher must give an answer; at the same time he must strive for the same objectivity that he would use in answering other questions concerning world views. It is not his task to lead the students in one direction or the other along a specific path, but rather to place material at their disposal, which will enable them to form their own opinion.

Pupils and Teachers

Through the manner of working and the human relationships to which one aspires in a Waldorf school, pupils and teachers often grow very close to one another. Is it not then inevitable that the influence, which at least some of the teachers have on the pupils should go beyond the pedagogical and human effect of the classroom and extend into the realm of one's general view of life? Since the Waldorf schools have no intention of becoming "philosophical institutions", this question must be taken very seriously. Naturally students will be more readily influenced by a teacher they like, than by one with whom they are ill at ease. However, it is also true that they will not really admire any teacher who does not completely respect their inner freedom. From about the seventh and eighth classes on and through the entire upper grades in the Waldorf school, one can notice again and again that although the philosophical differences between groups of pupils on the one hand and their teacher on the other become very deep, (even if these differences are mutually concealed, as is often the case) human contact, however, remains totally unaffected. People can admire one another greatly, even if they think in quite different ways. Naturally Waldorf teachers, like any other teachers, cannot prevent their pupils from taking on, in unthinking ways, small personal traits as well as more or less clearly conceived thoughts from those who instruct them. In this sense *all* education is "influencing".

If we allow the pupils to receive their knowledge from machines instead of teachers, in order to free them from all unauthorised or intentionally damaging influences, they are still, nevertheless, influenced by the very fact that they become bored. An upper school-boy from the Albert Schweitzer Gymnasium in Erlangen said of such teaching machines, "They're fun to play with. But they're less useful for learning, because one doesn't have to find one's own answers."

The essential thing is that the unavoidable influence does not work in a way that creates a uniform outlook and that on the other hand it encourages a development which is in harmony with the pupil's own personal disposition.

The First Eight Years of School

THE RIGHT TIME TO BEGIN

The Transition from Play to Work

The drawings and paintings of children in the nursery class are rather like the tracks left by a bird which has alighted on the snow for a moment and then taken flight again. It is a wonderful experience to dive into the world of colour but perseverance is not important. It is just the same with singing and movement and all other activities. Everything is play, the enjoyment of the experience of the moment and the final result is of no significance.

Seven-year-olds are very different. They are much more down-to-earth. If they are healthy and harmonious in their development, they can spend quite a time every morning hard at work. But they must have something concrete to work at, such as learning a poem, playing the recorder, painting a picture, shaping letters or figures. Their way of painting or drawing is very individual. Many children will sit patiently for a considerable time, surrounding a letter or a number with one glowing colour after another. Some will go on and on until they go right through the paper. The whole class will be one with their teacher in pondering about special moods of colour. What colours belong to January? Greyish-white and blue! And what about June? Perhaps green, red and yellow. And, of course, the forms must differ too in each case.

Some children can be extremely lazy and careless. It often needs quite an effort on the teacher's part to persuade them to finish covering their page. Gradually, however, one after another, the children grasp what is required of them and share in the joy of the creative process.

Psychologists are not always entirely in agreement over what can be demanded from the school-beginner. But on one thing there is little divergence of opinion and that is that it is one of the essentials that the child is able to sit still and apply himself to work.

The ability to concentrate implies such a marked change in the child's behaviour that we must indeed ask how it has come about.

Formative Forces

To understand Steiner's answer to this question demands more detailed consideration. This is essential in any more thorough presentation of his educational ideas, for it has far-reaching practical consequences.

He who has acquired powers of supersensible perception through inner self-training can observe certain formative forces which are at work in fashioning the child's growing and developing physical body. For those accustomed to see organic processes in purely mechanical terms, such as the passing on of a particular complex of chromosomes, such a statement may appear intolerable or nonsensical. But Steiner emphatically states that this phenomenon is open to empirical observation and that the inherited organism is considerably modified by the working of these formative forces.

As long as the little child is at the "infant" stage, during which growth proceeds at a rate incomparably greater than at later stages of development, these healthy life-bringing forces are clossely bound up with the physical organism. It is through their activity that the little child is kept in constant movement during the waking state.

Gradually a part of these forces is released from working in the biological sphere and becomes available as energy on a more inward level of being. While the body is now relatively speaking at rest, inner activity can unfold in the soul-realm.

It is now a question of training the memory, developing habits and inclinations, of strengthening the conscience and the character, of guiding fantasy and temperament in healthy directions. For these emancipated forces do not give up their formative character. They must still be active creatively. Formerly they were at work in living matter, in the organs and tissues of the human body, in the formation of the bones and teeth. The second dentition, beginning at the age of six or seven years, marks the final stage of their working on the physical body. They must now continue their creative activity on a different level. The young school child, as he sits bent over his copy-book, drawing away, can well be seen as a proof of their existence.

Continuing Characteristics of the Small Child

At the very moment, however, when such an activity comes to an end, the power of concentration disappears too. In the first class only one small disturbing event needs to occur to bring about complete disorder. Perhaps the children are told to stand up and one child happens to push his chair over. At once a number of lively members of the class will follow his example. The imitative process has immediately come to the fore. The characteristics of the small child are still just beneath the surface, ready to appear at the slightest provocation.

The still existing tendency to imitation can also, however, be made use of by the teacher. In his book 'Erlebte Padagogik', Rudolf Grosse gives an example of how these forces can be used in a pedagogical way. One day his own first class was not in the mood to settle down to work: "Since scolding and moralising are not very good teaching methods, I told them to stand on their chairs and jump off. This resulted in cheerful and noisy tumult. Again and again they had to repeat this, and then follow me stamping around the classroom, a lively procession in and out among the desks. Suddenly, I turned and said "softly". They joined in the game, the stamping ceased. Then I whispered "on tip-toe". Each tried to go on tip-toe, as silently as the teacher did, to his own place. I stood in front of the class, put my fingers to my lips and whispered again "quiet as a mouse". Complete silence! I kept this up for about two minutes and then praised them for their wonderful stillness. What was the result? They called

Photo copy

Illustration of a fairy-tale.

out the next morning, "can we be quiet as mice again?"

We can see in this description that the age of imitation had not completely passed. For quite a long time after the child enters the first class the teacher can with justification call on this element, especially in the learning of foreign languages.

As we remember, Rudolf Steiner makes it clear that children at the kindergarten stage do not pay much attention to what they are actually told to do in words but all the more to everything that actually happens or is done in their environment. But at the same time as the powers of their own inner life begin to unfold, they develop a capacity which will remain theirs throughout life, and is indeed one of the most important human faculties. This is the ability to grasp what another person says and to recreate it as part of one's own conscious soul life.

When is the Child Ready for School

The answer to this question is different from country to country. In France and Germany children start school officially at the age of six, although many French children begin a year earlier. In the English primary school, teaching of the three R's starts at five; in large parts of the USA formal teaching begins at six; in the USSR and the Scandinavian countries education starts at seven.

Many modern educational investigators derive from these various customs the idea that there is no such thing as a special age when children are "ready" for school. They base this on the fact that so far no physiological symptom has been discovered which would pinpoint any particular age for this transition. They say that the physical body is continually developing during childhood, that is from the age of four until puberty. Even the second dentition is apparently occurring earlier than it used to.

Strangely enough, the fact is seldom mentioned that Jean Piaget discovered a definite change on a psychological level at a special point of time: "The age of seven which coincides with readiness for education, marks a decisive turning-point in the psychological development of the child. Taking into consideration any aspect whatever of the soul-life, one can observe the emergence of new inner faculties, whether on the level of intelligence, emotion, social relationship, or individual actions."

This is the age at which children begin to be able to concentrate and work together in an orderly manner, for instance, to join in a game which is based on definite rules. The change which takes place in the thought-realm is no less striking. As we said previously, the child is not able to deal with abstractions before the age of seven. Here is the report of another experiment in addition to those referred to earlier: "Three differently coloured balls, A, B, and C, roll through a tube. The children have watched them starting off in the order A, B, C, and now expect them to come out at the other end of the tube in the same order. Intuitive thought is their sure guide. But what if we now incline the tube in the opposite direction so that the balls roll back again? The youngest children do not expect the balls to be in the order C, B, A, and are surprised by it. Once they have learned to predict this sequence, we turn the tube over by 180°. The child must try to grasp that now we get first the sequence C, B, A, and then A, B, C. But not only does it not manage to understand this, but when he has seen that A and C roll out alternatively, he also expects that the middle ball B should have a turn at coming out first."

Piaget adds that the child's inability to grasp abstractions depends on a definite inner condition: "It is simply a question of patterns of perceptions, or patterns of actions which are transposed to become mental concepts. They are pictures, imitations of outer reality." It would not be going too far to connect this tendency to a purely pictorial kind of thinking, with a marked difficulty in learning to read and write which can be observed in many children under seven, as we have earlier remarked.

It cannot be emphasised strongly enough that Piaget's observations are entirely in line with those previously stated by Rudolf Steiner. He too lay stress on the fact that the appearance of new inner powers takes place at about the age of seven, and that it is at this time that the child learns to live and work together with other children in quite a new way. It is now that the child is "ready" for school. Rudolf Steiner points out that to be taught to read and write before this age has as a consequence a weakening effect on the physical organism for forces are called on and used which are still needed in the realm of organic development.

THE CLASS TEACHER

On their very first day at school the children are met by their class teacher. From then on he or she will be there to receive them every morning for seven or eight years. It is the class teacher who gives them their daily "main lesson", which covers all main subjects in block periods and he may also take them for other subjects.

Apart from preparing his lessons, the class teacher has a number of other tasks; maintaining contact with the parents; attending the weekly teachers' meetings; giving extra help to children unable to keep up, for instance in writing or arithmetic; conscientiously marking the children's copy books, organising extra-mural activities and perhaps even sharing some administrative duties.

Why do individual teachers have to carry so many responsibilities? Does their teaching not suffer as a result? Have the Waldorf schools not noticed that we are living in the age of specialisation? Why should the children not be taught by another teacher from time to time, for instance in class VI or VIII by specialist teachers in certain subjects?

The class-teacher system certainly brings with it quite considerable problems. In some cases the class teacher has to spend large portions of his holidays studying the various subjects he is due to teach next term. He might even seek some private instruction from one of the specialist teachers. And if he finds that one or other of the subjects is indeed beyond his capacity as the children grow older, then a compromise can be made in class VII or VIII, a specialist teacher may be called in to teach his class for instance in physics or chemistry.

But in spite of the need for compromise on various occasions, the class-teacher system is maintained. Indeed it is one of the cornerstones of a Waldorf school's work.

In the lecture courses which Rudolf Steiner gave to the future teachers just before the first Waldorf school was founded, he described the tasks of the class teacher from many different aspects. These descriptions are so fundamental that further details will be given.

Keeping Pace with the Children

In 'The Study of Man' Steiner describes what the class teacher can do to keep pace with the development of his children: "He should review the physical development of the children and remember their appearance. Then at the end of the school year or some other period of time he should review their development again and observe the changes which have taken place." (2. 9. 1919)

In 'Practical Course for Teachers' he gave examples of how quite ordinary every-day occurrences can help the teacher to put to good use his intimate knowledge of the development of each child: "If for only a week you have been in the habit of eating a sandwich at ten-thirty each morning, you will probably find that already in the second week you are quite hungry for the sandwich at the time in question. So quickly does the human organism become accustomed to a rhythm. However, not only the outer organism but the whole human being is inclined to rhythm. Therefore, it is good in the whole course of life—and this is what one is concerned with when bringing up and educating children— to look to rhythmical repetition. It is good to remember that one can return to certain specific educational themes year after year. You should thus select certain themes which you work through with the children, make a note of them and return to something similar each year. This can even be done with abstract things. In other words: in the first year you teach the children to add up in a way which is suited to the child's disposition; you return to the subject of addition in the second year and teach them more about it; and in the third year you return to it again, so that the same activity is taken up repeatedly but in progressive repetition." (27.8.1919)

A further example: during the first year the class could learn a certan poem or verse, to which the teacher would refer in the following year perhaps speaking about it in a different way. For instance on an autumm day he could remind the children of an autumn poem they had learned one or two years earlier. Gradually the teacher grows accustomed to weaving these "progressive repetitions" more or less imperceptibly into all his lessons.

Such a way of teaching would not be possible without the existence of the class teacher who every morning, for seven or eight years, is there to receiye the children when they come to school, unless he is prevented by illness.

Seven or eight years is a long time, during which the children undergo a number of profound changes. And the teacher has to accompany them through these changes. In class I when the children live in the imaginative, dreamlike world of fairy tales, the teacher—like a mother—has to help them with all kinds of little practical things such as untying knots in shoe-laces, returning lost belongings etc. In class VIII he must command a reasonable knowledge of a large number of subjects and be able to speak to his group of teenagers with the authority of someone who knows how to cope with life in the world; his role has in a way become that of an older friend and adviser.

Self Education

Is it not likely that the pupils would grow tired of having the same teacher year in year out? This is something the class teacher must make great efforts to prevent. He has to try and develop and change himself according to the changing needs of his children. Some teachers find this surprisingly easy. For others it is a long and strenuous struggle, as many an example may show.

For instance, a certain class teacher was able, for the sake of his class, to overcome a serious phobia. The effort changed him so much that he was also able to make quite a new relationship with the children. Or there was the class teacher who could not draw and who spent night after night practising. Gradually the children in her class came to be known throughout the school as being the most skilful in drawing. Another teacher was a choleric who knew only too well that he could not always control his temper. So that his class should not have to bear the brunt of this weakness he would spend some time each morning chopping wood to "let off steam" before going to school.

The Community of the Class

Gradually through all difficulties and all joys the class and its teacher become welded together as a community. There are very rare occasions when this relationship of teacher and class is unfruitful so that either the teacher or one of the children has to leave but in nearly every case, even if there are many problems, the class community is of the deepest value.

The reason for this is quite simply that such a community enables children to grow roots. To be under the care of the same people year after year gives them a feeling of having found a home on earth. For modern children whose lives are so full of superficial meetings, making it difficult to develop loyalties to other people, this may be one of the most important experiences.

As already mentioned, there is a tendency in education today to split up the unity of a class simply for reasons of expediency: varying groups of pupils move from one classroom to another to be taught by different teachers. Teachers involved in this kind of work have

often expressed the opinion that i a worsening of discipline and weak children's feeling of security and of belol. to the school. Taken to its logical extre such a system could indeed have far-reaching harmful effects.

In Waldorf schools all over the world it is found that no other teacher is able to establish such a close contact with a class as the class-teacher himself. In moral and disciplinary questions it is his word which is heeded most seriously. If the class-teacher becomes ill, it is often difficult for another teacher to take over his class. Through his constant efforts to develop himself and through his deep bond with his class he becomes the person of greatest authority to them. It is difficult or even impossible to replace him.

However, as the class-teacher approaches the end of the class teacher period, he has to arrange his work so that the pupils gradually become more independent. The former strong personal link with the teacher is widened to include the whole school and this is the transition to the Upper School.

...ITY OR
...?

leads to
is the
...ring
...e

The principle of authority is often questioned nowadays. Many psychologists and young parents are of the opinion that it is good for growing children to be treated on the same level as adults as soon as possible. The desire to do the best for one's children by treating them as companions from an early age is understandable but in some cases the bold slogans of freedom and equality are used by parents to hide their own uncertainty or even their lack of interest in how their children are developing. These parents are more concerned with their own than with their children's needs.

It is also unfortunate that the word "authority" has collected overtones which link it with the ideas of constraint or dictatorship, or at best with the patriarchal customs of an age which cannot return.

In Waldorf schools, authority has nothing to do with these overtones. It is based on an experience which cannot be denied by anyone who works with children and who does not cling to theoretical speculations, viz. that it is important for children to be in close proximity with someone whose support they can feel and to whom they can look up. This feeling of security is a source of strength of which young children can never have enough.

It is this kind of natural authority which prompts younger children to settle any argument at home quite categorically with the magic words: "but my teacher says ..." Then as the years go by and they grow older they may no longer flaunt their admiration for their teacher quite so adamantly but it is interesting to observe how seriously they take anything that comes from a teacher they really love.

Rudolf Steiner points out that genuine authority can never be achieved or maintained by any external means. In one of his most basic statements about this he said: "It is most important that devotion and admiration for the teacher and love for the teacher should come about as of itself. Otherwise it is of no value. Any devotion which is forced or which is based upon the rules and laws of the school is of no value for the development of the human being. It can be experienced quite positively that when children are educated in accordance with their own being they are most likely to be devoted to their teacher." (9. 5. 1922)

Punishment

What Rudolf Steiner says about punishment should not be taken to mean that he is against everything which might be regarded as punishment or strictness. Teachers who try to educate according to the true nature and needs of their pupils, must come to understand that any wrong-doing of children and teenagers hardly ever stems from a conscious effort but is nearly always the result of some degree of thoughtlessness. And the therapy for thoughtlessness is a call to consciousness and reflection. "Many, many theories have been expounded on the reasons for punishment. But the only real reason lies in the knowledge that punishment should serve the purpose of harnessing the forces of the soul in a way which can extend the consciousness to areas hitherto untouched by it." (1. 2. 1916)

An awakening effect of this kind can never by achieved if the teacher himself acts impulsively, for instance by giving a child a box on the ear in anger. The effect would be no better if he waited until the following day and then caned a child in cold blood; in this case the punishment would be simply experienced as a form of cruelty.

There are signs that in pre-industrial society children were more robust and dreamy than is usual today. At that time corporal punishment administered by a respected adult may have had a salutary and awakening effect. But in our more problematical age a child who is hit or caned may all too easily gain the impression that the person administering the punishment is simply acting out of antipathy.

Today it is becoming more and more difficult to maintain discipline and to give undisturbed lessons. It is, therefore, more and more important for the teachers to consider what has just been said. It is, after all, a fact that those children and adolescents whose behaviour is most disturbing are usually the ones who have suffered most from environmental damage. Thus even if the teacher is forced to be extremely strict, he should never give his charges reason to doubt that what he really wants is to help them.

It is perhaps unavoidable in any school that a teacher provoked beyond his limits may forget himself and react too hastily. But what is important is that he should realise that any measures which are not basically helpful or therapeutic but are the result of hurt pride are educationally valueless or even harmful.

Some Practical Experiences

A number of Waldorf school teachers from different countries once met to discuss the question of "difficult classes". Exact descriptions were given of a number of upper school classes in which the children were either unwilling to work or actually rebellious. Various possible causes were examined and it was found that there was indeed a "lowest common denominator". In every case during their years in the lower and middle school the classes had had class-teachers who would not tolerate any appreciable opposition and who had enforced strict external discipline right up to class VIII. All had been well while the class-teacher remained in charge but in class IX the problems had begun to appear, in some cases quite rapidly.

Attention was then turned to examples of classes where the pupils had been particularly enthusiastic about work and had shown great loyalty to their teachers during their final years at school. Here too all the classes had something in common, viz. a class-teacher who had not been too insistent on external discipline but had been warmly appreciated by his pupils.

One example was particularly striking. A certain class-teacher had a very large class, as she liked to accept more and more new pupils. During her lessons the classroom was sometimes like a stormy ocean and when the class was singing the tempest seemed to increase in fury. The teacher often had to shout to be heard and though her lessons were rich in content, her presentation was not always systematic. Yet amid all the noise the relationship between teacher and pupils was warmly human. When her pupils entered the upper school there were large gaps in their knowledge. But then they started studying with great enthusiasm and learnt remarkably rapidly, often pushing the teachers faster then they had intended to go. Class discussions were of a very high standard, both as regards intelligence and human understanding.

Observations of this kind must, of course, be regarded and treated very cautiously indeed. It would be quite wrong to assume that Rudolf Steiner's educational principles presupposed any lack of discipline. All teachers and all classes are different. What is right in one case may be impossible in another. Every teacher has, and must have, his own way of solving disciplinary problems. But amid all the manifold individual variations there is an underlying principle which Rudolf Steiner did point out and which is shown in the examples given, namely that the only desirable form of authority is the one based on mutual sympathy.

From Trust to Freedom

Authority which is practised for the good of the children and not for the convenience of the teacher will not hinder their development towards freedom. On the contrary, a child who is able to experience steady confidence in those whose task it is to educate him, will find it easier to build up the inner calm and security which will enable him later in life to realise himself in a natural and relaxed way. The question "authority *or* freedom" is, therefore, not a valid one. Authority is a necessary stage on the way to freedom.

In the western world today there are probably many children who have to grow up without ever really feeling respect for an older person. To regard this fact as a positive symptom of the development towards freedom in our time is an error and also an exceedingly short-sighted way of thinking. For it is usually those people who as children were unable to feel respect and admiration in any form, who in later life are less capable of genuine feeling and of making warm, human contact.

THE IMPORTANCE OF THE PICTORIAL ELEMENT

One of the frequent prejudices held against Waldorf schools is that the children are told too many fairy tales. To answer such a criticism it is necessary to consider in greater depht the part which pictures, both visual and imaginative, play in the lives of young children. Many people will remember from their childhood days a painting or a book illustration which was created by an artist's imagination, and they may realise that such a picture affected them more deeply than a picture which was merely depicting outer nature. Perhaps they may still be able to conjure up something of the feeling—maybe of joyful warmth, or maybe a fearful shudder—originally felt. Children's love of pictures springs from the heart and is engendered by a longing to live in the realm of human feeling.

Why is it that children have such a strong desire for pictures which are not mere copies of earthly reality? It could be argued that their hunger for pictures merely corresponds to an adult's preference for stories in magazines or thrillers and the like. But there is more to the problem than meets the eye. The yearning for pictures in children is particularly strong during a definite phase of their development. Arnold Gesell has shown that the interest in comics begins to awaken in American children at about the age of six, that it culminates at about eight or nine, and that it begins to diminish at about ten.

Children have an insatiable appetite for pictures, which producers of comics and cartoon films have exploited to the full. Unfortunately, they tend to provide artificial stimulants such as Donald Ducks rushing about and speaking through their noses, or gangsters shooting with pistols, or death-rays from outer space. Children of about seven will quite happily act the story of Little Red Riding Hood, or perform it with their puppets. This engages them in a more genuinely imaginative activity. If their tastes have not been spoilt by too many sensational and fantastic films or comics, they have a deeply-founded preference for fairy tales and mythological pictures.

The Age of Picture Consciousness

In all cultural epochs and in the history of all peoples, there have been times when adult human beings experienced the same kinship with the pictorial element as children do today. The myths of ancient India, Babylon, Egypt, and those told by the Celts, the Teutonic tribes, and by the primitive races still in existence today, all bear witness to a stage of cultural development when people reverently accepted what their priests or medicine men told them about the creation of the world in wonderful, majestic pictures.

We can observe the gradual transition from man's old imaginative picture-consciousness to a more intellectually-orientated and clearly-defined thinking particularly well in the development of Greek philosophy and drama. Without wishing to press the comparison too far, we can say that our children go through a similar process of development. Children

117

have a kind of pictorial thinking which reaches its climax between the ages of six and ten and which then gradually changes into their newly-found interest in the causality of things, and into the ability to use abstract concepts.

Rudolf Steiner emphasised time and again the importance of meeting children's need to live in pictures. One of his more startling remarks in this respect was made in a lecture given in England in 1923 to a group of educationalists and others interested in teaching:

"What would you say if someone who in a restaurant had been served with fish were to carefully separate out the bones and eat them after placing the edible parts on the side of his plate? You would probably be afraid that the bones might choke him and you would realise that his digestion would not be able to cope with the fish bones.

Yet the very same thing happens, only on a different level, if instead of giving soul nourishment to the child in forms of living pictures which speak to his whole being, you teach him dry, abstract and lifeless concepts." (13. 8. 1923)

Critics of Waldorf schools who maintain that too many imaginative pictures are given to the children in the first three years at school, have not realised that the motives behind such practice are not merely "sacred cows", old fashioned ideas, or even a lack of interest in the realities of modern life, but that a consistent pedagogical principle is being applied in full consciousness, based on a knowledge of the growing child. Furthermore, such critics only look at one side of the curriculum, for in the third class, for example, special emphasis is laid upon lessons in practical life, such as the study of house-building and farming, and in Class IV the children are taught how to compose their first business letters.

If one wishes not to exhaust the children intellectually, but to preserve their healthy receptivity, it is essential to let them experience truly imaginative pictures. It has often been observed that pupils in Waldorf schools who had been taught in a particularly imaginative and pictorial way in the younger years, later on showed unusual readiness to learn and understand intellectual subjects. Such pupils not only displayed mobility in thinking, but a stable and balanced emotional life as well. In order to meet the child's natural demand for the pictorial element, it is essential to permeate every lesson with imaginative quality. There is no other way, imaginative pictures must be given their due.

In a Waldorf school, the Main Lesson (see the chapter on 'The Rhythm of the Day') usually includes a daily instalment of a single continuous story, carefully chosen to fit the soul mood of the class:

Class I — fairy tales
Class II — fables and legends. 'The King of Ireland's son' is aften told in English schools.
Class III — selected stories from the Old Testament
Class IV — stories from Nordic mythology
Class V — parts of Greek mythology and legends from Ancient India, Persia, Babylonia and Egypt.

Speaking about the importance of satisfying the child's hunger for imaginations, Rudolf

The teacher tells the children a story, and the children respond through their artistic activity. The child's picture is the spontaneous expression of what it has experienced through its teacher.

Two illustrations of the same fairy-tale.

Steiner went even further by linking a rebellious and anarchist attitude, so prevalent today, to this very same problem. Although his views may sound strange and even far-fetched to anyone who has not occupied himself with his teachings, they nevertheless show the depth of the problem involved:

"We live at the beginning of an era—and here lies very largely the reason for the turbulent character of our present time—in which the souls as they descend from the spiritual world into earthly life, through conception and birth, bring powerful images with them. What lives in the depths of children's souls are Imaginations which have been received in the spiritual world. They seek to come forth. Thus there are forces working in the child which will shatter him unless they are brought out through an imaginative approach in education. What is the result if this does not happen? Such forces do not vanish. They spread, gaining momentum, until finally they penetrate people's thoughts, feelings and will impulses. And what kind of people result from such happenings? They are the rebels, revolutionaries, dissatisfied people who do not know what they want because they want something which can never be found. If the world is in revolt today, then it is the heavens that are in revolt, — that is, the heavenly forces that are held back in the souls of men, being unable to appear in their true guise, are changed to their very opposite ... into strife and bloodshed ... No wonder that those who participate in the work of destroying the social order feel that they are doing something good ... Such is the serious nature of the truths which we should recognise today." (11. 9. 1920)

PICTURES BEFORE LETTERS

"The powerful prince comes prancing along and bows to the proud princess." The children of the first class are energetically repeating this sentence, stamping as they pronounce the sound "P". They have heard a fairy-tale about the prince and the princess, and re-experience it in rhythmical recitation. Then they draw the picture with coloured crayons, the prince raising his hand to doff his purple velvet cap and bow low before the haughty princess. Gradually the form of the letter P emerges from the figure of the prince with his uplifted arms. At last the children draw just the letter itself, but the story and the picture they have drawn or painted remain alive in their imagination. In a similar way the teacher introduces other consonants. The king raising his sword becomes the K, the tall tree with its outspread branches becomes T, the path over the mountains remains as the letter M. Vowels arise from bodily features each expressing a different mood of soul. Such movements are then arrested, as it were, in a fixed sign which becomes the written symbol for a particular vowel. Thus "outer" sounds (consonants) and "inner" sounds (vowels) are distinguished from the very beginning.

The powerful king is contracted to the pale thin letter K.

In this way the letter arises from the picture, and reading is derived from the activity of writing. All the letters are gradually introduced during the first school year, and the children learn to read only what the teacher and they themselves have written. Only during the second school year is reading practised in a more systematic way, and the printed word makes its first appearance.

Why do we adopt in Waldorf schools this lengthy and rather complicated approach to learning? Perhaps I may be allowed to recall the childhood memory of my own first writing-lesson. The teacher stood at the board and wrote the letters B and I. Then she turned to us and said "That is 'bi'". Quickly the thought shot through my head, "But that doesn't look like a 'bi'.* It just isn't true." I felt disappointed and as if I stood at the borders of an alien new world, which I must now enter.

The transition from the world of real things to the world of signs is more difficult for many children than we imagine. A bridge is made by engaging the child's imaginative faculties and presenting letters at first through familiar pictures. We are here speaking, of course, of the average school-child, not children who have special learning difficulties.

Rudolf Steiner emphasised that children should not be forced to learn to read and write before they are really ready for it,** and that then they should recapitulate the same process that is to be found in the old Egyptian, Babylonian and Chinese cultures, namely the transition from the picture-element to the sign.

It may be asked whether this slow process is not boring for the more intelligent children, especially those who have learnt to read and

write before coming to school. Everything depends on the ability of the teacher to make the pictorial character of the letter sufficiently interesting. Such problems soon disappear when drawing and painting, as well as the stories told, excite the children's interest. When children realise, too, that this is the way in which mankind first mastered the art of writing, they even feel a certain pride and respect for their own activities. A little girl in a Waldorf school, comparing herself with some cousins who had learnt to read more quickly at another school, remarked "Oh yes, they did learn to read, but they have no idea where the letters come from!"

Speed in learning has little worth. It is the depth of the child's experience that matters. How poor is the trivial content of the customary first Readers used in ordinary schools—of necessity couched in simple terms because the child is just learning to read—compared with the wealth gained from the teacher who speaks with creative imagination of the world both of every-day life and of fairy tale and legend.

The transition from the world of objects to that of abstract signs is a deep incision in the life of a human being. Rudolf Steiner was most emphatic that children should learn to read and write only when absolutely ready for school, and that then they should follow the same steps which were taken in the past by civilisations as a whole—namely, from pictures to letters.

Writing is here made to suit the subject-matter. The "winter" letters are angular and cold-looking. The "summer" letters are soft and rounded, and the colours warm and glowing.

** See chapter: "The Right Time to Begin."

* In Swedish "bi" is the word for "bee".

Januar is-
skjegg
smeller i
husvegg

Juni trår
dansen med
midtsommer krans

FAIRY TALES IN CLASS ONE

The educational value of fairy tales has come to be doubted. It is thought that they are not exciting enough for six and seven-year-olds and that they are too frightening for younger children. Some child psychiatrists "see red" when Grimm's fairy tales are mentioned.

However, in Waldorf schools fairy tales are regarded as one of the most important educational means available to parents and teachers, and a considerable amount of time is set aside for story telling. What is the reason for this?

Let us begin with a typical example: A phlegmatic little girl, aged about five or six, was told the story of Mother Holle by her mother. She heard how the good girl in the story always did her work in Mother Holle's house willingly and conscientiously, and how finally she was led by her mistress to a great doorway.

There a shower of gold fell upon her. Then the door closed behind her and she found herself near her parents' home, to which she returned. The lazy maiden, who faced a similar situation without, however, being able to cope with it adequately, was also led to the great doorway. But all she received was a shower of pitch. This picture of the two maidens returning home, one shining with gold, and

Illustration of a fairy-tale. Class 1.

the other covered with pitch, made a deep impression on the phlegmatic child. Slowly and emphatically she said, "I'm always going to be a good girl, too."

With drastic vividness not found in any other kind of literature, fairy tales reveal the inmost core of their various characters. In this way children receive a knowledge of human nature which they could not understand in any other form and which, at the same time, helps them to develop their feelings for right and wrong.

Though traditional fairy tales have undergone considerable changes in being passed from generation to generation and from one country to another, many of their characteristic features indicate that they were told originally by single, anonymous personalities. In addition to their poetical gifts, these original story-tellers must have had deep insight into human nature and great wisdom about the world.

Many fairy tales are real works of art, deeply ethical in their attitudes, free from all petty moralizing, and created for people who have not lost their childhood imagination.

The Face of Evil

But why should fairy tales so often introduce all sorts of loathsome creatures which do not exist? Should we not protect the children instead of burdening them with all sorts of wicked fairies, trolls, witches and giants?
Before answering this question, let us look for a moment at the way in which these creatures are described in fairy tales.
Fairy tales which still reveal the manner in which they were told by the story-tellers of old, have a simple and almost naive style with relatively few words. Their pictures are pithy but painted, as it were, with few strokes.

Details are sparse. Usually the representatives of evil reveal themselves only by their words and deeds.

The wicked stepmother in "Snow White" is able to deceive the king and many other people because she is the fairest in all the land. The wicked fairy in "Sleeping Beauty" dresses up as an old woman before tempting the princess to spin and prick herself with the spindle. The witch in "Hansel and Gretel" is a particularly striking figure. She appears to the two lost children like a friendly old woman who offers them a good meal and soft beds to sleep in. An unusually detailed generalisation is added to her description: "Witches have red eyes and cannot see far, but they have keen noses which can smell human beings when they are approaching." The witch's animal lust becomes only too obvious when she tries to entice Gretel to creep into the oven. But she gives herself away and, by a ruse, Gretel succeeds in pushing her into the oven instead.

The Scandinavian trolls are a race apart. The Norwegian fairy tale "The Troll Wedding" tells us how a young girl, who is engaged to be married, is living high up in the mountains, together with her cows. One day crowds of people come to visit her in her hut, led by the bridegroom himself. The people have brought her wedding dress, as well as table cloths and silver plates for the wedding. The festivities begin, but the dog knows instinctively that all is not well. Barking loudly, he rushes down the mountain to the village and fetches the real bridegroom who brings his gun and rescues his bride. She had not noticed that her visitors were trolls, but now she sees that all the fine food for the wedding feast is nothing but moss, toadstools and cow-dung.

Trolls can appear in all sorts of shapes and disguises: as small children, gnome-like adults, or as wonderfully beautiful women. Usually they have quite specific aims. For instance, they may want to entice certain people to follow them inside the mountain. Sometimes if someone accepts food and drink from them, he is condemned to remain with them. This is a very old theme which already appears in the Odyssey when Circe entices shipwrecked sailors to her castle and offers them poisoned wine. As soon as they have drunk, she turns them into pigs and does not let them go. Because they give in to their lower instincts, Circe is able to gain power over them. Those who have been spellbound by the trolls can be saved by their own, or by someone else's, spiritual awareness. Nevertheless, a sojourn with the trolls leaves its mark. Frequently those who return feel like strangers among their fellow men. Sometimes they may remain eccentric for the rest of their lives.

Grotesque characters such as trolls and witches with long noses or ears usually only appear in humorous fairy tales. Giants, too, despite all their fearsomeness, generally display some comical features. With the exception of dragons and devils, which impersonate evil incarnate, the forces of evil are described in many fairy tales merely as possessing the power to deceive men's eyes and in this way appear human so that they cannot easily be distinguished from ordinary people.

Fairy Tales and Real Life

Is all this not rather fantastic and "quite mad"? Not in the least. Anyone who has experienced how some adolescents are drawn into joining gangs indulging in drugtaking, robberies, or violence, cannot help being amazed at the similarity of these temptations in real life to those depicted in fairy tales. There are "bewitched" people all around us; there are others whose psychological make-up resembles that of witches and trolls in the way in which they exhibit primitive cunning, insinuating flattery, animal lust and boundless cynicism.

The terrible thing about the powers of evil as described in real fairy-tales is that they really exist.

Many people express the view that instead of telling children fairy tales we ought to prepare them for modern life. Children should be forewarned so as to be fore-armed. But if we look at the present situation, we can find countless children who have been overtaken by conditions of modern life all too soon and too suddenly and who have to face a life of fear and helplessness, of disillusionment and brutality.

If fairy tales are told in the right way, unsentimentally, without intellectual interpretations and without gory details, their witches, giants and trolls can help children to experience evil in the world before having to face it.

However, what matters most is that children should experience how the beneficent powers in the world rule supreme, and how they enable the characters of the fairy tales, be they kings or hunters, princes or soldiers, to develop virtues such as courage, perseverance, loyalty or a sense of justice. For in this way the "Happy End" imbues the children with reassurance and confidence that the evil in the world can be and must be overcome and that renewed strength and deeper happiness are the just reward for an honest struggle.

Choosing the Right Story

Children of the fairy tale age, i.e. between four and nine, can gradually be told an increasing number of tales from their own and from other people's countries. Those suitable for the youngest stage are the short and, if possible, humorous stories which can be told over and over again, preferably word for word, such as "The Millet Pudding" and "Star-Dollars". "The Wolf and the Seven Little Goats". "Sleeping Beauty" and "Snow White" are also possible at this stage provided their darker aspects are not made too dramatic but told in a light and almost "floating" manner. After five years of age children are able to follow stories whose leading characters undergo a certain development as the action unfolds. However, it is always advisable before choosing one's story to pay heed to the individual disposition of each child, to his background and also to the season of the year.

But what is one to do if, after all, a little five-year-old does feel frightened of the wolf or of some other monster as he lies awake at night? Should one calm his fears by explaining that there are no wolves roaming the land and that in real life there are no giants, goblins or witches? After all that has been stated so far, it would be obviously wrong to nullify the pictures of the fairy tale world after having given them to the child. This would seriously undermine his trust in what his elders have to say to him. On the other hand, life will not allow children to remain completely protected from experiencing the darker aspects of existence and, in any case, most children have their own instinctive glimpses of them. We must help them to come to terms with their problems. A song at bedtime, a prayer, or a little talk about something beautiful that happened during the day usually helps. A happy and much-loved story can drive away fears. One can tell children how each child has his guardian angel who will watch over him, especially at night time. One parent once gave his young son a wooden toy-sword, showing him how the hilt of the sword had the shape of the cross, and telling him how all bad creatures were afraid of this sign. "And if ever a nasty goblin should find his way into your room," he said, "you just show him the hilt of your sword and point the cross at him. You'll see how quickly he will disappear."

But would not the remark that a goblin *might* find his way into the child's bedroom make him more frightened than ever? It is difficult to tell, but what matters is that an atmosphere of loving trust should flow between child and adult. And then it is often quite sufficient to leave the bedroom door ajar as a gesture of nearness and a close link. Almost all children go through a period when they are afraid to go to sleep in the dark because they are plagued by disquieting thoughts. The serene light of a burning candle will also help them to go to sleep peacefully. If seven-year-olds should declare that fairy tales are "baby stuff", they merely imitate the attitude of people around them. If they meet adults who look upon the language of fairy tales as an expression of human culture, they will never voice such a statement. When it is story-time in Class I the children settle down in anticipation, quieten each other and listen with wide-open eyes. Sometimes they cannot suppress their comments. Hearing of the wicked deeds of a magician, a plucky and lively little boy might protest loudly: "Isn't he horrid!" Or the eyes of a rather timid and restless little girl might light up when she hears how the poor little mouse is finally changed into a princess: "Oh, how lovely!"

Sometimes the question pop up, "Is this story true?" But such doubts are rather fleeting, for the fairy tale soon claims full attention. If the teacher takes care to tell only stories which express inner truths in picture form, he can say with a good conscience, "Yes, in their way, fairy tales are true."

If a child brings into the classroom real scepticism picked up outside school, then the teacher will have to explain that the world of fairy tales is different from the world around us, but that it nevertheless exists.

Children who are used to hearing genuine fairy tales develop quite a feeling for their quality. Made-up stories which pretend to be fairy tales but are fantastic or too realistic, are often received with disappointment and dissatisfaction simply because they have no depth and because they are inartistic. An unfortunate teacher who once told such a story to her class was met with the remark, "And now will you us a *proper* fairy tale?"

When once one has really entered into the world of fairy tales and knows how much their pictures have to offer, one gains a real yardstick with which to measure the "value" of the picture-series in comic books, cartoon films and the like. One could compare them with overcooked tinned food which fills you up for the moment but soon leaves you hungrier than ever, or even undernourished.

INTRODUCING ARITHMETIC

The class teacher is talking to his six-year-old pupils in Class I: A farmer has made a large cheese which he cuts into ten pieces. He has promised three pieces to his neighbours and needs one for his own family for tea. How many pieces are left for him to sell at the market? (This question appeals to order-loving melancholics who like to plan carefully.)

The market is very crowded. Four big, fat ladies are pushing their way towards the farmer and each buys one piece of cheese. (Now it is time to direct a question to the cholerics, who are becoming rather restless.) Strangely enough, each lady has a husband and four children, all of whom like cheese. How many people are there altogether in the four families who will be having cheese for tea?

The pushing and shoving in the market place is getting even worse. A hungry boy cannot resist the temptation to pinch a piece of cheese and the butcher's dog runs off with another. After a while the boy's guilty conscience makes him return his piece of cheese. But the farmer is kind-hearted and lets him keep half of it. The dog, however, does not return, since he has wasted no time in eating up his piece. How many pieces has the farmer now? (The crowds of people and jumble of events suggest a whole host of further questions specially suited to the sanguine children.)

Now it is time to think of all the people who will have eaten some of the lovely cheese. (Here the phlegmatics, always at home in the company of people enjoying their food, can do their bit of steady adding up.)

This example illustrates how the teacher can involve the four temperaments even during an arithmetic lesson.

The four basic processes of arithmetic are always applied side by side. In this subject the teacher can move along fairly rapidly, in contrast to writing and reading lessons.

One thing is fundamental: numbers are generally regarded as a part of a whole (e.g. the farmer's large cheese). This can be done in many different ways. For instance, a certain distance between two places can be sub-divided into the required number of parts, or a king can divide his kingdom into provinces to be shared amongst his sons and vassals, and so on.

Such an "Analytical" approach stimulates the imaginative powers of the child. It is possible to sub-divide a duodecimal number in many different ways, whereas the opposite way of adding up the factors allows far less freedom (Needless to say it is essential to practise the "synthetic" approach as well). There is, however, one more point which should be mentioned here:

The All-Comprising Number One

Some ancient myths describe how, at the beginning of the world, the various elements were created out of one entity, such as that of Okeanos in the Greek and that of the Giant Ymir in the Nordic mythology. The totality sacrifices itself so that the parts can be created. When practising arithmetic, the teacher again and again returns to this same principle,

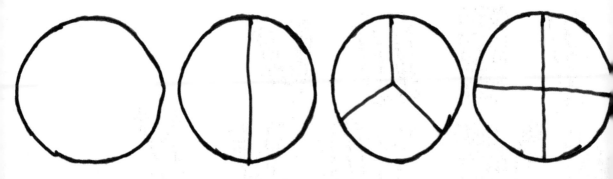

he starts with the whole which is then divided up to be given away.

Children feel quite naturally that the world is a unity. According to Piaget, the tendency to regard God as the creator of all things is found not only among children who have had a religious up-bringing.

In this way, arithmetic lessons can even provide an opportunity for exercising moral qualities! But they can equally well become a playground for little egoisms if one is not careful: If you get two sweets from Charles, three from Richard, and two from Mary, how many will you have? Somehow one easily slips into this kind of question in mental arithmetic instead of asking the same question the other way round: If you give Charles two sweets, Richard three, and Mary two, how many will you have given away? Why should this be so? It is because when counting, measuring or comparing, egoism tends to enter instinctively particularly when one appeals only to the intellect. For the intellect is by nature rapacious, it wants to conquer, it is greedy for new things. Feelings and willpower are needed to counteract this by selflessness. And yet, when dealing with numbers, an objective and unemotional attitude is called for. Such observations are not insignificant. Simply by the choice of his examples the teacher has it in his power to let moral impulses permeate his lessons quite imperceptibly.

Learning Tables through Movement

The best way of introducing children to the world of numbers is by letting them move to rhythms, which in any case are inherent in counting and in number-series.

In Class I, all the children might follow the teacher round the class-room counting in threes, with two tiptoed steps followed by a stamp and a clap of hands:

One, Two, *Three;*

Four, Five, *Six;*

Seven, Eight, *Nine;*

Ten, Eleven, *Twelve* ...

In Class II, the children recite their tables up to twelve to the accompaniment of appropriate movements, such as clapping or jumping, and their boisterous enthusiasm can make the class-room reverberate throughout the school:

Above: The idea that the parts derive from the whole is one that has a natural appeal for the child.

Above right: Some teachers like to use the Roman numerals when first introducing arithmetic, as they have a direct visual relationship with the fingers, and the Arabic numbers soon follow.

Below right: These flower-patterns can be used either for addition, multiplication, or division. Such a picture makes immediately obvious the relationship between the four rules.

Three is one times three, —

Six is two times three, etc.

As the numbers get bigger, the activity is lifted more and more into the thinking sphere:

Forty-five is *Five* times nine;

Fifty-four is *Six* times nine;

Sixty-three is *Seven* times nine;

Seventy-two is *Eight* times nine, etc.

There is no better training for the memory than learning tables by heart in arithmetic. Every series of numbers is meaningful and full of secrets which can be discovered later on.

For instance, one can start with the numbers in the nine-times table: 18, 27, 36, 45, 54, 63, 72, 81. When adding the digits of each multiple, the sum will be nine. Other discoveries can be made which fill the children with both wonder and enthusiasm.

Apart from recognising such laws of number, one must not forget to bring many examples from daily life. In Class III, the main-lesson periods of House-Building and Farming give many opportunities for weighing and measuring. The length, breadth and height of the class-room can be measured, the length and width of the play-ground etc.

Beside this practical aspect, the world of pure numbers remains important and fascinating.

For instance, the children in Class III or IV can be confronted with the following phenomenon:

$$
\begin{array}{llll}
1 \times 1 = 1 & & & \\
2 \times 2 = 4 & > 3 & > 2 & \\
3 \times 3 = 9 & > 5 & > 2 & \\
4 \times 4 = 16 & > 7 & > 2 & \\
5 \times 5 = 25 & > 9 & &
\end{array}
$$

The cholerics are now in the grip of the fervour of discovery. Surely at some point the "difference between the differences" must become larger than 2! They try out ever larger numbers:

$$
\begin{array}{llll}
10 \times 10 = 100 & & & \\
11 \times 11 = 121 & > 21 & > 2 & \\
12 \times 12 = 144 & > 23 & > 2 & \\
13 \times 13 = 169 & > 25 & > 2 & \\
14 \times 14 = 196 & > 27 & &
\end{array}
$$

But at last they realise that the world of numbers knows no compromise and nothing that is arbitrary. The laws are immutable and often surprisingly different from what one would expect. They are inscribed in the blueprint of the universe. In this way, one does not only awaken an urge for investigation in the children, but one helps them to develop their thinking in a fitting and healthy manner.

Doubling and halving.

FABLES AND LEGENDS IN CLASS TWO

Said the Mouse to the Elephant: "Did you hear how the bridge rumbled as we went over it together?"

Fables are usually very terse and concise. However, children are not likely to appreciate their striking worldly wisdom unless the ground has been adequately prepared by a conversation leading to the point of the fable in question.

For instance: Two men go up into the hay loft to get hay for the cows. One is strong and pitches huge bundles of hay down through the trapdoor into the mangers. The other is weak and only manages to throw down a few handfuls. But afterwards he boasts about the huge bales of hay which he has given the cows. The children understand the character of each man, the one strong but thoughtful and silent, the other weak but talkative and boastful. Later you ask the children to describe what an elephant and a mouse look like; and then you can tell the fable.

The frog who wants to look as big as an ox puffs himself up until he bursts. Bring unable to reach the grapes, the fox saves his face by saying that they are sour anyway. The stag, seeing his reflection in a pond, admires his beautiful antlers but deplores his thin little legs (see drawing). But when chased by a lion, his antlers are caught in the branches of a tree and he awaits his doom, realising that his deplorable legs could have saved him while his magnificent antlers were the cause of his ensuing death.

Fables show us human weaknesses in animal form and neither fur nor feathers can disguise this fact. Sometimes children will laugh, sometimes they are indignant. However, if a teacher were to tell too many fables, their laughter and indignation could easily turn to mockery. Therefore, fables need a counterbalance: stories which do not ridicule but which are uplifting. In contrast to human faults being exposed via the animal, children also need to look up to human beings who have overcome their animal nature and who, therefore, are able to tame wild animals whose mode of life would destroy man's orderly world. Such characters can be found in the myths and legends.

We live in an age in which legends, with their "senseless" miracles and pious talk, are usually looked upon as being utterly boring and anachronistic. Such an opinion is quite justified in the case of legends invented for sentimental or even mercenary reasons. But genuine legends spring from a different source and they tower above their false offspring like truly creative genius over weakness, resignation and despondency.

Offerus was a giant of a man, eleven cubits tall, and he wanted to serve only the strongest master. When he noticed his king making the sign of the cross at the mention of the devil, Offerus decided to serve the devil instead. Seeing the devil bow before a cross on the wayside, Offerus sought counsel of an old hermit who told him about the true Lord of the world. But how could he serve this Lord? Hardly by praying and fasting, since Offerus needed plenty to eat to keep up his physical strength. So he became a ferryman who car-

ried wanderers on his shoulders across the turbulent waters of a rushing river. One night Offerus heard a child calling three times. He took him on his mighty shoulders but the child's weight seemed to increase until, in midstream, the burden became heavier than any he had yet carried across. The child on his shoulders was Christ, who carries the burdens of the whole world. In the darkness of the night the child shone like the sun above the wild waters (see drawing). Thus Offerus, sinking into the water, was christened "Christ-Offerus", the Bearer of Christ.

St. Francis renounces his extravagant way of life and his promising career as a soldier. He becomes the minstrel of love, the lover of poverty and peace. He mortifies his body, "Brother Ass", but retains his good humour and his love of nature. He practises self control by fasting, thus all the better understanding the hunger felt by the animals: on behalf of the citizens of Gubbio he promises the man-eating wolf a permanent supply of food; humbly the fierce animal places its paw in his hand. St. Francis tames his own restlessness and loquacity, but he loves the chattering swallows and the cooing doves who listen to his sermons (see drawing).

Raniero di Ranieri, the crusader, journeys with his lighted candle from Jerusalem to Florence over mountains and through deserts. His heart changes as he guards the precious flame through all dangers and adventures. This is one of the most moving of Selma Lagerlof's Christ legends which the teacher could tell little by little over a period of many days.

Fables and legends have been told ever since the remotest past. They show us two sides of

How will this wily fox manage to entice the tasty bit of cheese out of the raven's beak? Class 2.

man's nature, and how these can become anced.

According to Blaise Pascal's wise premise; he who is able to unite and reconcile the greatest contrasts in himself is capable of achieving greatness. "It is dangerous to show men how much they resemble animals without also showing them their own greatness. It is equally dangerous to let them be aware of their loftiness without also pointing to their baseness."

THE OLD TESTAMENT IN CLASS THREE

The events, the language and the characters of the Bible stories are intimately interwoven with western culture. They can be found in the arts, in sayings and proverbs, and indeed they have become part and parcel of our world picture. Deprived of the Old Testament, children would lack one of the fundamental bases for understanding our past.

But these stories have far more to offer than a mere understanding of the historic roots of our civilisation, as the following incident may indicate:

A nine-year-old pupil in the third class of a Waldorf school was unable to attend school for a while and asked his father to tell him the Bible stories he was missing. The father asked the teacher which stories were involved

and then told them to his son as best he could. When he came to a passage where he had to mention the name of God, the boy was most agitated and interrupted him, saying "Father, you must never say 'God', you must say 'the Lord', just as the Bible does."

There is no other work in the whole of world literature which, from beginning to end, deals so thoroughly with the problem of authority.

The Old Testament—from which only a selection of significant stories is told—speaks at first of the whole of mankind, then of the Semites, then of the Israelites, and finally only of the tribe of Judah. But, throughout, the principal character is the same, the Lord God himself. Men break His commandments or even deny Him and He is compelled to chastise them. His punishments are often extremely severe but He is not petty. At times He even protects those who defy Him or those who commit sins. Not many of the characters in the Old Testament could approach the throne of the highest judge with completely pure hands.

Adam and Eve disobey His commandments and thus become the forebears of man who has to sustain himself by reaping the fruits of the earth.

The descendents of Cain, the fratricide, become the ancestors of cattle-breeding nomads, artisans and craftsmen. The arrogance of the attempt to build the tower of Babel leads to the scattering of the peoples and the birth of many tongues and hence to the spread of civilization over the face of the earth. Isaac's son Jacob wins his birthright by deception, thus becoming the ancestor of the twelve tribes of Israel. Through the falsehood of his brothers,

Joseph is led into Egypt, to be followed gradually by the whole of his people. Moses, who slays an Egyptian in anger, leads the children of Israel out of slavery. He meets the Lord on Mount Sinai and receives the tablets of the law, thus laying the foundation for the future religion of his people. Saul, David and Solomon are all problematic characters, and yet they are instrumental for the continuation of the work of God. With His immeasurable wisdom the Lord succeeds in bending the forces of defiance and of evil, thus making them serve the order of His universe.

The teacher can spare himself much moralising if he tells the stories of the Old Testament, whose pictures are quite different from those in fairy tales, fables and legends. The narrative style of the Bible is more complex and liable to varying interpretations. The stories do not always have a happy ending, but they are loaded with moral force.

When the children wax indignant about Adam and Eve, or tremble on account of the Flood, sigh with relief when Abraham is spared the command to sacrifice Isaac, or wonder at the revelation on Mount Sinai, rejoice with David, or clench their fists against Goliath and the Philistines, then they experience in great pictures the problems with which they are wrestling more or less consciously within their own souls—the new Covenant, which at their stage they have to enter into with their fellow beings, the experience of both reverence and resentment, of obedience and wilfulness, and, not least, the dim awareness that something new is happening in their own development. This is the crisis at the age of nine, the "new age of defiance".

STORIES RELATING TO INDIVIDUAL PROBLEMS

Stories illustrating the inner situation of an individual child or of a whole group can have amazingly far-reaching effects. In such stories children experience their own short-comings and the consequences of their actions with the same keen interest with which they usually follow the events and adventures of a well-loved hero, without, however, realising that they are looking at themselves. In this way it is possible to tackle personal problems or bad habits which would otherwise be very difficult to deal with. But it is most important that when listening to such a story the children remain completely unaware of the teacher's real purpose in telling it.

Among her group of seven-year-olds, a teacher once had a boy who often told lies. Thinking of him, she told her class "The Pearl of Truth" by Zacharias Topelius. In this story the Queen of the Land of Truth has lost an immensely valuable pearl down a deep well. One by one her subjects climb down into the well to search for the pearl. Anyone who has told a lie even only once in his life comes up again with a black ring round his mouth. Those who have lied frequently return with large black stains on their faces. During the course of the story the boy in question clearly showed that in fact he detested lies. Suddenly he blurted out: "I nev . . . always lie!" A moments reflec-

tion had turned yet another of the boy's lies into truth. The teacher apparently took no notice of this reaction and she continued with the story.

The boy's exclamation bore witness to a moment of deep self recognition. At about the same time his family moved house and their way of life also changed to a certain extent. The story contributed towards a healing process which eventually led to the boy becoming more harmonious and, as a result, more truthful.

If the teacher does not know of a suitable story, he should try to make one up. It need not be a poetic masterpiece! Steiner has emphasised that what matters is the teacher's effort to enter into the being and actions of the little "sinner". Though his story may be amateurish, his inner effort has a very strong effect upon his pupils.

One young and inexperienced teacher found that he could not control his very lively Class I. In despair he sent the worst culprits out of the classroom. In the corridor they found a coal scuttle and began pelting each other with pieces of coal. Some of the young scamps burst back into the classroom and there was complete chaos. As this was the last lesson of the day, some mothers began to arrive to collect their children and were thus witnesses of this dreadful scene.

This and similar experiences profoundly depressed the young teacher. He began to spend his evening trying to find a solution to his problem. Naturally his thoughts turned again and again to the wildest of the children. Gradually a story began to emerge as a result of his musing. It was about a youth who had been given the task of looking after the king's sheep and whose life would be forfeited if he lost any of them. But a number of the

In this picture the child has obviously delighted in letting the Tower of Babel grow higher and higher. Class 3.

Next page: The god Odin and his eight-legged steed Sleipnir. Class 4.

sheep took no notice of the young shepherd nor of his dog and ran far away. Others were scattered by the wolf. After several adventures and with the help of kind people he was at last able to collect all the sheep together again and bring them back to the king.

The children listened attentively to the story of the straying sheep. Some of them expressed their indignation about the stupidity and disobedience of the animals. The parallel situation in the class was obvious, yet the teacher avoided hinting at it and the children said nothing. Nevertheless, something had changed. A link of sympathy was at last established without which no work can flourish in any class. Of course, the behaviour of the class was far from exemplary even then, but a lasting contact between the teacher and the children had been made.

Stories of this therapeutic kind can still be very effective when children are approaching puberty. A boy aged eleven once had to face a difficult home situation caused by his parents' divorce. This, on top of his own personality difficulties, made him very aggressive. One day he picked up a stone and threw it at a former older pupil who had come back to the school on a visit. At the same time he sneered at the older boy, whom he knew well and actually admired.

The teacher decided to take "indirect" action in the hope of helping the boy to repent of what he had done. She was in the middle of a main lesson on geography,* describing the spread of local industry in one of the country's provinces. She now wove into the lesson a dramatic story about two men who had been good friends and comrades at work, but between whom enmity had gradually grown which finally led to a violent fight in the street.

The children were very indignant and the boy in question interrupted, saying: "I didn't do it like that!", followed almost immediately by: "I didn't really mean to do it!" The teacher took no notice and finished her story. The other children in the class did not notice what was going on, but after the lesson the boy went to the teacher and said: "I don't know why I did it, I'm going to apologise to him." To the joy and surprise of the older boy he really did conquer his pride and apologised. This incident contributed greatly to the boy gradually becoming more harmonious.

Those who create, prepare and tell such stories, really know what it is to share in the children's inner battles with the problems life brings them.

THE NINTH YEAR – A TURNING POINT IN THE CHILD'S DEVELOPMENT

Victor was nine. He had always been easy to manage both at home and at school. One day the parents had reason to complain to the class-teacher that Victor had suddenly become extremely obstreperous, refused to take part in the usual Sunday walk, and was most unruly. The music-teacher, too, had been having trouble. Victor had always been quite a support in the class, but now he had been blowing his recorder upside down, and doing many other silly things. Even his hand-writing had changed to a kind of miniature writing. After four or five months this phase passed. He became quieter again, and the unruliness came to an end.

At this age an intelligent child can gaze long and silently at an adult with the unspoken question as to what kind of person the adult really is. The unconscious feeling can arise in the child that the adult has been weighed-up and found wanting. In such a situation the child's behaviour alters from one moment to the next. All respect has vanished.

Children who have been forced to experience all too often in their own lives the effects of adult insecurity, such as continuous anxiety over the smallest indisposition, giving way to the most fleeting of moods etc., can just at this age find themselves in a real period of crisis. This can show itself in attacks of fear, outbreaks of temper, or other similarly striking symptoms.

At this age whole classes may put their teacher to the test. Earlier on children were simply noisy at times. Now they will make little experiments. How will the teacher react when a snowball is fastened to the ceiling just above the spot where he usually stands, and slowly begins to drip on to him? His weaknesses both large and small are noticed and give rise to comments. They are also aptly copied. It has also been observed that children of this age can secretly imitate and ridicule in a completely heartless way, the handicap of some child in the class. If the teacher feels personally injured, or reacts with stern or unconsidered disciplinary measures, a really difficult and unpleasant situation may develop.

What is it, that is actually taking place in the child's own being at this particular stage? Rudolf Steiner describes this phenomenon as a process of emancipation with consequences of greater import than we often realise.

Even if the original instinctive "I-experience", comes much earlier than this, actually in the third or fourth year of life, yet before the ninth year children are not able consciously to experience themselves as separate from their environment. The instinctive longing of the little child to identify itself with animals, plants, and stones, with wind and cloud and star, is often regarded as a kind of childish anthropomorphism, a more or less conscious attempt to "ensoul" the outer reality. Steiner maintains that such terms do not do justice to the entirely spontaneous and unintellectual element in the child's mode of experience. When Piaget describes how children before the seventh year grasp reality as an undifferentiated unity, how they are not in the position to distinguish between their own content of consciousness, and that of the objects in the world around them, and then how in the period from the eighth to the eleventh year they lose their anthropomorphism, and begin to look at things in a realistic way, then he comes very near to Steiner's conception, even if his manner of expressing himself is a little different. (Guido Petter, 'The Spiritual Development Of The Child In The Works Of Jean Piaget.')

During the first three years the teacher must pay due regard to this characteristic in his whole way of teaching. Earth and Sun, Plant and Animal must speak to each other as if they were human beings. Only in the fourth class does he pass on, step by step, to describing things "as they are."

It is this change in their relationship to the environment that causes so many children of this age to go through a period of alienation. The fact is that they can now observe their teacher with much greater awareness than before. But they are testing "authority", not because they want to shake it off, but because they want to make sure it really exists.

This remark of a nine-year old choleric, about a teacher of riper years who had mastered the difficult art of being strict and kindly at the same time, is typical for this age, "The old thing is alright–as long as you do what she tells you!"

Having saved up the realistic presentation of reality for this point of time, the class-teacher in the Waldorf school now has at his disposal a powerful weapon which he can use to overcome the difficulties. He has a whole battery of exciting subjects, which convey new knowledge. Local geography and animal study are taken in Class IV. General geography, botany and history in Class V. For now the children have reached the inner maturity they need to look with wide-awake eyes at the world of reality, armed and equipped with a desire for learning as yet unused and therefore keen.

ENVIRONMENTAL STUDIES

In the first years of school the souls of healthy children still live strongly in the world of pictures created by the human imagination. The instinctive wish at this age to follow everything in the environment with close interest can actually best be served by the teacher clothing the events of this world in living stories. Field and wood, stream and bank, house and garden, flower and tree, bird and fish, hold conversations with each other as if they were people. In the third class, when the children are nearing the ninth-year stage, begins another mode of approach. The transition can be found by the teacher when he speaks of objects and activities which are common to the realm of fairy-tales as well as the world around us, and therefore have something of an archetypal quality. For instance, he may speak to the children of the farmer and his plough, the carpenter and his saw, the fisher and his net, the bricklayer and his trowel.

Today or Yesterday

The objection could be raised that such an approach is in certain respects not true to the facts. Would it not be more in keeping to describe to the children the working world as it is today, in a straightforward and direct way? But whenever someone actually does this in a one-sided way, he is contributing to that unattached and rather conceited attitude which is so easily engendered in children today by our modern ways of life and thought. A well-known British jazz-singer was asked about ten years ago—and at that time he was still a very young man—which type of dance-music would in his opinion replace the sort then in vogue. He made it clear in his reply that he considered "rock 'n roll", which was then the height of fashion as a kind of culmination of musical development, the end of the road in

When the child is nine or ten years old he becomes awake in a different way to the world around him. It is important at this point to introduce subjects that provide full opportunity for his new faculties of observation and learning. In the third class different basic crafts are presented, and in the fourth class the study of the home environment. These are like doors through which the child steps out into the world.

the history of music. Life itself brings it about that in most cases our pupils come to judge the world according to prevailing modern standards. We as teachers must make it possible through our consciously directed efforts that they gradually acquire for themselves a humanly balanced approach to the world, with due regard to man's historical development. Our forefathers, who did their farming without tractors, fishing without trawlers and sounding devices, were neither stupid nor impractical in the eyes of their contemporaries. We have been able to achieve more than they did, because we, as it were, stand on their shoulders. We must feel gratitude towards them. Seen from this aspect, it is entirely in keeping with the times, when teaching a third class, to make use of many such examples which have either no special time association at all or belong to a past age.

For instance, the teacher describes the various types of grain and their special qualities and uses, for one is not quite a full human being if one cannot distinguish between wheat, rye, barley and oats. He describes how in earlier times corn was harvested, threshed, dried, milled and baked. He tells the children how butter and cheese were made, how meat and vegetables were preserved, how people manured and sowed their fields, and how they built their houses. It is a good thing if every child once in its lifetime can handle implements and materials such as a butter churn, a plough, bricks and mortar etc., or at least watch them being used. The crafts and skills concerned can be grasped by younger children because they are simple. They provide a suitable basis for the later understanding of complicated technical processes.

When building is the subject under discussion, one particular aspect, previously not so thoroughly dealt with, becomes important, the ques-

tion of weights and measures. The children's interest in this section of mathematics can be awakened when they are brought to realise, that in olden times measurements of length were often derived from the human body, for instance, an inch, a foot, a yard, a mile (the Roman "mille passus"). Later they begin to use the easier modern units of measurement, metres, litres, kilograms etc., which are however more abstract in their derivation. It is most important that these calculations, when one actually reaches this point, are exactly worked out. Pupils usually find great delight in measuring their class-room, houses, gardens and fields, in fact any area or cubic content.

In the fourth class, it is clear that the teacher must introduce new and lively themes to meet the increasing awakeness of the ten-year-olds. Now we come to a more detailed study of the child's surroundings. The history and geography of the town or village and its immediate neighbourhood are described. As a background activity to this study, excursions are made to farms, mills, factories, museums, churches, the town-hall etc., and the children draw or paint pictures of what they have seen.

Another significant experience can be introduced to the child in connection with this subject. He draws a picture of his own route to school, starting from the bed where he slept, and ending in the class-room. The houses, of course, must be rather small. One has to draw this as it would look to a bird or the pilot of a low-flying helicopter. For the first time the child draws a kind of map.

To watch a house being built is a memorable experience in the third or fourth class. It is not an easy matter to draw a map for the fist time. For how can you possibly fit in all the interesting things you see o your way to school in one and the same picture? Class 4.

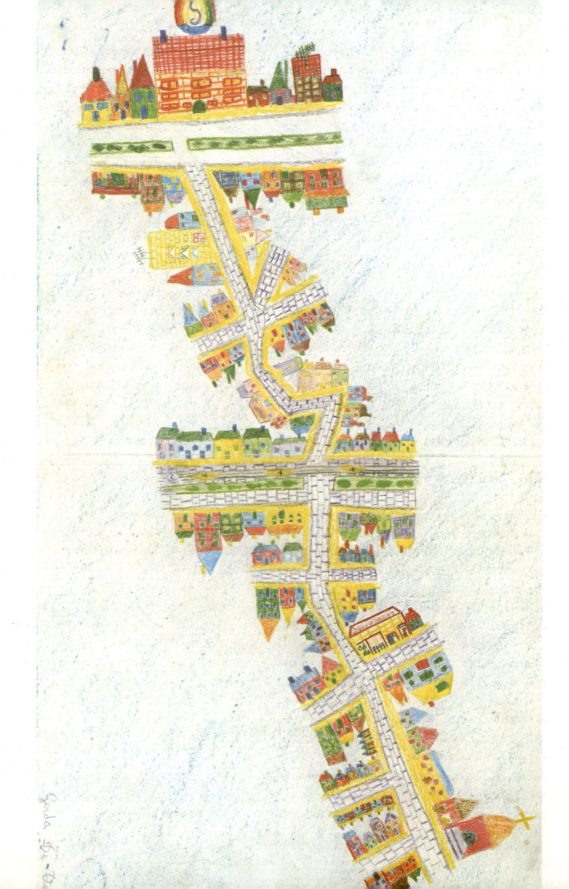

without the wind we human beings could not live.

Einmal Mörtel, Einmal Stein
Fügen wir der Mauer ein

Left: If the wind did not continually bring fresh air from the sea into the big industrial cities, human beings could not go no living there.

The work of the brick-layer is one of the archetypal crafts which can still see today.

STUDY OF MAN
AND THE ANIMAL
KINGDOM

To what extent is there kinship between man and animal, and what distinguishes the one from the other? In a preliminary discussion between teacher and children in the IV class, leading up to the study of elementary zoology, significant aspects can come to expression. A class-teacher narrates the following conversation:

"How would it be if we acted like animals?"

"Do you mean climbing a tree like a squirrel, for instance?"

"Yes, take that as an example."

"Well, we could climb the tree, of course, but we couldn't keep up with the squirrel."

"But Peter, supposing you tried to leap like an squirrel, you would probably kill yourself, for you can't fly through the air as he does."

"Yes, I could, if I had a parachute!"

"But you wouldn't have one!"

Now another child joins in: "When I was small, we always played horses, and ran about."

"How did you do that?"

"Well, we pretended to be horses, but of course we weren't really because we had no horses."

"George can be just like a fish. He can swim under water."

"Well, yes, but only for a little while."

"I couldn't keep it up for long."

"But you don't need to. You can take a submarine. That does better even than a fish."

"Yes, or have aeroplanes, jet-fighters, for flying. Even the birds can't keep up with them."[*]

Such a conversation may result in the children becoming especially interested in the differentiation between the limbs of the various animals, in comparison with those of man, and the teacher can follow this up in subsequent lessons, as the following examples illustrate:

The octopus propels himself along by expelling the water he takes in. Its so-called arms are not actual limbs, but rather like outstretched lips feeling around for their prey, which they then greedily engulf.

In the case of the mole, the fore-feet, which are used for digging, are short but very muscular, the toes are webbed and flattened out to form a kind of shovel, the bare palms are turned outwards. The mole can neither jump nor climb, and therefore he only creeps out of his burrow at night. Strangely enough, he is also a good swimmer. But digging is his greatest skill.

In the same way the seal, with its trunk shaped like a large drop and its legs transformed to flappers, belongs to the water in which it lives. Out of the water it is helpless and clumsy.

The woodpecker is neither a hunter nor skilful in flight. His claws are formed in such a way that he can hold himself firmly upright on a tree-trunk and drum at the bark.

The brown bear, despite its heavy build, is quick-moving and nimble. Carrying a dead

[*] Margarete Lundmerk, "På Väg mot on ny padagogik" (Nov. 2, 1966).

The eagle is at home in the air.

horse on its fore-paws, it can climb about on narrow mountain-paths. Equally well it can catch up with a running reindeer, and bring it to the ground with a single blow. Quite often it walks upright, treading the ground rather like man, with the flat of its foot. But its claws can never be retracted. Its touch is always aggressive.

Animals can in every case use their limbs only in a specialised one-sided way. It is their instinctive desires that dictate their movements, getting food, reproduction, or defence. Fore and hind-limbs are seldom differentiated.

Here we come to significant differences between man and animal. Man is not able to swim, run, or climb as well as the various "specialists" among the animals. But on the other hand he is versatile. He can make tools for himself, which nowadays often far outstrip the achievements of the animals. He can employ his hands for activities which he himself has consciously decided to carry out, activities which from a material point of view may seem unmotivated, and stand in direct contrast to certain instincts which he shares with the animals. He can perform hand-movements which are exclusive to the human race, such as making and controlling machines, writing, playing a musical instrument, painting and modelling. "There is no more beautiful symbol of human freedom than the human arm and hand."*

Animals and the Temperaments

Among the instinctive capacities, which the human being has in the age of childhood, and later to a great extent loses, belongs the ability to identify himself with the experience of a certain animal. The teacher can work with this, inasmuch as he characterises animals which bring to clear expression one or another of the temperaments. If he gives a lively description, it is a matter of course that the grazing cow will especially appeal to the phlegmatic children, the pouncing lion to the cholerics, and the leaping antelope to the sanguines. Maybe the melancholic children in the class, especially those with a hint of choler, will be drawn to the eagle.

But there are also animals which can be so described that they have an appeal to all the temperaments. The octopus or squid, was painted at the same time by the whole class. Just these pictures clearly show how instinctive and how varied is the approach of the different children in the class to the same subject. It is most essential that in this period children should not be led to draw in a naturalistic way, but should be allowed to express to the full their own inner predispositions. Whoever is inclined to think that the paintings done by Waldorf pupils have a common style should carefully compare this set of paintings of the octopus.

* Rudolf Steiner in a lecture of 28. 8. 1919.

Above right: Form and movement are reminiscent of early cave-drawings. Class 8.

Below right: A lion hunting for prey. Class 5.

152

BOTANY

Basic Conditions of Plant-life

Teaching about plants can begin with a conversation between class and teacher about the importance of the sun in the life of the plant. The children's attention can be drawn to the yearly variations in the sun's daily course in the temperate zones, the first sensitive reactions in tree and bud to the increasing daylight, the great changes that come with the warmth of spring. Without making use of abstract scientific concepts, the teacher can call on the children's own powers of observation in speaking of the difference between the parts of the plant exposed to the light, and those under the earth. How colourful and delicate is the blossom, how soft and full of sap is the leaf and stem, how strong and hard the white or brownish root.

The sun, however, is only one of the two decisive factors for plant-life. The other is the soil, and from the soil comes moisture. A wilting pot-plant which recovers its erectness and begins to grow again when it is watered demonstrates to the children the significance of moisture. The teacher may describe the leguminous plants, which in wet summers merely grow longer and longer without forming seed, and on the other hand the trees whose leaves after a dry growing season turn yellow and wither already in June. Pine-trees with their shallow roots can only exist in a moist soil, whereas the deeper-rooting firs can survive in a drier situation.

But soil-fertility does not only depend on water. Again in quite a simple but concrete way the teacher can show the children the differences in the structure and composition of the soil in different neighbourhoods and point out that where some plants need quite a special soil-condition, others will grow anywhere.

After dwelling on these more general aspects, examples may be given of particular plant-communities which the children themselves may have observed. For instance, what sort of plants do we usually find on a pasture, and which on grassland where no animals graze, on heaths or in bogs, on mountain-slopes or in fertile valleys, in different types of woodlands? What do we see growing on a rubbish heap, and what in a well-tended garden? What plants appear during the course of the changing seasons?

The child's growing awareness for the plant-world which results from such considerations

One of the factors that have contributed to the destruction of our natural environment is a general lack of knowledge of the basic requirements of the plant. Only when children at the right stage of their development get a real experience of how climate, soil and vegetation form an inter-related whole, will they have the insight later on to help in maintaining soil-fertility and a healthy plant-life in various regions of the world.

Above right: Sketch of a fern-clump.

Below right: The hard old tree-trunk performs the same function for the twigs and leaves sprouting from it as the mound of earth for the plants growing on its surface. Class 5.

Prickly
Shield

throws a new light on farming practices which were first introduced in Class III. The teacher can point out, for example, what a vast difference there is when the farmer ploughs up an old-established pasture where the soil has been kept fertile for years by the grazing animal and the growth of white clover, or when he cultivates a piece of ground, where man in his greed has exploited the soil through monoculture.

The Classification of Plants

But how can the teacher, when he wishes to remain in the realm of concrete observation, give the children some kind of survey over the wide range of plant-life?

One possibility would be to set side by side the different levels of plant-life (fungi, lichens, algae, mosses, ferns, flowering-plants etc.), with the stages of the child's development. The mushrooms, which while growing quickly are otherwise such undeveloped organisms, having neither leaves, stems or roots, can be compared to small babies. Flowering-plants with their greater differentiation and possibilities correspond to the schoolchild, etc. Such an approach, as suggested by Rudolf Steiner in his seminar lecture of 2.9.1919, is not just an arbitary comparison, but one that is especially stimulating and fruitful for the child. Dr. Gerbert Grohmann has elaborated and confirmed it from the standpoint of a trained botanist, and as the result of many year's teaching experience in a Waldorf school, in his books, 'The Plant' Volumes I and II, and his book about plants for children, 'Lesebuch der Pflanzenkunde'. (A Reader about Plants.)

Another way of achieving a similar survey would be to climb in imagination a tropical mountain, such as the Kilimanjaro. The different vegetational zones, tropical forest, mixed woodland, moss-lichen belt, permanent snow, come under revue, rather as if one were travelling from the Equator to the North Pole. Looked at in this way, the two hemispheres appear like two mountains joined at the base. Plant-study thus leads over into geography.

The Value of Plant Study

Such a wide approach naturally makes demands on the teacher. Not everyone has the necessary knowledge and connection with nature. Would it not be good, just in this case, to avail oneself of the various teaching aids? But which to choose? To examine a few wilting plant-specimens in the class-room would actually go contrary to the desired direction, namely to experience the plant-world in its natural context. To make botanical excursions for the purpose of methodical observation is a sure way to spoil the children's experience of nature. No book, no coloured slide, no film can stimulate so strong an inner experience or so lively a conversation as gathering together what the children have actually seen themselves, supplemented by the teacher's account of what is further away and less known to them. Such a course of plant-study certainly involves a long time spent in preparation by the teacher.

What is the real significance of this period of study? It is indeed a subject of the utmost importance. Rudolf Steiner has repeatedly impressed on us that the decrease in quality of agricultural produce is due to the fact that modern man has not acquired through his education a strong enough feeling for the importance of maintaining soil-fertility. As he says in a lecture of 14.8.1924, "If we wish to know how plant and earth belong together, then we must find out to what type of soil the single plant belongs; and how to manure the soil properly can only be learned by seeing the earth and the plant-world as a unity, and the plant as something growing within the organism of the earth." The problem here brought forward by Rudolf Steiner has become ever more acute. The enormous increase in the use of nitrogen in modern agriculture has been a potent factor in exposing farmcrops to the attacks of insect and fungus pests. In turn the use of poisonous pesticides to solve this problem is starting to cause damage to an extent that we are just beginning to realise, but do not yet fully grasp. Namely because he has not understood the natural connection between the soil and plant-life, man has destroyed to an extent probably never known before the productiveness of the earth. According to FAO statistics some 38 % of the earth-surface is covered either by desert or urban developments. According to R. Doane and G. Borgström, the corresponding figure for 1880 was 17 %. The increase in world-population adds to the problem. If the agricultural problems of the future are to be successfully tackled, not only farmers, scientists and authorities must take part, but also, because of the resultant cost, the ordinary consumer. Exploitation of Nature will gradually have to give way to a deepened understanding for the essentials of ecology on the part of a growing number of people. Will our children be able to think and act rightly in this sphere if the basis for this understanding has not been prepared through their early education?

Right and left next pages: The contrasting moods of lily and rose. Class 6.

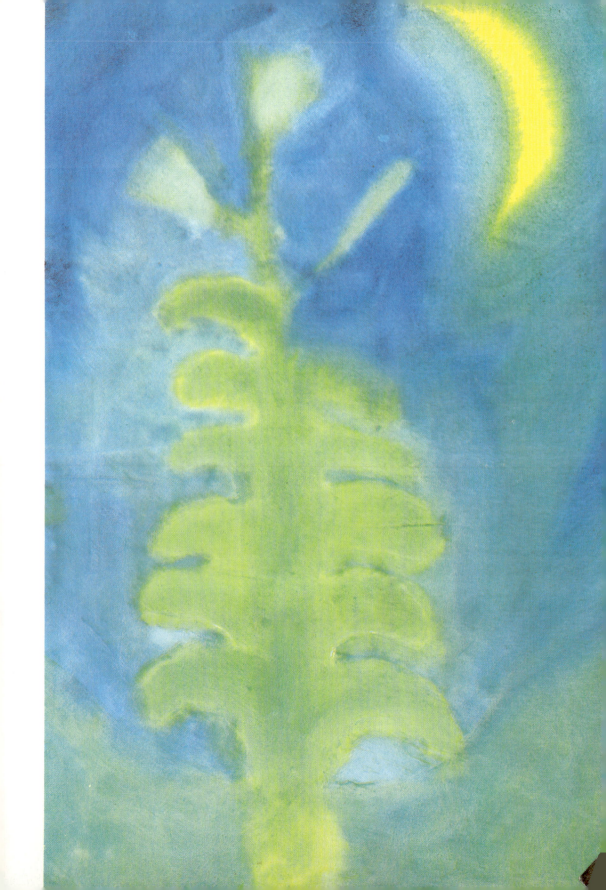

GEOGRAPHY

When in the fifth class, studies of the immediate environment pass over into geography proper, the children enter upon a realm of knowledge which in Rudolf Steiner's view is one of the most important:

"Teaching the child in this way, we place him into space, and he will begin to be interested in the world, in the whole wide world. And we shall see the results of this in many directions. A child with whom we study geography in an intelligent manner will have a more loving relationship to his fellow men than one who has no feeling of what proximity in space means; for he will learn to feel that he lives alongside of other human beings, and he will come to have regard and respect for them.

The teaching of geography is one of the most important means of ensuring a sense of responsibility in later life towards the natural resources of the earth and their fair distribution for the benefit of mankind as a whole, rather than to the advantage of political or industrial power-groups. There is hardly another sphere of study through which we can appeal so strongly, without the need to moralize, to the sense for "brotherhood" in economic matters, as the study of geography in early adolescence.

Above left: Fritjof Nansen's ship battling its way through polar ice.
Below left: Volcanic eruption.
The contrast of the subject-matter in these two pictures is shown in every detail of form and colour.

Such things play no little part in the moral training of the children, and the lack of attention to geography is partly responsible for the terrible decline in recent years of the brotherly love that should prevail among men." (14. 6. 1921)

The Effect of the Natural Surrounding

In what way does his natural environment influence man? What is life like on the shores of the Polar seas, where one sometimes has to cut a path through the ice with one's boat? How does one feel when living in a volcanic area, where one is faced with earthquakes or flowing lava? The attempt to experience inwardly the most varied conditions of human life provide interesting and important themes for artistic activity.

The drawing of maps presents quite a new task. The transition from a simple sketch-plan of the neighbourhood, as was drawn earlier, to an actual map marks an important step in the child's development. The map shows little or nothing of what we actually see around us. To understand its meaning, one needs an appreciation of abstraction. This is something that usually only evolves in the child by the eleventh or twelfth year.

The best way of understanding a map is to paint it oneself. Different elements, such as a desert, a tropical forest, or a mountainous region, demand differing artistic treatment. The following examples all concern northern Europe:

The origin of Holland as land wrested from the sea, and its present contours, can be strongly experienced in the intermingling water-colours.

In painting Finland as "the land of a thousand lakes", blue is much in evidence.

163

To depict Norway with its complicated structure of mountain and valley demands intricate detail.

Economic Geography

In Class V a larger area is taken which forms a whole either from a regional or economic point of view.

In Class VI the power of thinking is beginning to awaken and with it the understanding for the laws of physics and chemistry. Geography lessons must bring to the children facts that enlarge their inner horizon. They must be led into the realm of mineralogy, meteorology, astronomy, and especially to the consideration of the economic factors affecting the different regions of the entire globe.

Most Waldorf schools are in temperate regions with relatively congenial conditions for plant-growth, and intensive industrial development.

Of course, the children must learn to know their own surrounding in all its different aspects. But it is almost more important that they should become familiar with the details of everyday life and the special environmental problems of people who have to struggle for their existence, for instance in tropical regions.

Cultural Aspects

Economic considerations are continued in Classes VII and VIII, for at this age children delight in learning new facts, and often take an especial pleasure in statistics, graphs, or lists of names. Another new aspect too now enters in. The cultural traditions, the spiritual directions of the various peoples come more and more under consideration. It can be suf-

ficient for the teacher to bring to the class certain examples, which illuminate and characterise in a striking way the cultural climate of some particular region. In this context passages from various travellers' accounts of their experiences among the different races can be read and discussed. One or two typical examples can be indicated:

China

"It happened in Koulun, that part of Hong Kong which is built on the mainland. I found an antique shop there, where I hoped to buy a particular small object that I had been looking for. Hardly had I entered, in fact I was still standing in the doorway from where I could see the hundreds of objects with which the shop was crammed—although actually not the one I had come to buy—when the Chinese shopkeeper greeted me. Then he looked at me thoughtfully, but it was almost more a listening than a looking, though I remained silent. Then he said with a smile, as if it were the most natural thing in the world, "Sir, I believe you are looking for a small jade holder for joss-sticks?" I could only confirm this. It was exactly what I had in mind. Almost daily I had similar experiences while I was in Asia. It is a matter . . . of thought-reading." (From the 'Asienfibel' by Jean Gebser)

Has the painter here realized the stark differences between Norway and Sweden from the cultural, as well as the geographical aspect? Class 5.

"One day I was walking though the Liu Li-Chang, a street in the old part of Peking always crowded with people. A man of fifty or perhaps older, obviously a workman, was cycling home on his old bike. His progress was slow and laboured. Suddenly the front fork broke, and he fell to the ground. Not one of the men and women going along that narrow street either turned to look or stopped. They merely stepped aside to avoid him. No-one offered help. Slowly he got up again, his mouth was bleeding. This kind of indifference was typical of the old China." ('The three banners of China' by Marc Riboud)

The United States

"New York", a traveller there wrote about 1840, "is the busiest town one can imagine. Everything in the streets is rush and hurry. Even the carriages do not move at a walking pace, but trot or even gallop along! Everyone on the street", he continues, "keeps to the same tempo, as if they were frightened of being late ... Nervous tension is everywhere. All contemporary observers have noticed how Americans swallow their food quickly, and leave the table. Their jaws move incessantly, and the chewing of tobacco—the forerunner of chewing-gum—is a general habit."

Another traveller writes about the New Englander: "When his feet are still, it is his hands that are always busy with something, whether he carves a piece of wood or just makes notches in the edge of the table." ('The epic of America' by James Truslow Adams)

HISTORY

Today people are already speaking of youth "without a sense of history". Interest in historical relationships must first be awakened. For only out of an understanding of the past is it possible to do justice to the present and to shape the future. Instruction in history in the early school years takes on special significance here, because it often produces lasting and effective impressions.

The historical approach which is beginning generally to gain ground today was established in the curriculum of the Waldorf Schools from the beginning. Not the national but the human aspect is what must determine the educational horizon.

In class IV the children are introduced to the history of their immediate neighbourhood. In class V, however, this direction is not maintained, and national history is not the next step. The approach becomes immediately world-wide. But how can the interest of ten- or eleven-year-olds be kindled for the remoter aspects of the history of mankind? Where should the teacher start?

Stages in Historical Evolution

The earliest religions documents give an indication of definite stages in the development of the ancient peoples.

In the Bhagavad Gita the holy Yogi sunk in meditation is presented as the highest aim of man. In the Persian Zend-Avesta other virtues are pre-eminent: the industrious husbandman with his prosperous herds of cattle and flourishing crops becomes the ideal. In one of the Babylonian myths of creation, man's foremost task is to build temples to the gods. In Homer's epics, after the death of the valiant Achilles, the central figure is the clever Odysseus, who conquers Troy through his god-inspired cunning and overcomes the many trials and tribulations that beset him on his homeward journey.

These examples illustrate four great stages in the history of man. The first was the religious attitude of the early nomadic civilisations, wholly turned towards the gods and away from the earth. Then came the devotion to the soil of the first tribes to settle down and cultivate the ground. A later stage was the development of an artistic culture, as exemplified by the river-civilisations of the Middle-East and their great monuments. And nearer our own time came the Greeks, with their newly awakened powers of organising life through the thinking faculty.

This evolutionary stream, flowing from East to West, and in time giving rise to our own form of civilisation, had its origin in North-East India about 10,000—8,000 B.C. It proceeded by way of Iran to Mesopotamia and Egypt, where the first great works of architecture and early writing arose about 3,000 B.C., and ultimately spread throughout the whole Mediterranean world.

When the teacher of class V describes this development in a lively and imaginative way, he will find that the children become fascinated by this great canvas of historical evolution. The ancient myths and epics, which the children have heard at an earlier age, now assume a new significance as the backcloth of actual historical events.

Subjective or Objective Presentation?

There is always a problem when the subject-matter of a lesson is presented primarily through the teacher himself and not through textbooks, and this comes to the fore especially in the teaching of history. The question arises how far one can achieve an objective approach.

An actual example may illustrate how this requirement can be met in Waldorf teaching methods.

History teaching in class VII should comprise those events in the fifteenth and sixteenth centuries which justify one in speaking of the dawn of a new era: the Renaissance, the Reformation, the great new discoveries in the fields of geography and astronomy. It is obviously impossible to confine oneself to a mere catalogue of events and to exclude any feeling participation on the part of the pupil in the attempt to be objective. If you want to arouse the interest of thirteen-year-olds in Luther's 95 theses pinned to the church door at Wittenberg, in his appearance at the Diet of Worms and for his religious reforms in Saxony, you have to describe vividly the symptoms of decadence in the Church of his time and especially Luther's own bold initiative. How shall the teacher describe this? Shall he portray equally dramatically his religious narrowmindedness, his belief in the supreme power of the state, and his lack of understanding of what lay at the base of the peasants' revolts? Viewed historically, this would seem justified, but if this were too strongly emphasised, the children would not be able to sustain their admiration for Luther as a character.

This kind of situation presents a real dilemma. The prevalent idea today is that there should be no "heroes". Yet young people have an absolute need for personalities whom they can admire. If this is not satisfied in the classroom, and their enthusiasm for real things is not enkindled, then no other objects of worship are available except those put forward by advertisements and mass media, which soon lose their glamour and are exchanged for other "stars".

A class-teacher who faced just the problem cited above, approached it in the following way. First he described the Reformation in a sympathetic light, and presented Luther with an obvious undertone of appreciation. After a few days the whole class had adopted this attitude, and were loud in their denunciation of Luther's opponents. Now the teacher passed on to describing the Catholic world. He concentrated on the fierce battle that the Pope and the other Catholic leaders had to fight against the Turks. He portrayed in full detail the atrocities perpetrated by the Turks in the conquered territories, and the complete lack of help on the part of the Protestant princes. He also described vividly the brave and knightly Don John of Austria, half-brother of Philip II., who led the Catholic fleet to victory at Lepanto, in 1571. Now the mood of the class changed entirely. One of the indignant questions was: "But surely that must have meant that many people turned to Catholicism?"

If we wish as teachers to awaken in the children a sense for what is generally human and not just nationalistic, then we cannot take as a starting-point the glorious past of our own nation. The teaching of history must stand on a completely new basis. Even at eleven years of age the child can grasp the significance of a world-wide perspective, when the great cultural epochs are presented in a broad and colourful panorama against the background of actual historical events.

Next pages: Hannibal's march across the Alps. Class 6.

PLAY-ACTING

What is the significance of play-acting for the child in the Waldorf school? Of course, there can be all kinds of plays. There are the brief scenes recited in the first class by the high, wavering childish voices of seven-year-olds and, at the other end of the scale, we have the classical dramas of Schiller and Shakespeare, presented in the upper school with the youthful fervour of adolescence. It is often the custom that Class Eight plays some major piece before entering the upper school and that Class Twelve presents some outstanding classical or modern drama. Here, however, we shall only comment upon what is presented in the way of plays at monthly festivals.

What does Class II perform, for example? It might be a fable, or a legend, or a little poem which has been made into a drama. The class forms a chorus. One or several of the children wear little caps—and at once it turns into a dramatic presentation! Often they are all dressed up and then it becomes for them an unforgettable experience.

The most remarkable and perhaps most important dramatic presentations are to be found in the upper forms, somewhere around the fourth or the fifth. Formerly people were often of the opinion that in theatrical pieces with ten- and eleven-years-olds the neat little verses would no longer suffice, but it must be "proper" theatre with individual roles and dialogues. There is a lack of such plays; the existing ones are often incredibly banal and mediocre.

One soon realises that ten- and eleven-years-olds, even thirteen- and fourteen-years-olds, are only successful in carrying out individual roles in exceptional cases. Too frequently one must admonish them to speak "naturally": "You just don't *talk* that way in everyday speech." In a short time they have lost all desire to act. Very often the teacher then draws the false conclusion that plays and theatre are something you can do only with small children or with especially interested or gifted older children.

If eleven-year-olds (except those few who may be called "theatrically gifted") no longer wish to act after having taken part in "Robby and Fiffy and the Hidden Treasure" (title made up) then that does not necessarily mean that the theatre does not belong to this age level. It may also mean that they avoid this fare because it is unpalatable.

Children need "spiritual food".

It would be as difficult for an infant to receive nourishment from adults' food, as it would be for small school children before puberty to get any nourishment from certain types of "down-to-earth" pedagogical material slapped in front of them. As an artistic element of style, the prose dialogue is much too difficult to handle. Rhythmical speech in itself already possesses the quality of "spiritual food".

There is only one possibility of achieving clarity in such questions. One experiences how it works out in reality. For example, let us enter the fifth class and observe:

"Shame on you, sons of Argos, you children!
I trusted in you,

You who with brave arms rescued our ships!
But when you shun the danger of mortal combat,
Then the day has come
When the Trojans will compel us with force!"

There stands Hector, bathed in light, and there stands fleet-footed Achilles. And those children standing on the tower (of chairs placed on a table) must be Zeus himself, "the cloud-shaker", and lovely Hera. Here the Iliad comes to life!

Their eyes are sparkling and their cheeks are glowing. No one is embarrassed because no one need be ashamed if his movements and voice are not "realistic". The rhythm carries the voices so that the room resounds. It is quite sufficient if Agamemnon simply takes a step forward and brandishes his wooden sword a bit. All enemies fall like nine-pins at his attack.

Or let us take a look at Class Four, where they are dramatising Nordic mythology. The floors of many a Waldorf school have seen innumerable giants fall from the blows of Thor's hammer 'Mjölnir'. The choir first represents one character, then the other, and are responsible for all the props needed (a wall, a forest, a house, a street). Whoever momentarily does not act, simply melts in with the rest of the chorus. It can be very educational when one succumbs to the attempt to introduce naturalistic effects: it is immediately evident how strongly this goes against the particular demands of this type of theatre.

On the other hand a dramatic presentation can tolerate a touch of the drastic and comical. A class VI once practised a presentation of King Arthur and Merlin the Magician. Moreover they were acting in English and had learnt their pieces up to the dramatic moment when the sword in the anvil reveals its mean-

ing. Then the teacher thought that there ought to be horses on the stage. The class was deeply insulted when he suggested they drape material over hobby horses. But the teacher explained that the heroes would be able to mount swiftly and move across the stage using their own legs. Eventually, these stylised "suggestions" of horses were proved to be the only appropriate solution.

Stage properties too often show remarkable ingenuity. Yard-long gilded horns on Thor's goats, a painted cardboard sheet that represents the side of a ship in the Battle of Salamis, a seven-headed dragon with seven smiling blue-eyed childlike heads, each with a collar out of which a stuffed dragon appears—all this makes an unforgettable impression.

The Battle of Salamis! That was an unforgettable play! These children, who stood as still as candles while reciting their verses, were suddenly Greece personified, as one sees it in classical sculpture, and as one hears it in the epic of Homer. The whole chorus was clothed in white and had the character of a power of fate, in whose hand it lay to conceal events (when it grouped itself at the front of the stage) or to reveal them (when it drew the side curtains open). This unearthly element is the quintessence of what happens on the stage when children perform.

If these plays simply occurred once a year, for example, as part of a programme at the end of the school-year, then the impressions would be of no lasting value. Through the monthly festivals, however, the plays become an everyday part of the school. They must be rehearsed well in advance of the actual presentation, and the other pupils experience them as spectators. In this way the plays serve as an instrument of education.

Through looking on and participating, through words, gestures, rhythms, and motions of all kinds, feelings are awakened into existence, feelings which otherwise might have remained dormant throughout one's whole life. Viewed correctly, a feeling for style, for rhythm and form have significance for one's whole life, and not merely a superficial aesthetic effect for the moment.

GEOMETRY

In the Rudolf Steiner schools children are often taught to draw the most beautiful geometrical forms with the help of a ruler and compass, sometimes as early as the fourth or fifth class. Actual geometrical construction, however, is not introduced until class VI.

Most of us usually associate the concept of "geometry" with long and difficult series of formal proofs. Here, however, something quite different is intended. Geometry can be "experienced" long before one has to "prove" anything with it.

What happens when one constructs a regular eighteen-sided figure and connects each point with the other? What happens when one intersects the radius of a circle six times and draws circles around the six intersecting points with the same radius? Or if one uses the same principle to construct twelve or more circles?

What figures develop when one draws a system of "rotating" semi-circles into a large circle with each semi-circle having a different centre? Approached in this way geometry becomes a voyage of discovery in a world of forms of infinite richness.

However, how does one find the path from the poetry of construction to the prose of truth? The theorem of Pythagoras can serve as an example of how these two worlds may be bridged. If the children draw a rectangular triangle and construct squares on each side and cut both small ones according to one or other of the models in the accompanying pictures, they will immediately see that the collective parts of the large square can be discovered in the figures which have thus arisen. The pupils can be encouraged to form the basic triangles of the whole construction in as many ways as possible. The principle always holds true. The areas of both small squares always exactly cover the large quadrangle.

Although such assignments still remain completely within the realm of the pictorial-concrete, they can serve as a preliminary practice of what is to come later. One should not then go on to the actual proofs until the children have reached the stage of development in which the need to explain causal relations has awakened and with it the joy in abstractions such as are to be found in algebra. This stage begins only about the twelfth year.

Next two pages: The traditional intellectual approach to geometry has little appeal for the twelve-year-old, but to discover the laws underlying geometrical constructions by actually drawing them awakens enthusiasm.

THE TWELFTH YEAR

Linda always seemed to be a reliable character. Her notebooks and practical work were finished with care and attention. Her general behaviour was always good-natured and friendly. In her sixth school-year a striking change took place. It began by her experimenting with a number of quite different writing-styles: one with upright letters, one in which they slanted backward, one with letters slanting forward, one with large letters, and one with small ones; she even tried writing upside down. The next phase was experimenting with her face: eye shadow, rouge, new expressions, etc. During class she became more and more talkative and refused to sing or recite. Previously she had shown considerable agility in Eurythmy and gymnastics. Now these exercises have become a strain for her. If she is not actually busy with something, she prefers just to lie on the floor. Her moods and her limbs have suddenly become lethargic. Her moods change quickly, however, depending upon what is going on around her. A little joke is all it takes to make Linda happy again.

After the crisis of the ninth year, most children enter a harmonious period. Ten-year-olds are often very active and good-natured: "When a ten-year-old is at his best, he gives such a well-balanced impression that he appears as the finished expression of nature's creative powers." (Arnold Gesell, 'Youth, the years from ten to sixteen'.)

At the age of eleven and above all at twelve, the picture changes. The skeleton becomes heavier, and movements, especially in the case of boys, lose their gracefulness and become jerky and uneven. The tendency to rebel increases. The deep inner transformation, which appears as an accompanying phenomenon of puberty, has not only its dark side but also its bright side. Pupils of this age have a sense of responsibility and intellectual powers which the teacher need only encourage in order to see the beauty and strength of this period of life come to expression. Loneliness and true friendship, self-interest and devoted interest for others, death and love, which previously existed only in the unknown depths of feeling, now become a real personal experience. The independent life of feeling awakens and changes the relationship to one's own body, to the environment and to ideas and ideologies. It reflects itself in one's ability to love and be interested in the world, as well as in the ability to reason and to judge.

In these years more and more specialised subjects are taken up in the classroom; subjects which require independent thinking and individual initiative. Homework increases in its scope and becomes a responsibility which the young people begin to understand and appreciate.

SCIENTIFIC LAWS;
VISIBLE
AND AUDIBLE

Walter Heitler, the well-known physicist, writes about the effect of scientific thinking on modern man (in 'Industrielle Organisation, Schweizerische Zeitschrift für Betriebswissenschaft', No. 10, 1963):

"Today when we work in the realm of atomic science or cosmology, or even the most modern area of physics, the physics of elementary particles, this no longer has the least thing to do with human life. On the other hand intellectual thinking is developed to an exceptionally high level... If scientific thinking of this character is carried to an extreme and consumes a large amount of human activity, then it is perhaps understandable that it often, although not always, must be at the expense of other things, for example, the realm of feeling. *Here perhaps one can speak of a certain kind of destruction of the human soul. If one looks carefully enough one can actually observe this phenomenon.*"

"Of course, it is not so serious if this is limited to a small number of scientists. It does, however, become a serious matter if these scientists exert a decisive influence in public life. To some extent this is already often the case. But I would consider it alarming, if, as is perhaps partly the case already, this direction of abstract thinking were to extend over wide circles of the population—that is to say if one educates young people in this direction from the start, and if one sees to it that as many people as possible devote themselves largely to abstract thinking..."

"In America it has been suggested that physics instruction begin with the fundamental building-block of matter, that is with electrons, protons, etc. Then in school the atom is gradually built (naturally only in thought), and out of the atom comes the molecules, and out of the molecules finally a piece of chalk or a stone that falls to the ground. That is just the opposite of what I would most decidedly recommend. The point of departure should be phenomena as they are actually experienced; observation is then supplemented through experimentation, and only then are the abstract concepts developed. Concepts in chemistry such as atoms and molecules should only come at the end."

The First Lesson in Physics

A phlegmatic twelve-year-old girl, who is otherwise uninterested in her school work, comes home and eagerly places a number of conical glasses on the table, fills them with water to different levels, strikes them with a fork, and pours water in and out, until she has worked out a little tonic scale. "What did you have today?" "Physics, for the first time!" She beams with joy.

There are probably few subjects which have as stirring an effect as physics. Children often get very enthusiastic about it. Physics instruction begins in Class Six with phenomena from the most diverse fields of investigation.

It is good to start with acoustics. One can assume that most children have had some experience with musical instruments. Then one widens the field of observation by using unknown instruments. Only gradually does the physical treatment of acoustics develop from these artistic musical experiences. Experiments are begun and the most diverse objects are hung on a string, then struck to test their sound. The tonal qualities of different

Der Sand ordnete sich zu wunderbaren Figuren. Wir haben beobachtet:

Vierstern — Acht-Stern — Sechzen-Stern

Tiefer Ton — Höherer Ton — Sehr hoher Ton

der Grieß gliedert sich wenig. — der Grieß wird mehr geformt. — der Grieß wird noch stärker geordnet.

Some of the well-known Chladni sound-forms produced through the vibrations of various musical tones. Class 6.

types of wood or plates of the most common metals are compared and arranged according to sound and pitch. The children should be given the opportunity to make as many discoveries as possible themselves. Finally a string is spanned across a sounding-board, and in such a way that the vibrating part can be shortened or lengthened through a crosspiece that has been placed under it. The children who can play the violin will immediately realise that one can produce tonal intervals by shortening the vibrating string. For the others it will take a bit more time to make this observation. However, since this deals with a very basic experience, one should wait patiently to see what they can discover on their own. When does the octave sound? When you shorten the string by one half. If $2/3$ of the string vibrates then the fifth is heard, if $3/4$ then a fourth, and if $3/5$ then a sixth, etc. For the time being one can be satisfied simply to

measure. The number of vibrations—which, of course, the children cannot perceive immediately—are discussed later.

One can spread sand on a sheet of light metal which has been fastened in the centre to a board and stroke the edge of the metal sheet with a violin bow. The magnificent Chladnian sound patterns arise through the dancing grains of sand. Here too one finds great value in the fact that children experience how sounds can work creatively by producing forms in the sand. One draws as accurately as possible which figures arise from which sounds. The connection between the number of vibrations and the forms they produce is thus already visibly experienced at this point.

Then the field of optics is considered. As an example of a readily observable and impressive experiment one can show the pupils the Goethean archetypal colour phenomenon. The colour of a luminous or dark object changes strikingly when it is observed through an opaque or "cloudy" medium (coloured panes of glass, liquids, clouds of smoke). The following experiments epitomise the phenomena.

When you blow across the mouth of a test-tube, a note sounds that varies according to the amount of liquid it holds.
This picture shows how strongly the pupil has entered into the experiment. Class 6.

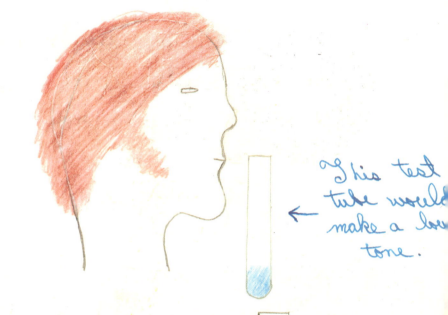

This test tube would make a low tone.

The tube with the lesser water will make a lower tone when blown on.

If you drop soapsuds in a transparent dish of water, a cloudy solution will appear. The light placed behind the dish will cause a warm colour to arise. If you place the light to the side of the container then you see a cold colour against a dark background. By joining light and opaqueness you see in one instance ruby red, in another a luminous blue. Now the teacher can remind the students that on beautiful evenings we often experience exactly the same phenomenon. The setting sun is a brilliant red while the sky on the horizon is a deep blue. Clear objects observed through an opaque medium appear yellow or red. Dark objects seen through a light medium appear blue. The children have thus experienced a law (an "archetypal phenomenon" in the sense of Goethe's theory of colour) which they most likely would not have arrived at through their own thinking, but which was readily perceived through the experience of their senses. Thus the powers of observation are strengthened. In the same term, or at least in the same school year, the pupils are given a first glance at the other areas of classical physics by conducting experiments in the theory of heat, electricity and magnetics. Mechanics are not discussed until Class VII, while in Class VIII some basic concepts in hydraulics, aero-dynamics and meteorology are developed, and all other areas are gone into more deeply.

The Path to Chemistry

At the beginning of chemistry instruction the students learn how the process of burning in different natural materials can take place in quite different ways. Why do some materials burn with a bright flame while others quickly turn into glowing embers? Why such dense smoke? Why does a flame make soot? One can set up a series of experiments to show the different ways in which fire manifests itself. It is astonishing to see the crackling flames of a hard log and to observe the hot intense inner glow of sawdust, though hardly visible from the outside (the heat that is developed in this way is so intense that ceramics could be fired by it). One calls forth the bright charm of sanguine children by setting fire to old dry reeds and watching them flare up quickly. Other children are more interested in watching the wavering bluish flames as they slowly and gradually consume alcohol which has been mixed with water. To begin with it is not the great scientific results that most excite the children. It appears more important to see that, if possible, every child can experience the way in which one's thinking can bring order into the often confusing many-sidedness of sense impressions. One can view these phenomena as polarities thus:

violent crackling, explosive burning
blazing, leaping flames
wavering, subdued consuming
hot glowing turning into charcoal

The material is not treated intellectually until the day after the experiment. The children raise questions, discuss them and propose further experiments. Through common research they are led to investigating the role of air in any type of combustion. They are led to the discovery of oxygen. The children also have numerous experiences from everyday life to relate to the issues at hand. Most of them have made a fire at one time or another and know how to put one out. Or they know how to start a fire in a damp forest. Chemistry can form a central part of the children's experience and remain so throughout their lives.

Right: Blast furnace.

skip hoist

Down Comer
hot gas outlet
to stoves

coke

Limestone

IRON ORE

STEEL
CASING

hot air blast
from stoves

SLAG

MOLTEN IRON

BLAST FURNES
CROSS SECTION

IRON

It can span the bridge to the wide world confronting them, including the industrial world.

Gradually one expands the study to include other processes of nature (the cycles of calcium and of water in nature) as well as to the industrial processes such as the manufacture of glass, the smelting of metals and their importance to our civilisation.

When the development of modern industry is described in the history lessons of Class Eight, then in chemistry special emphasis is placed upon that metal which—next to gold—has played the most important role in the history of mankind: iron.

Engineering and modern industry could only unfold to the extent that iron-production and

Mars, the God of Iron, looks down on Manhattan. This picture arose from the consideration of the role of iron in modern civilization.

technology made it possible. Without Court's "flame-oven" (invented 1783-84) the early industrial development in England would hardly have come about. Without the modern developments of steel production (The Bessemer Process, 1858; The Siemens-Martin Process, 1865; The Thomas Process, 1878) we would not have been able to build ocean liners, world-wide railway networks, cars, modern agricultural implements, or modern cities. Every person should know, at least in principle, how iron is produced in a blast furnace.

THE HEAVENLY BODIES AS WE SEE THEM

Is it true that the children of today—who become acquainted with modern space research at an early age—can really feel "at home" in the universe? At first glance this would seem without question to be the case. They "know" as a rule incomparably more about the moon, Mars, Venus, and our whole solar system than their counterparts of twenty years ago. That one calculates the distance to the fixed stars in terms of light years and that one recognises no limits to the universe, they have surely heard as well. But to what extent can one really feel "at home" in the cosmos of modern-day astronomy?

The uncertainty of space travel is depicted with uncommon fantasy in the modern verse epic "Aniara" by the Swedish poet Harry Martinson. "Aniara" is a gigantic space ship which is to transport several thousand people from the earth, contaminated through atomic warfare, to Mars which in the meantime has been made habitable. Through a mechanical fault, however, the space ship runs off course with the bow directed toward the constellation of Lyra out into the depths of space. Meteorites and burnt out suns surround them on their way. To the people on board the cosmos is an interminable cemetery, which their bodies will cross through on the way to some distant goal for fifteen million years.

Through such a "narration" we are made aware of how the constant reports on space travel really affect us and, above all, affect our children. There are two aspects to this problem. On the one hand, we are pulled into a dead, hostile world through the irresistible fascination of the situation in which we ourselves could physically exist only under the most artificial conditions. On the other hand we become somewhat estranged from the earth and its tasks through the powerful demands made upon our imagination.

If future mankind is to be spared from wasting a large part of its time in dreamy gazing at television programmes of the coming flights to Mars and Venus then we must try to arouse in our children as strong a love as possible for the earth and the responsibilities it presents.

Through its data on the moon, Venus, Mars and Jupiter, space research itself can make an important contribution. Never before have we had the occasion to be so fully and gratefully aware of the special properties of our earth, with its atmosphere and temperature conditions and its regular water-cycle. It is the task of the school to see to it that this insight does not remain merely theoretical. In the Waldorf school astronomy is a part of the geography instruction. It is only natural to compare the living conditions of the earth with those in the rest of the solar system down to the last detail. But perhaps even more important is the way in which we observe heavenly phenomena in the first place.

With twelve-year-old children a teacher can quite easily reach a rather unusual agreement: For the time being we shall decide to put as little trust as possible into any scientific authorities. We shall proceed only from what the senses and human understanding can tell us. We shall follow the courses of the heavenly bodies as we see them from the earth. We shall attempt to imagine the paths they take when viewed from the equator. What does the movement of the stars look like from the poles, from the tropics? We shall observe the phases of the moon and the changes of the sun's path through the changing seasons.

This "phenomenological" approach can be continued as a natural sequence in the higher classes. The pupils can be given the opportunity to draw the planetary paths, at least in part, as Ptolemy saw and comprehended them, in order to pursue historically the unfolding of modern astronomy.

They can witness in retrospect the moment when Copernicus, for purely geometrical reasons, hit upon the idea of drawing the planetary paths with a heliocentric construction; when Galileo first discovered the moons of Jupiter through the telescope and therewith offered visible evidence that there are heavenly bodies which describe non-geocentric paths; or when Kepler, while drawing the elliptical planetary paths, had the feeling of looking into the secret creation of God, the World Geometrician. Perhaps observing and intellectually comprehending the laws of heavenly movements and of the seasons form a necessary first step to *really* feeling "at home" on the earth as well as in our solar system.

The movements of the stars, as observed from the Equator, above—looking North or South, below—looking East or West.

Stjernebevegelser ved ekvator.
I syd: fra venstre mot höyre.
I nord: fra höyre mot venstre.

Stjernebevegelser ved ekvator
i öst: rett opp.

The Last Four School Years

THE AGE OF PUBERTY IN THE WORLD TODAY

Pamela is 14, but she looks 18. She is cheerful and unaffected. Around her mouth she has a determined look. The quality about her which most people think of is her unrestrained need for independence. At 13 she had a job as a stewardess on a large ocean liner.

Although she is quite gifted, in school she is, generally speaking, lazy and uninterested. Her parents are indifferent, that is, they make no demands. Pamela's relationship to her mother is not especially close. She understands her father, however, and they get along well. She likes to talk to him about all kinds of things. Although not especially pretty, she seems to be attractive to the opposite sex. Her behaviour is by no means reserved, rather somewhat uninhibited. At the age of 15 she suddenly wants to have her own flat. After some opposition the parents finally consent to her wish.

A twenty-year-old boy moves into the new flat with her. He is rather primitive and does not share her intellectual interests at all. Pamela gradually breaks off their "engagement". He moves away, but keeps coming back. She feels sorry for him, and renews her attachment to him. But soon she breaks with him again. On the telephone she shares all this with her father, but explains that she wants to handle this affair alone. Often, when she is alone in the evening, she 'phones her father. The hour is late and she is afraid of the dark. After some complications she succeeds in permanently freeing herself from the boy. She is not yet 17 years old.

Then follows the next step in her development: she begins to study Catholicism, reads, makes notes, attends courses. She loves discussion, but her thoughts are completely unoriginal. She simply repeats what she has learnt. At the same time her need to believe is great. Her eyes are filled with rapture whenever she listens to someone whose views she finds pleasing. If she is confronted with other ways of thinking, she withdraws into herself, becomes quiet and closed-up. At an age when intellectually gifted young people usually try to attain inner independence, Pamela quite willingly submits to an absolute authority.

At the age of 15, Pamela entered a Waldorf school. Both she and her parents felt that this helped her gain a new interest in learning. In spite of periodically distressing personal problems, she usually did her work enthusiastically.

Pamela's situation seems to be a special case, and yet in certain respects it is a representative one. One may notice especially the strong contrast between early maturity on the one hand (independence, the "engagement", the need for her own views) and certain "remnants" of childhood on the other (the need for fatherly contact, fear of the dark, faith in authority).

Accelerated Physical Maturity

Puberty is introduced through a series of decisive physical symptoms. The body grows rapidly, the muscles and bones are strengthened. Often there appears a gain in weight which is followed by a loss in weight. For good reasons it is assumed that all these changes are caused by the increased secretion of sex hormones, which usually sets in a few years before puberty.

Nowadays these changes begin earlier. It is a matter of a whole group of phenomena which have been described unequivocally in the industrialised areas of the world. These phenomena seem to have begun to appear during the last century and were investigated scientifically in 1935, when E. Koch, a medical officer in Leipzig, first verified their existence statistically.

People are taller than in the past. The average weight at birth is higher. As a rule, the second dentition and sexual maturity appear appreciably earlier. Many psychologists talk of an accelerated intellectual development as well.

What is the cause of all this? Here opinions differ greatly. Scientific discussion has been especially lively in Germany. A group of researchers, including W. Lenz, maintain that the only important cause of early maturity is the increased consumption of fat and protein. According to another theory, one which the pediatrician B. de Rudder has energetically advocated, the phenomena are not to be explained solely on the basis of nutrition. Rather are they due to the entire process of urbanisation, especially the unprecedented increase in sense impressions, both in number and intensity, which influence the child. The representatives of this theory have naturally pointed to the fact that an increase in body-height in small children (as opposed to an increase in body-weight) continued independently of the lean years of 1945–47, according to research done in large German cities.

Even if the causes of this acceleration have not been conclusively explained, their results are visible for all of us: children "grow-up" faster nowadays.

Is it really so simple? In order to shed light on these questions we need to look at the problems from a different perspective.

Physical and Spiritual Maturity

Since the decisive physical changes in puberty occur before the psychological, one would almost believe the latter to be of secondary importance. Many psychologists make this assumption. According to Rudolf Steiner, however, this is not the case. He points out that as early as the twelfth year, or even sooner, the natural gracefulness of the young child gives way to jerky and awkward movements in boys, and a certain heaviness and lethargy in girls. He emphasises that the very same inner powers which had manifested themselves as a kind of "musicality of the limbs", now undergo a metamorphosis and appear transformed as new capacities in the area of the life of feeling and imagination. In the "Education of the Child in the Light of Anthroposophy" he describes how the biological changes occur whenever these inner powers free themselves from the body and gradually awake as spiritual capacities of a kind not apparent earlier.

For Steiner this is the essential aspect of puberty. The physical capability to reproduce corresponds to the capacity on the spiritual plane to reflect inwardly, thus experiencing and understanding what is alive in the whole of humanity. The purely physical attraction to members of the opposite sex is only the limited expression of a wider capacity for love, which—when it develops in a healthy way—manifests itself in a deep interest for everything in the world. Where this interest is lacking, because of the emphasis on the physical instincts, one finds a stunted spiritual development.

Steiner considered the expression "sexual maturity" far too narrow and wanted to see it replaced by the term "earth-maturity".

The inner powers with which the teacher is concerned in children of this age can often express themselves with surprising strength in healthily developed personalities. Whoever has a serious conversation with a sixteen or seventeen-year-old can sense a maturity which a few years earlier was not at all present. Then the young person was still childlike in his thinking. But now there are few questions in the area of science, art and the humanities which do not arouse this keen interest.

There is one phenomenon above all which is striking among highly gifted adolescents. Their awareness of time and its demands, their acuteness of thought and ability to formulate often attest to a consciousness and an inner materity which are impressive. However, these same individuals often become very "mixed-up" in their mutual relationships, especially on the erotic level. The awareness of their rich inner endowments and the idea, prevalent in wide circles, that sexual maturity is equivalent to adulthood, often causes them to overestimate their level of maturity and leads them into situations which can create difficult problems. The case of Pamela is typical.

However, there are other groups of young people in whom the discrepancy between physical and psychological maturity reveals itself even more clearly. The frequent teenage mania for clothes, hairdos and pop-music, and their manner of social intercourse, carries with it a certain charm or is at least entertaining. Even the elder generation may feel this. Such manifestations often originate in an understandable opposition to the narrow-mindedness and lack of fantasy of the older generation. But the sudden appearance and flux of new styles in fashion also has another side which is of no little importance. The press, the radio and the television broadcast these impulses with enormous power. In their thoughts as well as in their free-time many young people nowadays busy themselves to a great extent with things "one must do" because "everyone does them". Thus an instinct for imitation is nurtured and preserved; an instinct which actually belongs to the early childhood years.

Not only the relatively harmless teenage styles, but also the really serious anti-social symptoms are spread and intensified through thoughtless imitation of patterns of behaviour which are picked up from the mass media or the immediate surroundings: joy-rides in borrowed or stolen cars, teenage crimes, sexual aggressiveness and misuse of drugs and alcohol.

Problems of Puberty and their Connection with the Education of Small Children

The case-histories of criminals or other social perverts are, as a rule, tales of fundamental human qualities which have been neglected through an inadequate upbringing and education, and show in most cases a lack of spiritual contact with the immediate surroundings during the earliest years of childhood (cf. the investigations of René Spitz). Many other less serious problems of adolescence can be viewed as "illnesses of deprivation" which also originate in early childhood.

During a pedagogical course in Holland in 1924, Rudolf Steiner touched upon this problem. He emphasised how various attitudes can be preserved throughout later life, although these attitudes actually belong to an earlier age and are usually outgrown under normal circumstances. Two such attitudes are the readiness of the pre-school child to imitate, and the need for authority that is present in the child before the age of puberty. The physical body continues to grow, but the spiritual element, at least partially, remains at a level which is much more childish than the biological age would indicate. In another lecture of the same year, Steiner gave an example of how such a retardation can come about. When the capacity for abstract thinking is awakened in man at the advent of puberty, the thought processes must receive constant nourishment from a richly developed life of will and feeling. If a young person suffers from inner impoverishment because the deeper levels of the soul are insufficiently developed, he gropes in a void with his newly-acquired intellectual capacity. He does not then orientate himself in his new environment with the help of his thinking but rather through imitation and belief in authority. "It gives him an instability which causes him to engage in all kinds of mischief, to imitate all sorts of things in the early teens, whatever suits his fancy. Mostly it is something which does not please the others who, as it happens, are more concerned with the utilitarian aspects of life. He does it because he was unable as a child to live properly in the element of imitation. All this occurs at an age in which he really should have some measure of self-control. Thus we see many young people past the age of puberty wandering about, looking here and there for some kind of support and thereby dampening the experience of inner freedom." (17. 4. 24)

It can hardly be doubted that many young people suffer from true spiritual impoverishment and thereby find themselves in a situation which reminds us a great deal of the one Rudolf Steiner describes above. Should his diagnosis prove to be correct, then it would be high time to reconsider the education of the child. To have models to imitate during the pre-school years and an authority to respect during the elementary school years are deeply-rooted needs, which exist within every human being and must be satisfied during childhood if the desire for imitation and a lack of judgment are not to follow him through the rest of his life. If by a "free" education one means a pedagogy which seeks to influence the child as little as possible and thereby neglects to fulfil these two basic needs, then the paradoxical result of such an education is a lack of inner freedom.

What the School-Years Can Mean

Can the schoolwork itself contribute to a more harmonious development for those children who suffer from spiritual impoverishment as a result of that which they experienced or missed out on during their early childhood years?

A concrete example will serve to shed light on this question.

During the first years of his life Martin was greatly neglected, until he finally came to a foster mother, a sincere and intelligent woman, who was very kind to him. However, because she was out at work, there was little extra time to spend with him. He often roamed about in the streets.

The foster mother wanted him to have more personal attention and was advised by a friend to try to send him to a Rudolf Steiner school. Martin was healthy and mature enough to begin school and was admitted to the first class. The look on his face was evidence of the neglect he had experienced in early childhood, but also revealed the alertness of his keen intelligence. In arithmetic he was one of the best pupils. On the other hand, his speech development made very slow progress. Only in the fifth class did he learn to read. From time to time he was rough or cruel to his classmates. However, he enjoyed school and after a while became quite cheerful and open. His temperament was decidedly sanguine. When he was sixteen years old his foster mother died under tragic circumstances. Martin now stood alone in life, but was taken in by a very stable family. He seemed to recover quickly from the death of his foster mother. However, the results of childhood neglect now became obvious, most especially in his unconcealed egoism. He loved chocolate and was, for example, perfectly capable, while a guest in the house of a strange family, of sneaking into their larder before the meal and completely devouring the entire chocolate dessert.

In his crass conception of life, he considered subjects such as mathematics, science, modern history, current events and practical crafts as worthwhile. Although extremely lazy, he often achieved surprisingly good results, thanks, among other things, to his extraordinarily good memory. His ability to express himself in words remained rudimentary. He had no physical defect which might affect his ability to read and write, such as dyslexia, but he simply neglected his written work. His spelling and sentence construction were often hair-raising. He was completely uninterested in the artistic subjects, sometimes downright insolent in these lessons. In classes in which the instruction did not directly interest him, he would often sit with his mouth open, even occasionally sucking his thumb, and with a passive facial expression under his short-cut, unkempt hair. His moral concepts were few, simple, and confused. If he considered it necessary, for example, he would lie unashamedly "to help my friend out". Outside of school he associated for a while with a circle of friends who had certain criminal tendencies. It later developed that he avoided being drawn into any kind of punishable misdeeds. Since he was easily-led, there was a period when people wondered whether his development would ever take a turn for the better. Above all, everything in him revolved around his deep need for personal contact. He never withdrew into himself. If a group of his friends were talking with a teacher in the corridor, Martin would always go up and join them, put his hand on their shoulders, and enthusiastically join in the conversation. The teachers knew how important it was for him and gave him as much of their time as they could. Several years after leaving he once said, "The school was my home."

As early as class twelve the first signs of a change could be noticed, a change which gradually took root. Martin became markedly industrious. He began to develop a consideration for the needs and problems of others. Sociability turned into cordiality. His interests broadened widely. He pursued cultural questions intensively and critically and became a constant theatre-goer. He was accepted at the university, lived very modestly, and was a very successful student.

Summary

The stories of Pamela and Martin can no more "prove" the specific value of Waldorf education than can other accounts of individual cases. They can, however, help to shed light on the practical objectives of the work in a Waldorf school.

There certainly can be no doubt that Pamela acquired more serious work habits after she had changed over to the Waldorf school. In other respects her life could not be changed very much. Her experiences would probably have run their course, even if she had attended another school. With respect to Martin, however, it must be said that his experience in the Waldorf school seems to have been of greater significance. Moreover, it was important that he had attended the Waldorf school from the first class onwards. The later school years are by no means insignificant. If he had left the Waldorf school after the eighth class, for example, then the effects of his school years would certainly not have been so profound and would not have carried him over crucial periods to the extent that they did.

One cannot repeat often enough that Waldorf schools exist for healthy children with normal talents and that they are not institutions for "problem children". But here, as in other ordinary schools, there must be a place for children who find themselves in difficult circumstances. It is quite clear in such cases that a Waldorf school has a greater impact if the child can enter it early, preferably in the first class, if he can go through the "crises" of the ninth and twelfth years under the protection of the loving authority of his teachers and with the companionship of his classmates, and if given the proper "spiritual nourishment", he has developed real and independent interests and thus prepared makes the transition to adolescence. For the crises of puberty must be controlled before they break out. It is often difficult or impossible to help students who only enter the Waldorf school for their last four years.

The description of Martin also confirms another principle. The most important thing for the inner development of the older pupil is the continuous contact with responsible adults. At a time when the spiritual process of maturation is, for various reasons, easily obstructed or distorted, this contact is more essential than ever.

BLACK AND WHITE DRAWING IN CLASSES 7 AND 8

Young people of the age of 14 or 15 find themselves in a period of contrasts. At the start of painting in black and white they immediately experience both polarities as phenomena which they interpret in themselves as symbols of light and darkness. The pupils learn to master the world of light and darkness by differentiating various types of light (the light of the sun and moon, street lights etc.). The final achievement of this training is learning to do a human portrait.

Above right: Exercise in shadow-construction.

Below right: An imaginative drawing arising from the inner experience of light and darkness.

To experience the surrounding world and especially the people in it as "black" or "white" is one of the characteristics of adolescence. It can be helpful in these years to bring this to an objective experience through the use of charcoal.

Lotta

FROM CLASS NINE TO CLASS TWELVE (THE UPPER SCHOOL)

There are important mental abilities which usually do not awaken in human beings until they reach their teens; for example, the ability to develop special interests of their own and personal taste, and the striving for independent judgment in important questions. The constant readiness to imitate, which was discussed in the previous chapter, and which without a doubt is an important factor in the contemporary development of civilisation, makes it difficult for the individual to develop and maintain the above-mentioned capacities.

Are the prophets of doom right when they predict that the mass-media will, slowly but surely, produce mass-people, who have nothing but collective impulses? How is the individual to find his own life-style in face of this stream of strong, often suggestive influences?

The instruction which is imparted to the pupils in Classes 9 to 12, that is in the Upper School, can in this respect be a significant help.

A "Scientific" Education

Strictly speaking, one can arrive at an independent judgment on a question through an attitude which may be described as scientific. No prejudicial opinions may be entertained, no emotions may disturb quiet observation.

One does not need to be a scientist to adopt this principle. It is enough if one strives to live and to think in a really modern, that is in a conscious, manner. To this extent, our epoch can justifiably be called an age of science. How many people are there today, however, who actually live in such a way that they take a position on knowledgeable questions, which concern themselves, without passion, without being led astray by their favourite thoughts, by catch-phrases with no substance, or by the "results of research" which in reality are only weakly-supported hypotheses? It is a tragic irony that the unheard of scientific advance which more than anything else has led to the erasing of old beliefs, at the same time has brought about a belief in authority which, for its blindness, can be compared to the old forms of religious belief.

Instruction in the upper classes of a Waldorf school will contribute to laying the foundation of an attitude to life which, not only on the surface but also in the depths, is scientific in the sense in which it is meant here. The very first steps along this path are, as we have seen, already laid down in the last years of the class-teacher period. There are fundamental changes in the teaching methods which go in the same direction, but which lead significantly further.

The teaching is taken over by specialist-teachers who have been appropriately trained in their own subject. At this level the teacher no longer has a self-evident authority. To be sure, it is important that the pupils have a respect for his specialised knowledge and pedagogical capabilities. The teacher must be ready, nevertheless, to explain fully whatever he says both on an academic and on a human level. All statements may be queried, and all serious questions are worthy of detailed consideration. The classes, therefore, often consist, for the most part, of conversations and discussions.

The natural science periods (biology, climatology, geology, chemistry, physics, mathematics etc.) are of course particularly suited to exercising the powers of observation and thinking. The experiments of the teacher and the pupils play a fundamental role in teaching right on into the twelfth class. Great precision is necessary in carrying out experiments, otherwise the results can be quite misleading. When conclusions are being reached, no step should be taken which is not confirmed through the observed phenomenon.—In mathematics, as far as possible, the pupils should, above all, understand the operations which are being carried out; the practice of actual mathematical processes which is of course important, takes second place.—In the cultural areas of history, the history of art and literature, and geography, the situation, at least in part, is quite different.

When one, for example, speaks of social, economic, and political questions, of individual destinies and works of art, then the listener, especially through a lively description, can be personally moved. Basically, the task is often one of helping the pupils overcome purely subjective sympathies and antipathies and, on the other side, of instilling in them a feeling for human destiny founded on knowledge, to which they were previously oblivious and which would have meant little to them at an earlier stage. In other words, one strives for an objective approach even in the sphere of emotions.

The material which is offered to the students in the upper classes is very comprehensive. Their independent effort is increasingly called on in writing and illustrating the subject-matter of their lessons in composing essays, and preparing talks. In addition, in the eleventh and above all in the twelfth class individual projects are chosen and carried out. Some pupils choose a subject of study from the realm of arts or crafts, while others investigate a scientific problem or plan a special series of experiments.

Experience has shown that those students who have attended a Waldorf school from the beginning have, on the whole, a good foundation for work of this kind. A claim on their intellectual powers has not been made prematurely, and they have not been forced to take in an excess of abstract knowledge. They look forward with excitement to the new subjects and new vistas of knowledge which await them in the upper school. As a rule their attitude is that of the alert critic, not of the tired sceptic. Their involvement becomes especially active when, for example, light can be thrown on human and social problems through scientific facts. Their desire to form their own conclusions in questions of knowledge often leads to the pursuit of scientifically orientated interests in their spare time.

Some General Aspects

In the year 2000, according to some current predictions, science will play an even greater role than it does today. If we want to prepare our children for this "knowledge explosion", there is no other possibility—according to the prevailing view—than to give them "thought models" without any detailed explanation; that is, hypotheses or theories, the scientific foundation of which can hardly be grasped by the pupil. The whole emphasis of learning is thus shifted into a different direction. Teacher-training, textbooks, aids and teaching methods, are already orientated towards this end in the highly industrialised countries.

In the face of this development we are justified in asking if, with such a method of teaching, one does not force upon the pupils, perhaps even without consciously striving to do so, a ready-made view of life. To be sure, one can maintain that modern scientific research finds itself in a constant state of change, and on these grounds alone (assuming that the results of such research are adequately presented), hinders the rise of a fixed view to the world. One can hardly deny, however, that the present development is moving along on definite, even more complicated courses, which determine not only the methods of investigation, the definitions and the theories, but also the questions themselves, and which strongly influence our conception of man and the world. When just such avenues of approach become to an ever greater extent the subject of a more or less automatic and unquestioning "learning", then the danger of an intellectual lack of freedom is obvious.

The goal which the upper school teachers of the scientific subjects in a Waldorf school place before themselves is a "phenomenologically" orientated instruction, which prefers to characterise rather than reduce to definitions, and which makes it possible for the pupils, at least to a certain extent, to understand and evaluate the foundations of various modern representative "Models of Thought" and scientific views.

Of course one might ask if the instruction in natural science at a Waldorf school, which received its spiritual foundation from Rudolf Steiner, is not in danger of becoming one-sided in another way. In addition to the viewpoints which have already been mentioned in the chapter on the idea of freedom, it should here be pointed out that the anthroposophical view of the world, which for the teachers forms the foundation of their concept of life, is broadminded and tolerant, not only in the sense that it acknowledges the validity of other ways of thinking but also inasmuch as it offers real help in penetrating and understanding other thought-systems. A thorough elaboration would lead too far, but one brief example may clarify what is meant. A history teacher tried to give his Class Eleven pupils an idea of Marxism. He had immersed himself so intensely in his subject and displayed such enthusiasm, that for a while the pupils believed he actually was a Marxist. Such a successful presentation, of course, is not always achieved, but one can nonetheless try to realise one of the most important goals of the entire learning experience in the upper school; to teach in such a way that the teacher not only opens the door to various avenues of approach but also makes it possible for each individual to become actively involved to a certain degree.

The Social Community of a Class

The question arises how, in a school in which there is no streaming according to intellectual ability, the teacher can carry on the lessons in a way that nevertheless makes increasingly high demands on the abilities of the gifted pupil.

One of the basic tenets of Waldorf education is that every child with normal abilities should in principle have the chance to attend school for the full twelve years. Experience has shown, however, that certain pupils who take a full and active part in lessons in the lower and middle school, for various reasons are not able to follow the work of the later school years. Most of these young people either leave school and learn a trade or continue in one of the so-called practical courses which have been set up at various Waldorf schools. But even among those pupils remaining in the class there are right up until the twelfth class considerable differences in individual ability and working potential. It should be emphasised that the Waldorf schools find this quite an acceptable situation. One must realise, however, that as a result of this there will be a wide range of actual achievement. Gifted and energetic pupils, after having completed the required courses, are ready for the university. Others, although they still reveal certain weak spots in their knowledge, have as a rule reached a good general level of education and are, therefore, able to meet satisfactorily the demands of modern life.

The pertinent question is naturally whether the intellectually bright child is not held back by his classmates whose gifts lie in other directions. It can certainly happen that a teacher has to go over something more than once for the sake of a child who has not fully understood, and thus the pace of a lesson may be slowed down. On the other hand this can serve to counterbalance a certain egoism and ambition on the part of the most highly gifted pupils, whose abilities can be challenged by being given special tasks. On the whole it can be said that the progress of a class is not seriously hindered by the presence of those pupils who are gifted more practically or artistically rather than intellectually, as long as each is taxed to their limits. This, of course, is only possible when a teacher really knows the individual capacities of his pupils, as is the aim in a Waldorf school.

Can the opposite not happen, however, that those who have no direct inclination towards scientific subjects are discouraged by the performance of the others? This danger is certainly there but the curriculum is so widely based that every pupil can find a sphere where he can hold his own and find satisfaction. It is important to the pupils as well as to the teachers to learn to value each individual according to his own innate talents, especially as they will soon be part of the wider social life in the world.

The Role of Art in the Upper School

Throughout the upper school, instruction in eurythmy, recitation, painting, drawing, modelling and skilled crafts still serves to counterbalance the scientific and intellectual demands of the curriculum. Art finds a new meaning in the life of a human being at this age-level. He can now, more consciously than before, work his way into the materials which are used in the different forms of art (tones, sounds, colour, wood, clay, metal, etc.). "History of Art" is a subject in itself in the curriculum of the upper school. Many pupils occupy themselves with art during their free time. Gradually they become more and more aware that life is becoming richer and more diversified, that there are definite psychological-aesthetic laws with which they can only become familiar to the extent that they are artistically active and observant. At the same time the possibilities develop to understand, enjoy, to make sound judgments, and in time—regardless of one's choice of occupation—to develop an individual taste and life-style.

MATHEMATICS AND GEOMETRY

Class Nine

By the time they make the transition into the upper school, if not before, the majority of the pupils become aware of how important it is to have a thorough knowledge of mathematics. They realise that the door to more theoretical and practical vocational training is only open to those who have a good mathematical grounding and indeed that mathematics is regarded very highly in modern society. This could be regarded as a fair wind for the awakening of new and specialised interests arising out of this subject. However, the teacher must resist the temptation to make too much use of this tendency. Throughout the school years mathematical instruction should be regarded as serving to develop the personality and should be regarded even now not as an end in itself.

The meaning of mathematical exercises has perhaps been most beautifully expressed by Plato. In "The Republic" he writes: "Through mathematics an instrument of the soul becomes refined and, as in a purifying fire, it is awakened to a new life force, while other activities destroy it and rob it of its power to behold, whereas it deserves far more to be maintained than do a thousand bodily eyes, for through this faculty alone is truth perceived."

But how far removed are the sixteen-year-olds from such a way of looking at things.

"What use is that?" is a typical question. These young people sit there in the classroom with their newly-awakened intellectual powers and yet under pressure to do something practical in the world. Still it is not difficult to engage them in a problem which is not at all directed toward the practical—as long as the proposed exercise addresses itself to their process of inner development.

The problem of the Hanoi towers can serve as an example for an exercise which at first directs itself to deductive reasoning and then leads beyond that. A Hanoi tower consists of a number of perforated stones which are arranged on a vertical pole. The largest stone is at the bottom and the stones become successively smaller until the top one is reached. In addition there are two bare poles at one's disposal. The question is: How many individual stones must be rearranged in order to build up the tower on one of the empty poles, under the condition that a larger stone should never be placed on top of a smaller one?

We assume that we have four stones. It does not take long for the students to discover through trial and error that $X = 15$ and that is how many rearrangements are necessary to build up the tower as required. The class will at once query how many moves are necessary for any given number of stones. Several of

Through geometry we learn to combine thinking with seeing. To achieve this we must cease to think of the point as a pin-prick, the line as a bar, parallel lines as railway tracks. We only begin to have a true experience of geometry when we can wrest our concepts away from the sense-perceptible.

Right: Various geometrical forms, drawn first from the view-point of Euclidean geometry, when we see them as we usually do as finite areas; then from the view-point of projective geometry, when the corresponding form reaches to infinity. The effort required in the latter case is greater, but the results are more interesting.

Vad gör en linje med ett plan? Delar det i en del.
Vad gör två linjer med ett plan? Delar det i två delar.
Vad gör en punkt i ett punktfält? Ingenting.
Vad gör två punkter i ett punktfält? Ingenting.

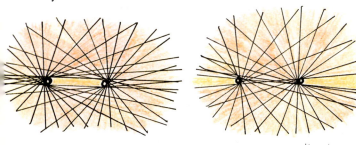

Två punkter i ett linjefält kan "dra isär" eller "dra ihop"
linjerna. I det ena fallet går alla linjer utanför punkterna,
i det andra emellan. Men eftersom punkterna är oändligt
små täcks i båda fallen samma yta.

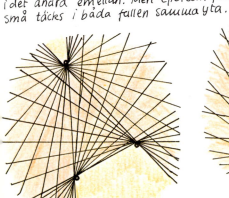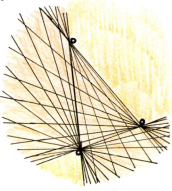

Här "delar" 3 punkter ett linjefält på 4 olika sätt. (Olika aspekter på fältet). I alla fallen blir
den orange ytan en trehörning.

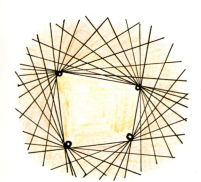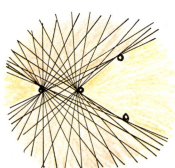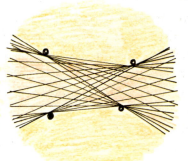

Med 4 punkter blev det egendomligt nog fyrhörningar av de orange ytorna.

them investigate how things work when there are less than four stones and conclude: one stone requires one rearrangement, two require three, and three stones require seven rearrangements. Is there any characteristic regularity in the numerical sequence 1, 3, 7, 15 that points to a general formula? And when this clue is found does it lead in the right direction? Is the assumption correct? The students test it in the case of five stones—yes, the rule is correct!

But how are we to prove the rule for a given number of stones? We cannot just keep building larger and larger towers. This method of helping oneself in the physical world through trial and error can only be useful up to a certain practical point. We must think, we must seek intensively for a decisive point until we can master in thought infinitely large towers. What is this decisive point? So we investigate how the number of rearrangements increases, when we increase the number of stones by one. The five-stone tower must be so constructed that the four-stone tower is built on the second pole. After that the fifth stone must be placed on pole number 3. At last we can build the whole fourstone tower on this pole. The number of rearrangements, therefore, is $x_5 = x_4 + 1 + x_4 = 15 + 1 + 15 = 31$. The same situation prevails for a tower with any number of stones: we can take the step from four to five, from five to six, and so on to infinity. From this discovery we can write the formula for the number of rearrangements of infinitely large towers.

The greater the pains. the greater the reward. The students learn that through a process of thinking they can reach a conclusion that is unreachable by technical means (even through the fastest computers). They have also learned to observe their own thinking. They learn to realise when they are thinking correctly and when they are thinking incorrectly. This realisation is essential. One feels that one is consciously and securely standing on the firm ground of truth when one lets a problem speak within oneself with its idea-content, when one perceives in oneself the objective nature of the problem.

As a rule the pupils in Class Nine cannot achieve such a conscious awareness of thinking, some not even in Class 12. The important thing is that, each one according to his individual capabilities, they come to realise more and more what clear thinking is.

In Class 9 the pupil feels an increasing need to stand on his own feet. Figuratively speaking, the teacher steps more and more to the side and the subject, in corresponding measure, comes to the fore. How suitable the practice of mathematics is to emancipate oneself from dependence on parents! For each person must find the truth for himself. In mathematics, however, differences in the pupils' abilities play an important role. How can the dreamy pupil who is not very intellectually inclined play a part?

The teacher must find a whole spectrum of problems, from the simple to the complex. As the technical expression goes, he must "be able to differentiate within the framework of the class". In class they practice counting again—but in other systems than the decimal one. That which has become routine in this system is now to be mastered through a constant practice with the binary system. This has a liberating effect. And there are exercises of every degree of difficulty, from addition to finding the square root and the different rules of division.

Permutations and combinations, examples from the theory of probability including those to do with life assurance, give the pupils ample material for exercising the powers of thinking. In geometry, through the study for example of various curves, there are similar possibilities.

Do experiences with finite curves such as the circle or the ellipse help us when we come to consider curves that run to infinity such as the parabola and hyperbola? The surprises that meet us here can be significant and instructive. The pupils gain insight into the certainty and ease with which analytical geometry with its equations solves such problems. A purely geometrical approach is as a rule more time-consuming but on the other hand it is rewarding. Quite apart from the end result important discoveries are made during the process and the pupils' interest is maintained throughout.

From the Tenth to the Twelfth Class

In Class 10 two major sections of the curriculum are brought to a conclusion. The climax of metrical plane geometry is the study of trigonometry. The pupils, who until now have had to be satisfied with dealing with special triangles and other geometrical figures, can now work with any kind of triangle with the help of the trigonometric tables and the slide-rule. The pupils gain a deep satisfaction from the practical application of trigonometry in surveying. Here they learn how the theodolite provides precise angles for the net of triangles which give the developing map stability and precision.

The second section of the curriculum leads into logarithms. Negative numbers, fractions and the number zero set new tasks, developing naturally from previous work with indices. The question is then always asked if the "old" rules of counting still hold good for the new

field into which the students have now ventured. This proves to be possible, and indeed there is even more to it. We look at the four rules in a broadened perspective and, at the same time, we learn the technique of mastering problems that would otherwise be too time-consuming to work out.

The joy the pupils experience in learning how to work with more precise instruments deepens their interest in exploring new areas of the mathematical edifice. After the satisfaction of mastering plane-geometry in the tenth class, comes the possibility of building up geometries for curved surfaces. As practical goals we can consider calculating distances and areas on the globe, problems in navigating by the stars, and the problem of projecting the globe, or a part of it, onto a plane, thus drawing a map of a spherical area. The class is thus presented with entirely new situations and must learn to appreciate that it is not impossible to project a spherical area with exactitude. It is interesting to observe, for example, that a map of the ocean is not the projection of a spherical area, but rather a carefully calculated copy, created so as to show the correct angles; thus it is "angularly true" and intended for finding the proper navigational course.

Questions relating to the concept of infinity can widen one's inner horizons. Perspective drawing helps in grasping this difficult idea—so does the concept of limit and the elements of Georg Cantor's theory of sets. Are there more points than numbers on a straight line? And how is a straight line or curve "made up" of points? The questions of the "infinitely large" and the "infinitely small" go back to the paradoxes which Zenon of Elea formulated 2,500 years ago.

Closely related to this chapter of knowledge is the concept of function which is practised and expanded, the function as an instrument of causal thinking which was unfolded and crystallized mathematically by Galileo, Newton, Leibniz and others. The concepts of speed and acceleration become capable of general application and make it possible to work out maxima and minima, an achievement which later, as for instance in critical path analysis, helped to further the perfection of technology.

Studies of the concept of infinity and function theory lead to abstract thought inasmuch as the problems are removed from the sensual-visual world. It is unavoidable that many pupils must be content in such areas with a general orientation and with certain basic principles. Perhaps in some pupils an aversion to the X, Y, Z of equations may arise. They can gain a new interest through constructive tasks, as in the important field of projective geometry. A number of French mathematicians (Poncelet, Brianchon, Carnot and other pupils of the great geometrician Monge) became absorbed by the possibilities of geometrical construction at the beginning of the 19th century and wanted to show that one can progress further by these methods than by the abstract equations of analytical geometry. Carnot wanted to "free geometry from the hieroglyphics of analysis".

Thus projective geometry was developed in the course of the 19th century. It provides the teacher with excellent material. It is surprising that it is not more widely used in general education. Projective geometry provides the pupils with exceptionally good opportunities for studying problems and relationships from different aspects. In comparison with the usual atomistic way of presentation, which thinks of a plane or line as made up of points, projective geometry presents the point as concept bearing planes or lines. The planes and the lines, as well as the point, can be looked at as primary archetypal elements.

Whoever has experienced how often young people tend to see a situation in terms of black or white, and often with deep conviction, realises that an important task of the school is to teach the children how to arrive at sound judgments. An important part of such training is that the pupils view problems from different aspects, and best of all from diametrically-opposed points of view. Projective geometry offers an excellent opportunity for practice in this direction in which all pupils can take part. When the Frenchman Desargues laid the foundation of this kind of geometry in the 17th century, he approached problems that had been raised by laymen, chiefly by artists. These painters were looking for methods of creating perspective. "The science that Desargues created is now one of the most beautiful branches of mathematics–perhaps because it was engendered by art", writes Morris Kline in 'Mathematics in Western Culture'.

If we wish to avoid talking past one another in everyday conversation, or when we are trying to understand certain scientific results, then we must make clear to ourselves and to others the basic concepts from which we have built up a train of thought. In science the following question often stands in the foreground: Which axioms or primary phenomena do we use as the basis? As objectively as possible we strive to recognise what is happening in the field of our investigation—be it a process of nature, an experiment, a psychological or historical occurrence. In Class 12 in a Waldorf school the pupils gain a wider perspective in

The "growth" of a pentagon—an exercise in projective geometry. Class 12.

the different subjects. In mathematics we learn how one can derive different geometries (Euclidean, non-Euclidean, analytic, synthetic etc.) and also different kinds of algebra (generalised, Boolean, Vector algebra etc.) through a skilful selection of basic axioms. Thus the researcher chooses the tool that is appropriate for him. In this connection students become familiar with examples of how a mathematical creation that for a long time was only considered "literature" for a few curious people, suddenly became a valuable tool in several fields of research. We refer here to Boolean algebra in logical analysis, calculation of probability and network problems in electricity.

In conclusion one can say that the teaching of mathematics consists of the two elements of instruction and practice. The more intimately these two aspects can be joined, the greater will be the interest and output of the pupil. In the long run perpetual practice leads to a mechanical kind of activity, while continual instruction disregards the intense desire for action on the part of the pupils. When it is a question of dealing with proofs and deductions, it is a golden rule that what can be directly experienced form a middle way between an exact but pedantic description and a more general survey which, however, may be lacking in the necessary detail.

Parallel with the solving of actual mathematical problems go informative conversations which provide insight into the way in which mathematical laws underlie nature and also the form of the human body. The chief significance of mathematics lies in the fact that it leads to a capacity for pure thought and to confidence in such a way of thinking, i. e. to that type of thinking that we work out for ourselves through an activity which is at the same time both subjective and objective.

PHYSICS

Class Nine

In physics during Classes Six, Seven and Eight the pupils have studied certain elementary phenomena of acoustics, optics, heat and mechanics (including hydrostatics and aeromechanics) and have become familiar with a number of their practical applications. In Class Nine, from both practical and theoretical aspects, the pupils learn to understand certain facts about heat and electricity sufficiently to have a complete understanding of how the steam engine, combustion engine, the telephone and other basic inventions function.

The way one may proceed in Class Nine can be demonstrated with an example from the theory of heat. Boyle's Laws on the pressure and volume of a gas serve to show how mathematical laws arise from the observation of the behaviour of matter. Matter does not react arbitrarily to the impact of heat. Expansion, the absorption of heat, the melting and evaporation points, and the boiling and freezing points are specific mathematical values which are characteristic for the different materials. Substances that are added to a specific material may raise its boiling point or lower its freezing point; indeed, a shifting of the boiling point may occur in certain cases that seems at first inexplicable.

The astonishment of the pupils over such natural phenomena is especially important and fruitful at this age. Strangely enough, water—the substance that is the most plentiful on the earth—is an exception to expansion through heating. The fact that it has its greatest density at 4° C makes it possible to prevent living things from freezing when the cold is especially bitter. Of special significance is the remarkable property of liquids to boil at ever lower temperatures if the air pressure is decreased. Graphs of changing saturation pressures can easily be drawn. It is especially interesting to note that, while all these curves appear to start out from the so-called absolute zero of temperature, on the other hand they collapse into a point, the critical state of matter. Gas or liquids are no longer to be distinguished, the heat of evaporation is zero. Nature itself sets a point for each liquid below which it cannot become gas and over which no gas can become fluid.

When we work with such laws and try to bring the pupils to a proper understanding of them, we soon realise what a subordinate role mere arithmetic plays. Even if technology and industry pass by the qualitive aspect of phenomena in heat theory and prefer to employ scientists who have a good command of mathematical physics, one should still realise that here is a task that, although underestimated, is pedagogically fruitful.

An especially interesting—but at the same time difficult—phenomenon is that of latent heat. Although the temperature does not indicate it, matter may take in considerable quantities of heat that nevertheless do not manifest themselves as increased heat. Instead this heat transforms the state of matter. Thus, when it snows it does not get cold, because latent heat, the heat of evaporation, is released and warms the surrounding area. Or we freeze when we are wet, because the heat that evaporates the water escapes from the body.

Expansion usually follows when matter is heated. Thus a body takes in heat and reacts with an expansion in volume. But what happens if the volume is expanded without an increase in heat? It gets colder. It is not always easy to make this clear to the pupils, but it is

an analogous occurrence; any expansion in volume requires heat. If the volume is expanded, for example, through the release of gas from a pressure-tank, but the gas is *not* at the same time heated, then it loses inner energy and gets colder. Carbonic acid snow can easily be produced in a warm classroom.

Gas, on the other hand contracts when it is cooled. A decrease in volume therefore means a decrease in heat. This, of course, explains why a gas gets warm under compression. Heat is released. That means that a solidification, contraction or a forming tendency corresponds to a loss of heat. Conversely an increase in heat corresponds to rarification, expansion, and a dissolution of form. In this sense one could even speak of heat as the opposite of heaviness: Heat works outwardly from matter, making things lighter, more rarified and less formed. Heaviness contracts, solidifies, and shapes.

How can heat be measured? Strictly speaking, it cannot. The following affords some insight into solving the problems of the nature of heat. One measures heat by its effect on a given amount of water. If one gram of water is heated one degree centigrade, then we call it a "thermal unit of one calorie".

Here one can introduce a number of calculations that can usefully be carried out in the course of a mathematics lesson. Here too we meet one of the fundamental principles of Waldorf pedagogy. The most important aspect of such study is to arouse a living interest in the phenomena of natural science and to cultivate an understanding of relationships. The mathematical aspect is of secondary importance.

Thus the whole theory of heat can be developed without ever actually explaining what "heat" is. The question of whether it is heat that moves molecules or whether the movement of molecules manifests itself as heat, should wait for a few more years. This question is actually best suited to Class Eleven. In Class Nine we should remain with those phenomena that afford sufficient occasion for wonder and experiment.

Class Ten

This age is devoted to classical physics in all its beauty and exactitude. The mathematical foundations have been well prepared. Trigonometry, quadratic equations, properties of the parabola and the ellipse, progressions, proportion, logarithms and slide-rules form the basis for an understanding of the physical laws of Galileo, Kepler, and Newton.

It is the awakening of expanding human thinking that, like the planetary spheres of Ptolemy, unfolds itself farther and farther into the cosmos. His geocentric conception of the universe is being supplanted by Copernicus' heliocentric interpretation. Why? What happens here?

The pupil experiences the greatest of the new thoughts. They are clearer, more logical, the modern mind finds them more satisfying than the earlier ideas. With the help of the most perfect geometrical figure, the circle, Ptolemy painstakingly explained the paths of the planets. The pupils draw and construct some of these interesting figures, which of course manifest themselves in the heavens to our eyes in the same way as they did then. For millenia these movements have been the same. But man always views them from a new standpoint. Copernicus views them from a universe with the sun in the centre. That is easier to imagine, the human spirit can grasp this because in the meantime man has become familiar with varying speeds and distances. How are the many stars supposed to make their daily course around the earth? And all equally fast? Sober thinking finds it hard to conceive. But even Copernicus could not think otherwise than in circles, and it was only Kepler who, through his own particular destiny, met the great observer of the stars Tycho Brahe at just the right moment and was able to show that all planetary courses are ellipses. The biographies of such personalities are especially suitable to make the new element in man's physical conception of the world clear to the pupils.

In Kepler's life this proof was a major event. Divine harmony was complete, for the harmony of the spheres became manifest as beauty through the mathematical laws. The cosmos proves the existence of God; it is not mere accident that prevails in the universe. All is well-ordered. The pupils apply Kepler's laws to the moons of the planets, even for artifical satellites, and see that the laws are correct.

Man has mastered the movements of the heavens and knows in advance that should a new planet appear, its course will not be arbitrary. A certain distance corresponds to the time required for one revolution. On the other hand, if the planet has a specific orbital period then its distance from the sun is determinable.

At this point in the study of physics a pupil may ask that very important question which has had significant consequences in the his-

In Class 11 emphasis is laid on exactness in technical drawings in the Physics lessons, for now the pupils should become familiar with the form and function of machines used in everyday life.

Above right: A D.C Generator.

Below right: An electric motor for both direct and alternating current.

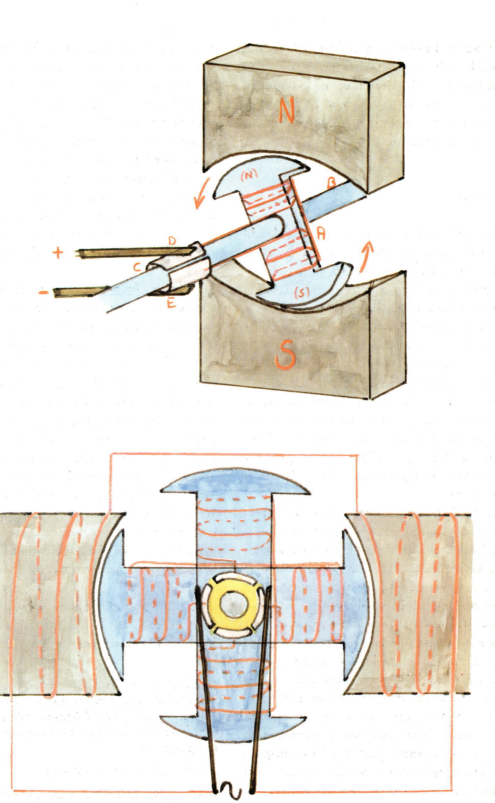

torical development of human consciousness. Now that the movements in heaven and, through Galileo, also certain movements on earth have been made fully clear to man, and now that the almost religious experience of a world-order streams through the soul, the question arises, *Why* are these laws valid? What is the *cause* of these movements?

At this point in the development of physics Isaac Newton steps in. The falling apple through which, according to an anecdote, he became aware of the phenomenon of gravity, "down to earth", can really be a kind of symbol for the development of a more human consciousness. Nothing divine is recognised as the cause any longer, only so-called gravity. It is forces that move bodies, it is forces that stop them, it is forces that hold the planets in their courses or throw them off course. The forces of inertia, gravity, friction, the centrifugal force, these are the foundations of Newtonian mechanics.

Newton's Law of Gravitation becomes the universal law of the cosmos; without ever having been there we can calculate the mass of the sun and all the planets. This feeling of the triumph of knowledge is the note on which the physics period in Class Ten can be concluded.

If time allows, the equations of motion and the laws of forces can be further developed through the parallelograms of forces and of velocities. The ability to calculate, however, should not come before the understanding of qualitative physical laws. Here too there are many possibilities of adapting the subject-matter to the different members of the class as is clear from what has been said earlier. The study of surveying and of geography strengthen the conviction that man is the central point of the universe—this time not geocentrically in the sense of the physical earth, but rather through his powers of thought. Newton placed the human intellect in the centre of the universe. From our vantage-point on the "dust-particle earth" we can calculate the most distant galaxies and assign our solar system its appointed place.

Class Eleven

In this class, if not already before, the teacher must decide what to choose from a virtually unlimited amount of material. A vast variety of experiments stands at one's disposal. An enormous industry is continually busy building apparatus and machines in which, directly or indirectly, the laws of electricity are applied in practice.

How much should a person today know about electricity? In the course of a few weeks of study the teacher must present the essentials of electricity and its uses in such a way that all pupils—among them perhaps even future specialists in the field—can get something important out of it for life. Each pupil, for example, should have a thorough understanding of the telephone, the radio, the electromotor and the generator. In his daily contact with these things a person has a feeling of security if he has at some time investigated them thoroughly. It is not, of course, necessary to burden the pupils with all the details of electronic theory or of the mathematical aspects of physics which are an essential for electrical engineers.

This is an exciting study. Through releasing gas into rarified space and with the help of so-called cathode-rays, we work out the one concept; of electricity as electrons, that is particles in motion. Through the study of electric and magnetic fields we come to the other concept of electricity as a movement through space of electro-magnetic waves which takes place most easily even through an empty space, through a vacuum. They move with the speed of light in all directions, millions of them, without interfering with each other. The "empty" space of the universe turns out to be pervaded by electro-magnetic fields. It has the property of letting electro-magnetic waves pass through it unhindered and unlimited. Waves or particles—what is electricity in reality? At this important point we learn the significance of the Goethean way of observing such phenomena, without asking "What is electricity?", but rather "How is electricity produced?", and "What does electricity do?" Everywhere we are confronted with polarities in this field of study, electricity never manifests itself onesidedly. There are always two poles, we call them positive and negative. Faraday indicated these as the production of electricity on glass and resin respectively. Changing electric and magnetic fields condition and produce one another in a constant interchange. Particles and waves appear as a polarity and so do capacitance and inductance. An impressive illustration of the latter is the oscillatory circuit, which as a result of the polarity of inductance and capacitance gives rise to the phonemenon of resonance by means of which we are able to pick a single one of the millions of electro-magnetic oscillations, as happens in radio. Another example is the polarity of metals, which produces voltage in the Galvanic pile, in the photo-cell or in the thermo-couple.

The teaching of electricity is the study of tension, of duality, of polarity. The discoveries of Oersted and Faraday, for example, can be seen at work in the microphone and telephone-receiver or in the polarity of an electro-motor and electro-generator.

The phenomenon of electricity is many-sided and far-reaching. What, for example, can we measure with electrical meters of any kind? Everything except electricity. We measure heat (or more precisely the expansion of a heated wire) or we measure the magnetic force that arises through electricity. The electricity as such seems to disappear the moment it is produced. It is transformed into heat and energy. Electricity is invisible, we possess no sense-organ for it, and the moment it is created it transforms itself into other physical forms. Even the electrical fields of static electricity do not manifest themselves as pure electricity, but rather as mechanical forces. Even a battery contains no electricity, and in so-called electric sparks we find glowing matter. Above all else, however, we should not withhold from the pupils of Class Eleven the duality of phenomenon and theory. We should make a sharp distinction between those experiments that represent a part of the world that can be perceived with the sense-organs and such pictures that reflect concepts, ideas, hypotheses, and theories. In textbooks experiments and theoretical concepts are often mixed, and in describing experiments that have been carried out we should take pains to distinguish clearly between actual observation and theory. The methods of research on the one hand and on the other the modern scientist's view of the world are a continuing undertone in the classes of the upper school.

The unity, the harmony of Class Ten has now been definitely lost. Class Eleven is dominated by polarity, duality, tension. Is it then impossible to gain a clear insight into the nature of electricity? Perhaps this period of study can close with just such a question.

Class Twelve

The phenomena of geometrical optics such as those of mechanical waves serve as an introduction to the study of physics in this class. Reflection, refraction and diffraction, polarisation and interference are properties of light, which bring clarity to a number of phenomena we meet every day. At the same time they form the basis for an understanding of the significant role which the dualistic conception of light has played in the history of physics. A man such as Newton adhered for a long time to the so-called corpuscle theory, although the undulatory theory (wave theory) of Huygens had already been accepted by most people. It was only after the additional evidence presented by Fresnel and others concerning the phenomena of diffraction and interference that the followers of Newton finally gave up the idea of particles. Light "is therefore a wave". But in which medium? A wave could only be conceived as being analogous to a wave of water. For this reason ether was invented. But the human mind was not entirely satisfied with this invisible, unweighable "substance", until the further paths of research into electricity and optics finally met: Maxwell explains light as an electromagnetic oscillation and classifies this oscillation among those already known. When x-rays could finally be made subject to interference, all known waves arranged themselves in the electro-magnetic series.

This unity of phenomena, however, did not last long. It was Max Planck who made the decisive discoveries. And the quantum theory which quickly arose no longer leaves any doubt: light must be thought of as particles (photons). Thus in the end, light also manifests itself dualistically; it manifests itself, according to circumstances, either as wave or as particle. The difficulties of comprehending physical occurences finally reaches its climax when we describe to the students the development of the model of the atom to its present state of knowledge. Even matter itself shows interference characteristics and must, therefore, also have the characteristics of a wave. Wave mechanics arises. Dalton thought out the first model of the atom, and this set off an interesting line of development. If we want to know how one really attempts to observe the behaviour of atoms, Rutherford's famous experiment can be considered as an example. He sent rays through a thin gold foil. In this way the rays were deflected at several points, so that Rutherford identified electric concentrations with the idea of an atomic nucleus. "Rutherford discovered the atomic nucleus." Rutherford's idea is still valid today. The atom consists essentially of nothing. Niels Bohr then proposed a new concept of the atom, which took into account the new phenomena of quantum physics. Heisenberg says about Bohr: "It was immediately apparent that Bohr had achieved his results not through calculations and evidence, but through intuition and guesswork." Bohr himself says, "The point of departure was not the idea that the atom is a planetary system in miniature and that one could here apply the laws of astronomy. I have never taken it that literally. But for me the point of departure was the stability of matter, which from the viewpoint of modern physics is a pure miracle ... Because of the stability of matter, Newtonian physics, within the atom, cannot be right; it can at best occasionally give a clue. And no clear description of the structure of the atom can be given, since such a description—just because it is to be clear—must make use of the concepts of classical physics which, however, no longer suffice to describe what is happening."

Heisenberg asks: "Will we ever be able to understand atoms at all, then?" Bohr replies: "Yes, but at the same time we shall learn for the first time the meaning of the word 'understand'" (Heisenberg, "The Part and the Whole").

Despite these realisations the students of Bohr and Heisenberg in thousands of textbooks have described the atom model in such a way that it has become absolutely real for the student. The chemist, for example, works very well with the concept of the atom which in theory is already outdated, but which still completely satisfies his requirements. The task of the school, however, should be to awaken in the human being a strong experience of the secret, well-structured nature of matter and to bring him to a closer understanding of the problems of really comprehending matter. "Even when modern science speaks about the forms of the atoms, the word 'form' here can only be understood in its most general meaning, as structure in time and space, as a symmetrical property of forces, as the potential of linking up with other atoms. In the case of the atom, concept and the thing itself will no longer be separated because the atom is actually no longer either" (Heisenberg).

It is not necessarily so that something as complicated as the atom will be better understood if we make a "simple model" of it. To be sure, such a simplification often leads to the possibility of calculating physical processes; on the other hand, however, it carries with it a tendency toward unreality. For every "model" presentation has its limits of validity and can turn into a lie, if we are not conscious that such limits exist.

With respect to this, Walter Heitler remarks, "I find it unjustified when teachers try to present higher, abstract areas of science in simplified form in the high schools, when such areas can only be properly understood at the university level."

We should never forget that many pupils hardly ever return to a study of physics in later life. The picture, the impression we pass on to them of the modern difficult fields of scientific conceptions of the world should be impressions for life. Even those who later do take up the study of science should be fully aware of the fact that the greatest of today's researchers are still wrestling for understanding, a fact of which those working only in the field of applied science are often quite oblivious.

CHEMISTRY

How is it that we daily come into contact with chemical phenomena, that chemical processes of many different kinds take place in our own organism, and yet many of us remain strangers to fundamental concepts of chemistry throughout our lives? Does this have something to do with the difficult nature of understanding chemical phenomena or does it derive from our methods of teaching?

Nowadays teachers, parents, and not least of all pupils, are confronted with such questions more than ever before. In many Western countries a revision of the chemistry curriculum and teaching methods is being carried out with the object that chemical processes can be grasped ever more quickly. Especially American teaching methods hope to achieve this by making the pupil conversant at an early stage with the world of models and formulae which, it is assumed, is as real as the physical world. Any experiments performed mainly serve as demonstrations and proofs of these more abstract concepts.

What effect does the teacher in a Waldorf school bring about when he immediately introduces the children in Class Seven to a wide range of actual phenomena? He sees to it, for example, that the phenomenon of fire is not limited to the more or less controlled flame of the Bunsen burner. Does he take the children to a forest fire? Perhaps not just that, but he does make it possible for every child to have the opportunity of holding his breath before the crackling noise and consuming force of a fire and to be carried away by the greatness and beauty of the experience. Chemical phenomena constantly threaten to overwhelm us. That is their nature. Therefore, it is necessary to arrange the phenomena through thinking, to relate them to one another without, however, denying them their validity as pure phenomena. Through experiments on a large scale the teacher awakens wonder. Then the pupils will also long to understand what they have observed. The experiment in school is more readily comprehensible than the direct experience in nature. It is often especially instructive because it answers a particular question which we may be asking about the world around us.

It has cost humanity a great effort to reach an understanding of a number of chemical processes. If one did not let the pupils partake in the basic discoveries they would miss important experiences. It is, therefore, essential that the teacher gives the pupils ample opportunity for discussion and carrying out their own experiments.

Right into the upper school the teaching of chemistry does not only add to the pupil's body of knowledge but also furthers his inner development. In the course of experiments the great chemical polarities of acid and alkali reappear again and again. But there are opposites also of other kinds, such as the metallic and the non-metallic elements.

Now, to be sure, many experiments and a good deal of mental effort are required to bring the different phenomena together in an intelligible way. Is an alkali always connected with a metal? Have acids always to do with oxygen, as Lavoiser thought when he called it oxy-gen? What part do non-metallic substances play in the chemical interaction of matter? One tends all too quickly to deduce rules from experiments, only to find soon afterwards that there are various exceptions! In such a situation a hypothesis offers an easy way out, and with the help of corollaries to this hypothesis one can still for a bit longer tolerate the exceptions. Is there a methodical way of building up a concept of nature, in which such exceptions can have their proper place? This would have to be a way free from any hypotheses, a way which takes special account of all the exceptions to the general rules.

Upon close examination Lavoisier's ideas about the role of oxygen in the formation of acids did not prove generally applicable. After all there are the hydrogen halides which are compounds with all the distinctive properties of acids and yet come into being without the participation of oxygen! Which substances in such a case are giving rise to acid-formation? Fluorine, chlorine, bromine, and iodine, elements of a special character, whose nature one can learn to know more closely just in this way, that is through observing their exceptional behaviour. In fact they constitute a special field of chemistry.

In this way, especially in Class Eleven, the need gradually arises to come to a careful classification of all matter and also the essential chemical processes. There are different possibilities of arrangement, and each in itself can show something interesting. If one looks at the periodic system of the elements or other groupings, it becomes increasingly clear that nature manifests herself in polarities, and is enhanced through their mutual interaction.

Many students can comprehend this *intellectually* without any great difficulty; however in an unstreamed class it is often necessary to present pictorial examples. The essential element of a picture is that it reveals its validity on more than one level. After the relationship of alkalis and acids to other natural phenomena has been worked out, the teacher can with the greatest caution pour concentrated sulphuric acid into a solution of sodium hydroxide. Both are crystal-clear liquids to look at and yet as they mix their opposition becomes apparent. The mixing of the two results in a harsh hissing sound and violent dangerous splashes. The mixture quickly heats up and boils wildly and noisily. Only gradually do things quieten down. One notices that many pupils feel relieved once the tumult has subsided. Finally it becomes completely still. After a period of cooling down, a salt precipitates out of the solution. Out of the chaos arise well-ordered crystalline forms.

Just as in the course of the history of chemical discoveries, the need arises also in the teaching of chemistry to arrive at a careful terminology and readily comprehensible classifications. On the whole usual chemical symbols are quickly grasped and learned by the pupils. In their eagerness many even make a game out of it. To be sure, an understanding of the ratio required in chemical reactions is more difficult to master. Yet the interaction of chemistry and mathematics offers interesting and important opportunities to learn about proportions.

Even in other fields of the study of nature, such as biology, proportions are a significant factor. Chemical formulae are above all an expression of relationships between weights and ratios which can be derived from them directly. But it is by no means easy to grasp this intellectually. That is why at this stage the more abstract concept of models in chemistry made their appearance. Even in school chemistry today the didactically far simpler way is chosen, using the atomic models which have simply to be accepted without being fully understood. An understanding of the origin of these models requires hard-won experience in experiments and an advanced mathematical knowledge. An important question faces the teacher at this point: Can his pupils remain free in respect of what they are being taught? Through the premature introduction of models which are not properly derived, the child is led to a false belief in authority, from which it is difficult for him to free himself. In some schools this starts as early as in the kindergarten. Such a method runs counter to the basic scientific object in view. In addition, nature herself recedes even further from the child's experience.

The history of modern chemistry reached a decisive turning point at the end of the nineteenth century. Even in the first half of the century the genius Faraday had striven to present phenomena. His experiments are often true discoveries, because they reveal the true being of nature. In Faraday's presentation there is much that can be learned of value to the teacher, for example, in the field of electrochemistry. We experience the effect of certain forces in chemical reactions, but still have no direct sense experience of the forces themselves. Even here there are models (for chemical compounds) which offer themselves as a substitute for physical reality. Chemists such as

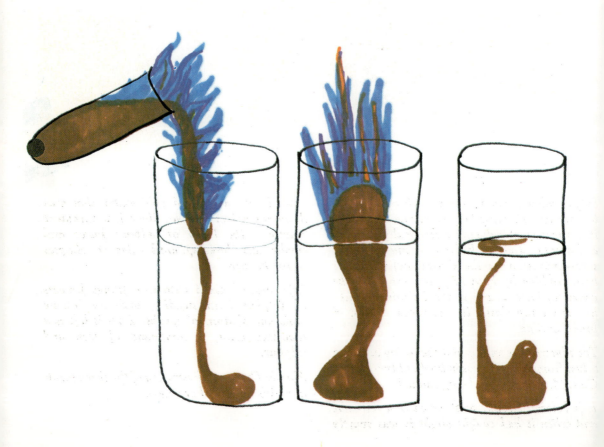

Svavlets 3 modifikationer i fast form.

Smell, colour, sound—the wealth of observable phenomena must be put on one side when it is a matter of reducing a chemical process to a formula. This path from a multitude of sense-impressions to the abstract definition has been trodden by humanity as a whole in the course of history, and in the Chemistry teaching of the top classes it is retraced at least in broad outline.

The illustrations on this and the facing page are taken from the main lesson books of two girls in Class 11. Sulphur was being studied.

Left below: Sulphur was heated in a test-tube and when it had caught alight it was swiftly poured into a glass of cold water that was illuminated from below. There is a turbulent reaction. The lump of sulphur hisses and smokes and flares up, until at last it collapses to the bottom.

Left above: Mixed with iron filings flowers of sulphur burn steadily, with an intense glow and showers of sparks. What is left is a lava-like crust, a compound of iron and sulphur.

Above: This is an illustration of the three forms in which solid sulphur occurs.

Wilhelm Ostwald observed the transition into the world of not directly provable hypotheses and tried to avoid this way. However the chemistry of today is no longer comprehensible without the use of hypothetical models. Therefore, even in a Waldorf school it is justifiable, indeed even necessary, to present this approach in appropriate instances. Moreover, from the study of such one-sided thinking which tries to get behind the phenomena, one can learn a great deal. At this point one also encounters the social problems of which many pupils are already aware. The world of synthetic preparations, which are usually no longer part of cycles of nature and act as poisons, raise questions in the minds of everyone. But it is not just a matter of rejecting modern technological chemistry. Chemistry will still continue to develop, perhaps even in completely different directions. For this to happen, however, greater insight is needed into the interaction and metamorphoses of matter in the ecological context. We also need more precise knowledge of the subtle effects these interactions have on human beings, a knowledge which can only gradually be acquired.

This awareness leads to an appreciation of the dilemma of modern chemistry, a dilemma which will gradually become apparent to everyone. Chemistry gives us a great deal of power, but it estranges us from the world, in so far as it is not in harmony with a conception of nature as a whole.

GEOGRAPHY

Classes Nine to Ten

Modern space research has shown us that the old dream of physically inhabiting other planets (for other than scientific purposes) must definitely be abandoned. The earth is our dwelling-place and will remain so. At the same time it has become increasingly clear that through our actions we have, in many respects, profoundly influenced those conditions which are necessary for the continuance of organic life. Moreover, we are even in a position to destroy these essentials through the use of physical and biological weapons. The question of the inner attitude with which we regard our earth has never been so important as in our present age.

The geography teaching in the upper classes of the Waldorf schools is designed to contribute towards a genuine and scientifically well-founded appreciation of events concerning the entire earth.

While regional geography has provided most of the subject matter in Classes Five to Eight, the pupils in the upper classes gradually come to consider processes which encompass the whole earth. The lessons must be planned in such a way that the pupils are directly introduced to the manifestations of nature. Geology is treated in the ninth class. The instruction in the school room must be supplemented by excursions such as, for instance, taking the whole class on an extended visit to a geologically interesting mountain range. Through the process of erosion one can clearly see that the face of the earth is forever changing. Plants and trees transform stone into fertile soil, the flowing waters reshape the landscape.

As the opposite of the processes of disintegration, the form-building processes of the mountains are operative within the earth. They create as is were the backbone of the continents. The mountains in those countries which border the Pacific Ocean have a primarily north-south orientation, while the mountains of the Alpine configuration run mainly in an east-west direction. Through this, seen from a global perspective, there arises a kind of cross. A comprehensive description of the powerful events which have produced the present countenance of the earth is for pupils of this age extraordinarily fascinating.

In Class Ten the pupils busy themselves on the one hand with the actual surveying of a small, limited region. They make their own maps. On the other hand they view the whole earth from a broad perspective. Through the new physical discoveries, the notion of the earth as merely a dead body, at least in practice, is clearly obsolete. Even in the lithosphere, the earth shows a mobility which is now clearly evident and which still continues in a vertical direction as well as a horizontal one, for instance the rising of the Scandinavian peninsula and the continental drift. The more we move away from the actual surface of the earth, the more intense the forces involved seem to become. First the

Next page: In Class 9 the complex formation of the Alps is studied. These three diverse pictures illustrate the same geological cross-section.

Extreme right: This illustrates the work in surveying carried out in Class 10. The pupils make exact maps such as this as a result of taking levels and measurements themselves. They are often justly proud of such an achievement and feel they have mastered a new skill.

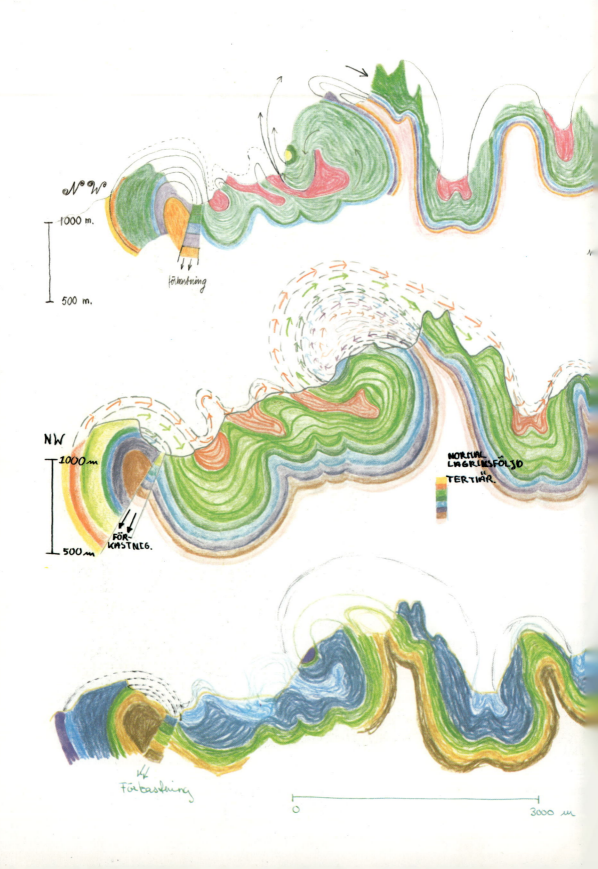

N°W

1000 m.

500 m.

förkastning

NW

1000 m

500 m

FÖR-
KASTNEG.

NORMAL
LAGRINGSFÖLJD
TERTIÄR.

Förkastning

0   3000 m

THORSÄTRA SKALA 1:400

pupils study the shape of the continents. They learn among other things that the earth shows a distinct polarity in the land and water hemispheres; they sketch and paint not only the heights of the mountains but also the depths of the sea; they experience the great ocean currents and through their own artistic work gain an understanding of the living picture of the wide range of plant-life which covers the earth's surface. Atmospheric phenomena, too, are thoroughly studied. The outermost layers of the earth's environment show us further intensification of activity. It is not only meteorites, but also other substances that are constantly penetrating from outer space the realm of the earth. Also in the magnetosphere there is a constant interplay between the cosmos and the earth. While the earth loses hydrogen in a constant stream out into space, it receives daily a supply of cosmic substances at the rate of 1,000–10,000 tons. From its outermost layer to its core, the earth reflects an intelligent organisation. It is an organism.

Such perspectives are designed to awaken in young people a sense of responsibility to the earth and its functions.

Mineralogy is often a favourite subject of teenage pupils especially if they can make practical field excursions and collect their own specimens.

BIOLOGY AND
THE STUDY OF MAN

Of all the conceptions we carry with us through life there are few which affect our actions so profoundly and permanently as the way in which we view the essential being of man. Let us try to put aside all secondary considerations and turn our thoughts solely to the essential question: What is man?

Is he a product of his social environment? This is the conviction of the Marxists, and from this follows the idea of the right of the Collectives to shape the existence of the individual.

Is he an incurable egoist, ruled by his impulses and desires? This conception lies at the basis of the capitalist system, in practice if not in theory. In the modern consumer society industrialists and advertisers plan ways in which the consumer can be "steered" by the help of "needs" which are sustained by advertisements and indeed are partially created by them in the first place.

Is he a specific combination of genes? Today this is the usual scientific interpretation and one which is increasingly gaining acceptance among laymen. Such a conception, however, also has its dangerous side. If it should become possible to manipulate our inherited characteristics, then from such a viewpoint this would be justified.

There are also other interpretations which can lead to far-reaching practical consequences: "Man is what he eats."—"Man is a higher animal."—"Man is a naked ape."

For the very reason that our own conception of the human being can lead to profound lifelong consequences for ourselves it is especially important that not only teachers but also textbooks used for self-study avoid premature judgments.

Concerning Rudolf Steiner's knowledge of man, which lies at the basis of his pedagogy, many readers might ask the following question. Does it not often happen that Waldorf teachers themselves present the students with similar preconceptions such as "Man is an immortal being of soul and spirit who goes through repeated earthlives"? To this one can only answer that if that happens then it is just as unpedagogical as all other cut-and-dried definitions.

Children and young people have the right to experience how their own conception of man gradually evolves in its manifold complexity out of an almost unlimited richness of phenomena. One of the teacher's most important tasks is so to direct the work that each judgment that occurs and each consequence which is drawn is suited as far as possible to the material under consideration and the age level of the pupils.

The Curriculum

The actual study of man begins in Class Seven with a general survey of the basic aspects of health and nutrition. Anyone who has ever read a book on medicine knows the danger lurking here—the reader comes to think he has every illness in the book! In puberty this anxiety is often very pronounced. It is important, therefore, that these questions be discussed as early as possible. On the other hand, below Class Seven most children would hardly be in a position to grasp the subject at all. Instruction in this sphere can be a real blessing. Never before and perhaps never again does a person eat so much and so quickly

KIDNEY. (CUT LONGITUDINALLY).

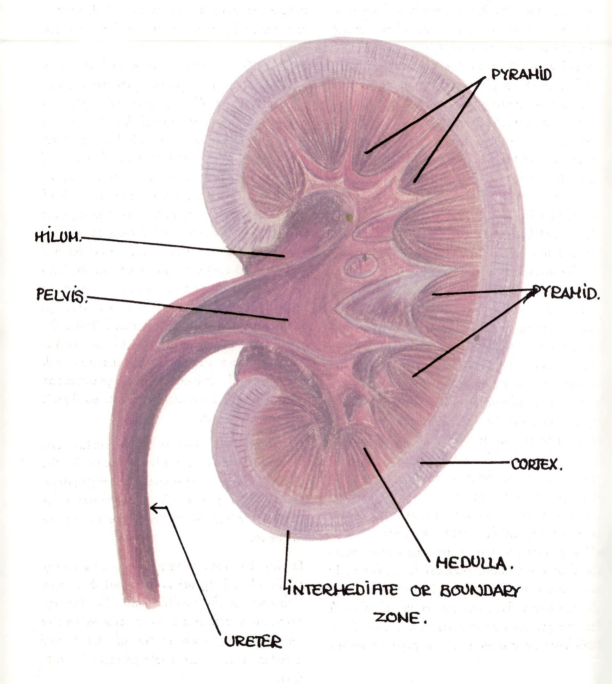

PYRAHID

HILUM.

PELVIS.

PYRAHID.

CORTEX.

HEDULLA.

INTERHEDIATE OR BOUNDARY
ZONE.

URETER

as he does at this age. Much better than long sermons on chewing, the quality of food and the like, is to describe in a lively and interesting manner the process of digestion through the mouth, the oesophagus, the stomach, the intestines, the liver, the blood and the kidneys, and to let the pupils work out the forms and primary functions of the most important inner organs through their own sketches. Whoever has once realised how the different organs react to unchewed, badly prepared, indigestible, spoilt or even poisoned food, will be able to develop a healthy feeling for these organs for his whole life.

In Class Eight the children are advanced enough to complete a new and important step in the study of man. They have in the meantime become acquainted with a number of elementary mechanical laws. Often with a keen interest they now discover how such phenomena have their counterparts in the human body: in the human eye, the leverage system of the skeleton, to name just one or two. The conclusion which can be drawn from this should not be that all functions of the human body can be explained in mechanical terms. One should formulate far more carefully what arises from direct observation and not go further than saying that there are certain activities in the human body which are understandable in physical terms.

The curriculum is such that the upper school teacher who becomes responsible for the study of human physiology and biology in general in the ninth class, can adjust the class work to the previous knowledge and needs of the children; he can also fill in gaps or review

In the upper school the illustrations gradually become more precise and include exact anatomical detail.

and expand on especially important sections. He can weave in descriptions of animals and nature and compare the ways in which animals and human beings are related to their environment.

In Class Ten a new stage is reached; the functions of the human soul and spirit are brought into the picture. What actually takes place in the physical and conceptual life of a person when he picks up a pencil? Through such simple examples the structure and function of the nervous and muscular systems can be illustrated. In addition the different levels of consciousness are considered; the waking state in which we can perceive and think about such an act; the dream state which pervades our feelings and emotions and which are perhaps also associated with it; the totally unconscious state of the functions of the will through which we carry out the act itself. While the different organs and systems of the human being are now described in connection with one's inner life, it is clear that the presentation on this level is much more complicated than it was in Class Seven.

Cytology is discussed in the eleventh class. Now is the time to study, for example, the division of cells, regeneration, propagation, heredity and ontogenesis. Also the numerous problems raised in modern genetics can be discussed.

During the course of this school year a survey of the plant kingdom is begun which is then continued in the twelfth class. The biology curriculum culminates in a comprehensive survey of the main species of the animal kingdom and of the whole process of evolution.

The Big Question: The Relationship Between Man and Animal

One of the most important of all problems is directly related to biology teaching in the top classes: What is the actual relationship between man and animal?

This question is by no means merely theoretical. It arises naturally from the life experience of the pupils. In his early childhood as well as in his early teens a human being often has the fundamental need of identifying with the animal world in one way or another. In one Class Nine a girl asked the question: "Why does the hedgehog have spines?" Without realising that he himself was a good illustration of this very problem, a boy well-entrenched behind a thick shock of hair and a leather jacket answered: "Why, to be able to roll himself up and defend himself, of course."

A decidedly choleric pupil always wanted to give talks on the rhinoceros, never forgetting to describe the outbreaks of wrath of this not exactly gentle animal. A small shy girl, without any outside motivation includes in her nature-study notebook a kind of "spiritual self-portrait", a picture of a shy doe. A phlegmatic child depicts in his notebook a careful and deeply-felt portrayal of an orang-utan which, resting lazily in the branch of a tree, enjoys the delicious fruit around him. This instinctive way of feeling oneself into the animal world can, of course, also express itself in a far more primitive manner.

What can a biology teacher say in summing-up this whole problem if he wishes to proceed in a purely phenomenological way of observation?

When Ernst Haeckel, at the end of the last century, graphically wrote down his thoughts about the descent of man, without any qualms he wrote the names of the different ape-forms on the family tree which leads in a direct line to the human being. Since then a great deal has happened in evolutionary research. The Belgian paleontologist Louis Dollo has shown that specialised organs cannot revert and then redevelop in another specialised direction. Man, however, is in many ways extraordinarily unspecialised. Here the teacher can remind the pupils of the lessons in Class Four where the hands of the human being were compared with the corresponding front limbs of mammals. That the human being therefore could stem from ancestors who evolved in their way of life and their bodily development a marked one-sidedness in the construction of the head or the extremities, for example, is not biologically conceivable. In modern "family trees" the names of the primates therefore have for the most part been placed on side-branches; and it is assumed that both humans and primates have descended from common ancestors. However, since even the most recent finds have provided no certain key to the appearance of these ancestral forms, recourse has been had to ancestral 'models' that understandably vary considerably from one scientist to another. It appears highly possible that the coming decades will bring far-reaching changes in the conception we have of our origin and evolution.

But what about the obvious relationship in the psychological sphere which has so often

In the study of Biology in Classes 11 and 12 the pupils become aware of the typical form or gesture of a certain plant or animal, whether it is more outwardly visible or more inwardly felt.

The changing moods of colour and form bring to expression various aspects of the cuttle-fish.

i vattnet kan bläckfisken för-
svinna från platsen. Då en
skräck uppstår, den känner
sig hotad tillgriper den denna
metod.

Octopus.

Armar, tentakler.

sugkoppar.

stora ögat

ganglier, koncentrerad nerv-
cellsanhopning. ögat kappslas
in.

skal, kalkbit under
huden, en slags
ryggrad.

mantel-
håla.

gand

mun, käkar. I munhålan
ligger en radula med tänder
grupperade i regelbundna
tvärrader. Det finns även ett
par kraftiga, spetsiga kitin
tänder, som
tillsammans
(bildar) liknar
en spetsig
papegojnäbb med
vilken den slavs-
ar i sig födan, mjukdelarna.

En slags tratt i
mantelhålans slut i vilken vatten drivs ut, bläckfisken simmar då bakåt. Framåt kryper den
genom att ta tag med sing sugkoppiga armar.

andlöppning.

magen.

gdlar i mantelhålan vilka syre-
sätter blodet.

been pointed out in modern behavioural sciences? In the human being there are certain obvious "animal needs" (sexual and territorial impulses) and in many animals a number of "human" traits (self-assertion or aggression). Through his powerful technology, however, man is incomparably more dangerous that any kind of animal. If one is really serious about putting man and animal on an equal footing then the consequences are very far-reaching. Then the most important goal of our education would have to be to learn to contain the especially dangerous impulse of aggression through sport or other harmless physical activities and to direct all lower instincts into other areas.

All such questions lead unavoidably to the realisation that we stand before a decisive alternative. If we regard man as a mere creature of instinct, then he needs constant spiritual, economic, and political directives. However, if we view him as a self-conscious Ego, capable of self-control and self-development, then it becomes meaningful to strive for such great goals as freedom, loyalty and democracy.

What right do we have to speak of man as an ego-being? This question can certainly be taken up in biology classes, perhaps by means of detailed comparisons between the functions of the instincts in man and in the animal. Nevertheless, this is a problem which science alone can never answer. Just by discussing such an important question of human existence one realises what a vital part the humanities play within the school curriculum.

HISTORY AND SOCIOLOGY

In Classes Eight and Nine the pupils—above all the boys—are eager to learn as much as possible about the time they live in. The history instruction for these years is designed to meet such a need. In Class Eight history from the 16th century to the present day is discussed, with special attention being given to economic history, that is the great technical discoveries and the development of trade and industry.

In Class Nine the same period is dealt with again, but this time the cultural, social and political events stand in the foreground: the rise of the modern national states, the history of colonialism, and the struggles between the Europeans and the other races, and the social developments of the era. Anyone who has no idea of these foundations cannot really understand what is happening in the world of today. When the hunger for modern history has been satisfied, at least for the time, then from a new perspective one can look back again at more distant times. In Class Ten the cultures of the ancient world are again taken up, but now from other vantage points; the significance of geographical and sociological connections for the particular life-styles of China, India, Persia, Mesopotamia, Egypt and Greece. In these, as in the following epochs, their connections with our own times are pointed out.

In Class Eleven medieval times are the main study. This goes parallel with the history of literature. Above all, attention is paid to the different cultural, historical and religious currents.

In Class Twelve when the pupils survey the whole course of history, they can draw comparisons and consider cross-sections of particular aspects, in order to appreciate what is characteristic of any given period. Of the many special studies that might be undertaken, we shall present only one as an example.

The social life in ancient Egypt and in the Sumerian city-state was thoroughly centralised: the priest-king, who was looked on as a god, was not only the chief priest and thus the leader of the whole cultural life, he was at the same time the supreme judge and war-lord and —at least in the earliest historical period—the owner of all property.

In the subsequent course of development, we see how gradually worldly rulership becomes separated from the priesthood. Kings and priests now stand opposite each other as two separate powers—sometimes as enemies, for instance, Consul and Pontifex Maximus in ancient Rome, Emperor and Pope in medieval Europe. During the transition to modern times, with the rise of the town, its guilds and corporations, a third powerful social factor, the growing economic life, begins to play an important part in the historic process. The beginnings of a "three-fold" ordering of society, in which the spiritual, economic, and political institutions find themselves in a certain balance, were destroyed or weakened through the powerful Absolutism of the 15th, 16th, and 17th centuries. The unified conception of the priest-state repeats itself but now in a more secular version. With the advent of the French Revolution the power of the prince begins to change into the power of the people. The rise of democracy, which in many respects in certainly necessary, has as its tragic consequence that disagreements between kings become enmity between whole nations. With the advent of industrialisation and modern communications, the democratic state of today acquires those economic and spiritual means by which it can become a threat to other equally well-equipped states. This leads to the confrontation of great powers in the modern world.

From such considerations it becomes necessary to consider the different concepts of society which attempt to overcome this problem. There is Marxism, for instance, the dialectic logic of which anticipates the dissolution of the modern state; a world-federalism which would bring together all power-blocks into one democratic universal state; the belief in a balance through mutual fear which enables the different states to hold one another in check by skilful diplomatic and technical manipulations. Rudolf Steiner's idea of a three-fold social order, would neutralise the danger of the "super-powers" by carefully-planned emancipation of both the economic and the spiritual life from the tyrannical domination of the centralised state. Which view best suits reality and which can best help in our present situation? The pupils themselves will have to decide that. The task of the teacher is to point out clearly the problems of the modern world and also the most important suggestions which have been advanced as a solution.

The main task of the teaching of history in the upper school is, of course, to present the wider perspectives. Often there is not enough time left to go into the personal destinies of individuals. Nevertheless the consideration of biographies is of the greatest importance. By means of such studies to which the pupils themselves may contribute in the form of reports, one thing becomes very clear. The inner being of a man—however one may judge his deeds— need not remain a passive onlooker of events that are coming to pass more or less automatically. It carries its impulses into the historical process and can, if the conditions are right, give a new direction to a whole stream of events. But it can also remain inactive and thereby miss a decisive opportunity.

Such brief biographies, which bring to expression a tragic human problem as is often the case in modern history, can call up in the pupils unexpectedly positive reactions. A boy whose emotional life had become severely disturbed as a result of a difficult early childhood and who consequently completely neglected his school-work, one day heard about the life of Bismarck and the severe depressions that accompanied him throughout many years of his political activity and the effects of which he mastered only with the greatest effort. A few days later the pupil came up to the teacher and said: "That Bismarck—he was a remarkable fellow!" After that he pulled himself together and during the rest of that period produced excellent work.

Romanesque and Gothic cathedrals.

THE ARTS IN
THE UPPER SCHOOL

As their powers of thought develop in various spheres, many of the pupils in the upper school are no longer satisfied merely to learn the method of certain artistic techniques. They want to know the reasons that give rise to them. A study of the different forms of art is taken as a main lesson period, in the same way as the sciences. Literature and poetry are treated in this way in Class 10, and music in Class 11. In other chapters of this book this is described more fully.

The Visual Arts

In the ninth class the life and work of Leonardo da Vinci may be the theme. The teacher reports briefly on his accomplishments in the most diverse fields (painting, drawing, sculpture, architecture, poetry, music, botany, mathematics, mechanics, anatomy), and describes his almost unique ability to hold in memory an impression perceived only once—for example that of a human face—and then to reproduce it with a sketching pen in the minutest detail as if the object were present in the room. He may end with an aphorism in which Leonardo's dry wisdom in earthly matters comes to expression in all clarity: "Whoever cannot achieve what he wants should want what he is capable of." To be confronted with extraordinary human greatness can fire one with enthusiasm but it can also be a sobering experience. A pupil comes with a question which reflects the whole uncertainty of the age of puberty: "How is one to know what one is capable of?"

It is not easy to answer such questions. Nor is it always necessary to do so. Often the most important thing is to engage the young people in the classroom on a purely human level so that important questions concerning life in general can spring up spontaneously.

The teaching of art in Class Nine deals with the history of the visual arts from ancient times as far as the period of Rembrandt. In studying the transitions from one direction of style to another the teacher can draw attention to significant riddles of human development. In the sombre and massive Romanesque architecture and the boldly-conceived Gothic cathedrals which in their upward thrust seem almost to overcome the forces of gravity, two contrasting moods of soul are reflected. A wide spectrum of feeling-perception comes to expression in the development of painting. The imaginative picture world of the medieval artists with its background of piety and devotion is followed in the south by the overwhelming enjoyment of the world of the senses expressed in the paintings of the Renaissance and in the north by a deepened and often very problematical landscape full of inward feeling as exemplified by the works of Grünewald, Dürer, and Rembrandt. The dramatic contrasts between light and shadow in Rembrandt's paintings can provide a basis for interesting colour studies.

History of Architecture

In Class twelve the history of architecture is the subject of study. From the vast field of available material one example will be given here, which can lead to an understanding for the problems of modern architecture.

233

The Spanish architect Antonio Gaudi (1852—1926) saw in the straight line the expression of human reason, in the curve the reflection of the activity of the creative deity. He sought his inspiration in nature, in the teeming richness of the living strength of the realm of plants, and thus created a bold, often fantastic, world of form. The brilliant and remarkable impulse which came to expression in his art was carried to an extreme and lost itself in the non-architectural, naturalistic plant-ornamentation of Art Nouveau. In energetic reaction to this manifestation of decadence, Le Corbusier (1887—1965) at a specific phase of his creative work condemned the curve altogether—he called it the "path of the donkey"—and wanted to create spaces in which the straight line ruled alone as an expression of reason. With his one-sided striving for rational utility ("the house is a dwelling-machine"), he became the founder of modern functionalism. The use of computers and of prefabricated building components have carried such ideas to an extreme, which threatens to force the town-dweller into living in a uniform, completely soulless space.

The attempts undertaken in the last few decades (not least of all by Le Corbusier himself) to "humanise" modern architecture once again by introducing a strong element of movement, bear witness to the difficulty of finding a valid alternative to the language of form generally used today.

Are we condemned, therefore, to decide on one or the other of these two chief directions in architecture, or is it possible to find a middle way? This is the point at which it is appropriate to mention the direction taken by Rudolf Steiner in this field. He was of the view that the activity which was to take place in a house should come to expression in the whole shape and structure. Whoever wants to build "functionally" must not only seek solutions which are flawless from a technical aspect but also are the expression in architectural terms of the soul and spiritual needs of the person who is to live or work there. Accordingly, in the second Goetheanum he wished to realise an architectural impulse which could be described as a "search for balance": an effort to bring the movement which is manifest in the individual surfaces and lines to a unified and harmonious whole.

Opposite right: In the Art lessons of Class 9 one of the tasks set can be to work through colour-relationships at the problem of the contrast of light and darkness, as it comes to expression in Rembrandt.

Next pages:
Pupil's drawings from the History of Architecture in Class 12.

"Falling Water" designed by Frank Lloyd Wright in 1936.

Windyhill House, Kilmacolm, designed by Charles Rennie Macintosh 1899–1901.

Goetheanum in Dornach, designed by Rudolf Steiner and built 1925–1928.

"Falling Water"
Connelisville, Pennsylvania 1936-37

WINDYHILL HOUSE, Kilmacolm 1899~1901 (Norra fasaden)

THE HISTORY OF LITERATURE

Why do we actually need poetry? Do we not live in a time in which reality, in many respects, surpasses all fiction, and in which the real problems of our fellow-men must be incomparably more important than the fictitious fate of any hero in a novel? What is the point of a thorough study of the fields of poetry and the other aspects of writing, or the history of literature in a contemporary curriculum?

One could, of course, answer the question by saying that only modern literature is considered in order to show how the problems of our time forcefully come to expression in just this medium. There is no doubt that many young people would welcome such an approach. Others would realise more or less clearly that the perspective which one gains through such a procedure is not entirely true. The question is really this: Is the literature of the past a cultural burden which we drag along from generation to generation only out of conservative regard? Or have perhaps the classical writers something to say to us which can hardly be found in contemporary writing? Actually the great problems of our time are not experienced and artistically expressed in all their ramifications only by modern authors. The literary material which is used in the upper classes of the Waldorf school shows very clearly that the motives and personalities of writers of the past can often be especially relevant and interesting for young people of today.

In teaching literature, just as in presenting historical development down to modern times, individual writers and their works of the end of the 18th and the beginning of the 19th century are considered. Gradually the students realise how exceptionally rich such a study is for an understanding of our own time. As the storms of the French Revolution and the Napoleonic Wars broke out over Europe, many people thought an epoch of apocalyptical upheaval had begun. These decades, chaotic though they were from a political aspect, turned out on the cultural level to be a true "Golden Age", an age in which an almost unique wealth of musical, philosophical and, above all, poetical gifts came to expression at the same time in Europe. Of loneliness, human conflict, broken promises, anxiety, fear of death, doubt in God and the world, as well as of war and famine, many of the people in this era knew a great deal, perhaps no less than the artists of today. But they often had to the highest degree the ability to formulate their suffering and deep inner problems in artistic terms, which in form and content were landmarks then and will remain so for some time to come. An outstanding example is Goethe, who in this context should not be looked at as a German, but rather as a European cultural figure. In dealing with such material, most important human questions will often be raised.

A brief example will show how impressive the intense intellectual activity of the leading cultural figures of that era can be for the pupils to meet with. A teacher in a literature period in Class Nine had described how Heinrich von Kleist, with his strong sense for the real consequences of Kant's theory of knowledge which is so full of resignation, decided to give up all research and to devote himself as a poet to the "beautiful illusion". One pupil found this view of life in which there was no way of achieving a knowledge of true reality ("the thing in itself") simply unbearable. Her arm shot up quickly and she asked with deep feeling: "How did Kant himself actually die? Did he commit suicide?"

The seriousness of life which comes to expression in such a period finds its counterbalance in the treatment of humour and humorous poetry. Rudolf Steiner recommended Jean Paul's observations on this subject as a point of departure in this class.

In Class ten the pupils are about sixteen years old and experience the transition from a life-style closely bound up with the family to that of an independent person. The main theme in the study of literature now depicts the same change, as it has come about too in history, especially in the Old Norse poetry. In

In much of modern literature there is the underlying theme, expressed with many variations and often with genius, of despair over the inability of modern man to find a way out of his difficulties. This pessimistic attitude is often considered, especially by young people, to be honest and in keeping with the times. If in abeyance to this opinion we restrict ourselves mainly to 20th century works, it is impossible to give a true picture of the development of the art of literature, and the ways in which human beings have faced their problems in the past. The perspective becomes even wider and more realistic, if we also introduce the literature of different nations as well as of former ages.

This girl of Class 11 has drawn and painted scenes from Wolfram von Eschenbach's epic of Parzival in the style of medieval illumination.

Vid Arthurs stad stod ståtlig riddare: Iter i sin röda rustning. Iter föll för svekfullt spjut, Parsival bort i röda rustningen.

Intet ord av medlidande kom över Parsivals läppar vid åsynen av den lidande sjuke Amfortas.

Bäste vännen Gawan ut på egna uppdrag. Fann till slut sin borg och hustru: Schastel marveil och orgiluce.

the oldest version of the Edda, Gudrun decides in the battle between her husband and the scions of her own clan in favour of her blood relations, although they had once slain her lover Sigurd. In the later sagas and in the "Nibelungenlied" we are told how this same personality—whether she is known as Gudrun or Kriemhild—carries out a terrible revenge on her own brothers because of her murdered husband. Between these two interpretations of an ancient motif there lies a powerful historical change; the experience in which the human ego frees itself from the bonds of blood relationship and becomes an individual in its own right. A similar ancient Germanic motif, which comes to expression in the Edda and especially in the Icelandic sagas, such as the saga of Burnt Njal, is the striving of the individual to remain steadfast in the face of loneliness, sorrow and death. In such scenes one can glimpse the birth of an ideal which later, in ever new metamorphoses, reappears in Western history, the strong emphasis on individualism.

In Class ten one period of teaching is devoted to the basic literary forms. The different schools of creative writing, poetry and its various metres and styles from ancient times to the present can here be observed as representative of the different states of consciousness in the different epochs. In the construction of dramas, epics and lyrical poems, certain basic artistic and psychological principles of each age can be discovered.

In Class eleven the point of departure is a study of medieval literature, above all that epoch which stands out in the world of knightly tales as an early and powerful parallel to the story of Faust: Wolfram von Eschenbach's "Parzival".* Parzival's course of life goes from the simple-mindedness of childhood and youth, through uncertainty, defiance and doubt to a

spiritual rebirth, to a deepened and satisfying experience of the self. The journey through life which Wolfram depicts in his epic has something which is valid for everyone. Whoever studies these three stages more closely can recognise them as possibilities at least in the life of every human being. Pupils and teacher can now both see how many authors of the past there are who have basically remained at the level of "simple-mindedness" their whole life through, how many modern authors have never gone beyond the experience of "doubt", but that there are also a group of important literary personalities who have lived through the earlier stages and then, towards the end of their lives, in one way or another have reached the stage of "spiritual rebirth". Faithfulness to the chosen goal determines one's destiny, the path of individual development, in spite of all obstacles in the way, and the single human being who has trodden this path can eventually be of service to mankind as a whole.

In Class twelve, after a survey of earlier literature, modern literature is discussed. In many schools this activity begins with Goethes "Faust", who can be taken as the prototype of the struggling modern man. Nietzsche, Ibsen, Tolstoy and Dostojevsky can then form the transition to modern literature, which encompasses both the sufferings and the greatness of our own era.

The selection of examples may vary, but it will always be such as will acquaint the pupils with literary creations which are a genuine expression of their own period and, at the same time, point towards the future.

* In Wolfram's "Parzival", the hero progresses through "Dumpfheit" and "Zweifel" to "Saelde". These expressions have been rendered into English in the present context as "simple-mindedness", "doubt", and "spiritual re-birth".

DRAMA IN
THE UPPER SCHOOL

In one of the upper classes—the tenth or the twelfth—a complete, full-length drama is undertaken. The pupils now experience what it means to work not out of the natural love of acting of younger children, but out of a conscious artistic feeling for style. The experiences which both the producer and players may undergo is related by the drama teacher of the Waldorf school in Stockholm as follows:

"A key word in the classical theory of drama was: 'sympathy'! To creep into a role, to become so deeply involved in it that you suffer to the same extent as the person you are representing. The beginning of all love is interest. Compassion is enhanced interest. At this point a pedagogical problem arises. How can the teacher help the pupil in such a way that he does not tire but maintains his interest in the part he is playing. One will succeed in this is one can continually discover new shades of meaning and new nuances of expression. Then the role becomes a real character, it comes to life. This interest, which can grow into compassion, is something different from the amateur interest of wanting to get on the stage to act out one's own self. The sympathy which is spoken of in the ancient theory of drama goes much further—a suffering which passes through a dramatic climax and reaches a release, a solution. The Classical Theory of drama also spoke of catharsis, of purification and refinement as the final phase of the dramatic experience. These concepts have been interpreted in many different ways in the course of the centuries... But in the dramatic work of the twelfth class the pupils can get an idea of what this actually means. Indeed, each pupil will perhaps notice that in struggling with a certain role he has become a different person. The class as a whole may go through a change because the pupils get to know one another in quite a new way. The pupils stand in a more objective relationship to their own personalities as well as to those of their comrades. In the course of this work much has come to pass —in fact, a kind of catharsis." (Louise Björneboe in "PåVäg", the journal of the Swedish Waldorf schools, No. 2–68.)

Only after puberty is the pupil able to represent on the stage a personality totally different to himself. This new experience can bring about what young people especially need, namely the ability to participate in the destiny of others to such an extent that now and again they may forget their own personal problems.

Next page: An exercise in drama. Classes 10 and 11.

Below: "A Sleep of Prisoners" by Christopher Fry.

MUSIC

Whoever has been present at a monthly festival in one of the larger Waldorf schools knows that the choir and orchestra play an important part in the life of the school. If it is one of the schools in which a real musical life has developed over the years, then the pupils in the upper school play some of the symphonic works of the great composers. In musical education, of course, an attempt is made to get even the relatively "non-musical" pupils to sing in tune. The purely "phenomenonological" study of the nature of different intervals and keys plays an important part. Characteristic folk-songs from different parts of the world are practised—often in connection with particular subjects of study, such as history or geography. In order that the pupils may come into a direct and living contact with music-making, which then becomes a lifelong interest for many of them, the musical examples, as far as possible, are given through live instrumentation or song. The question of the effect of technical aids (records, amplifiers, etc.) becomes a central theme of conversation.

Side by side with the practical experience, music theory and especially the history of music is a particularly important factor in Class eleven. The characteristic elements of different currents and styles give occasion to touch on central questions of the world of art and of human life.

The archetypal dichotomy of 'Apollonian' and 'Dionysian'* elements in ancient Greece, elaborated on by Nietzsche, was experienced first of all in the realm of mythology, and then made its mark in the whole Hellenic cultural life, especially in music. In the musical development of the West one can see this polarity come repeatedly to the fore. During epochs in which the 'Apollonian' mood predominates, there are still individual artists who represent the opposing element, for example, G. de Machault in the musical life of the 14th century, and Monteverdi at the beginning of the 17th century. The 'classical' Western music belongs to the treasures of cultural life and has as such been cultivated in a continuous tradition. The great masters of the Baroque and Rococo period, including Mozart, viewed music—to use the well-known phrase of E. von Hanslicks—as a "play of forms moving in sound". Their basic attitude to art and to life in general is, in spite of the intensity of feeling expressed in their music, essentially 'Apollonian'. One of the first to represent a radical approach was Beethoven. He was in full command of the whole range of traditional musical forms, but again and again consciously broke through them, especially in his last period of creativity.

In the following period the affinity developed between music and poetry, as for example in Weber, Schubert, Schumann, Berlioz and Liszt. In the operas of Richard Wagner the endeavour to blend the different arts, drama, scenery, instrumentation and song, reached a climax and in its power and universality achieved an effect on the audiences which went beyond anything known hitherto. In his last years Wagner strove intensely for release from the world of passion and emotion. Did he actually

* "Apollonian"—related more to the life of thinking and outer form, hence "classical" in a musical sense. "Dionysian"—related to the inner life of personal feeling and impulse, hence connected to what is called the "romantic" school.

achieve this in Parsifal, or is it true, as is often maintained, that even in the purely sacramental parts of his opera an unbridled emotional element comes to expression? Since the Parsifal theme is a kind of red thread in Class eleven, such a question can well be dwelt on.

With few exceptions—among which especially Mendelssohn and Bruckner should be mentioned—the basic nature of the Romantic composers can be described as predominantly 'Dionysian'. In modern music we discern evidence of the 'Apollonian' element which, however, finds its source of inspiration not primarily in the sphere of religion, as with the old masters, but rather in the realm of science and technology. In the case of Schoenberg this tendency often appears in a more mathematically structured form, in the case of Hindemith and Stravinsky more as a naive musical form. It becomes clearer and clearer that once again a radical change is taking place in the world of music. With all their modern freedom of form, contemporary composers seldom look on their work as products of personal creative artistry. They do not create finished compositions; they "give an account of some musical material". Their human attitude is often unassuming and experimental.

It is also worth while studying the music of such more distant cultures as those of India an China, although they stand outside the main stream of Western musical evolution.

PAINTING

After working in black and white in the eighth and ninth classes, the pupils in the tenth class return to colour. The following words of Rudolf Steiner can serve as a guide for the present task: "One should realise that we do not have to set up a special kind of painting for the children, but when one finds that they, in some way, are going to grow into painting, then the principles must be derived from a living painting-art, not from pedagogically contrived methods. The real artistic element must be carried out in the school, not a reasoned thought-out process ..." (Lecture of August, 17, 1923).

The examples of paintings reproduced here show how one can try, without directly following any one style, to penetrate the world of colours as great modern artists have done. They have grasped the characteristic nature, for instance, of blue and of yellow, of the warm and the cold colours, the powers of form and expression which colours themselves have latent in them. Goethe's "Theory of Colours" is an inexhaustible source of inspiration for this experience. It gives rise to free colour compositions.

The experiences in working with watercolour in painting in the lower school have

Free exercises in colour as a revival of painting after the period of working in black and white tones.

Above: Cold and warm values of the colour blue.

Below: Tensions in the sphere of yellow.

been by no means exhausted. The technique of layer-painting produces new and especially interesting colour-effects. Each shade of colour is applied separately and has to dry. It remains transparent: that is, what has already been painted shimmers through the next veil of colour. The new creative possibilities thus available stimulate the fantasy. The picture takes shape as a process of evolution from colours, not as a preconception which one has in mind from the beginning.

In Class eleven the attention of the pupils to their environment is directed in another way. The young people now experience the colours in their surroundings as eloquent phenomena! Still-life and figure painting are practised. The "Impressionists" and the "Expressionists" with their diametrically opposite basic human attitudes are represented in the pictures. The goal of this study of painting is reached in Class twelve when the pupils paint the human countenance.

More free colour-exercises.

Above: Three-colour harmony with variations.

Below: Cold and warm elements of red, beginning to form a composition.

The School in the Modern World

THE INDUSTRIALISED SCHOOL

In the early 1950's a number of sociologists in the USA evolved an idea which has since become wide-spread and which will probably have a profound effect not only on the future of the school itself but also on the future of mankind in general. They began to look upon education and training in terms of the economic life. It appeared to them that these aspects should not only be considered as "consuming" capital and human effort, but also as an investment which promotes an expansion of the economic life (Torsten Husén, Skola för 80-talet/The School of the Eighties). Soon a new university course was established on the "Economics of Education". A new way of viewing education arose: the universities are the producers of knowledge, the schools are the distributors. The American researcher, Fritz Machlup, in his recent book has shown that the "science industry" in the USA, both at school and research level, has recently been expanding at nearly twice the rate of the other industries. However, another point of view is possible. The schools may be viewed as producers too, if one imagines that the goods produced consist of a certain number of pupils who annually reach the end of the production line and are labelled with "price-tags" in the form of examination certificates.

Planning for the Future

Following the example of other industrial projects, people have tried to view these questions of production in a long-term and global context. In the description of the futurologists there are certain points which have become key questions in the minds of the educational experts. If no great world catastrophes occur, the course of development in the industrialised countries will run somewhat as follows. To an ever greater extent machines will take over the work of man. As the number of factory-workers decreases, so the number of office-workers increases. The need in the professions for an ever-increasing theoretical knowledge, the increased free time, the exagerrated growth in research, the increase in population, and the growing demand of modern man for insight into all fields of life and knowledge will lead to an ever-expanding "education explosion", which will leave its mark on all aspects of human society. To have attended school and acquired knowledge will, to an even greater extent than now, be regarded as the most prominent status symbol.

We find ourselves in the middle of this "explosion". During the years 1950—1965, the number of full-time students in the world was greater than the total number of students over several centuries.

In countries with centralised school systems the authorities have been confronted with insurmountable tasks. It is a question of seeing the entire development in advance and guiding it into the right direction. Overall planning, research, teacher training and building programmes all require painstaking and costly investigations and a vast increase in the number of officials and experts to deal with these tasks.

To treat the whole school-system as one large production unit, which can be organised in a rational way like any other, would appear as a useful avenue of approach in the present situation. The teaching methods which stand at the centre of the educational discussion today seem to have developed almost exclusively from a utilitarian point of view, and are aimed at making this actual "production machine" more effective. Some of the consequences of this system will now be described.

Educational Consequences

Since research and technology and, therefore, also life in society are becoming ever more complicated, in the future the professionally orientated, as well as the general education, will have to provide factual information in a far greater measure than hitherto.

Overall development in the present age is characterised by rapid changes and thus demands of large sections of the population that they continually carry their education further. The most important task of the schools, therefore, cannot be merely to dispense knowledge as such, but rather to "teach the art of learning".

Since the teacher is the most valuable "factor of production", and yet the scarcest, his duties should, as far as possible, be taken over by teaching aids, by new kinds of textbooks, instruction sets, teaching machines and television. The provision of test-papers can be taken care of by the authorities or a central curriculum bureau, and corrections and grading, at least for the most part, can be handled by computers. Step by step the teacher ceases to give instruction himself and changes his role to one of merely guiding his pupils and organising and supervising their work.

Since oral instruction on the part of the teacher necessitates a relatively small group of pupils, whereas the showing of films, the provision of materials, and the setting of assignments can equally well take place in large groups, Torsten Husen says the school class as we have previously known it, approaches a slow death. The classroom is replaced by a set of flexible learning-units with suitable equipment. Each pupil has to learn to work more and more on his own and not concern himself with what others are doing. Human relationships and social contact are no longer part of school experience. In all highly-industrialised countries authorities and educational experts are engaged in setting up guidelines for the "industrialisation" of the school. The comprehensive school plans speak of school units with a minimum of 2000 pupils, in order that each unit with its differentiation into numerous subject-groupings can be properly organised and be economically viable. And what will become of the human being himself, of mutual relationships, and of the most essential sphere of learning—learning to understand one's fellow-man?

The civilisation of the present affects the existence of all of us. If parents do not consciously create another form of existence within society, then the effects will be most severe on small children. They will be exposed to far too many one-sided sense-impressions and, at the same time, receive insufficient stimulus for the life of feeling and will-activity. The industrialised school with its excess of teaching aids and its absolute lack of community-building impulses is in danger of driving these tendencies to extremes. The feeling of alienation and isolation which many pupils must experience in such schools becomes more wide-spread and is felt more strongly than ever before. This appears as the inevitable consequence of such a school "reform", and many people are beginning to realise it.

In schools where the new methods have not yet been introduced to any great extent, there are countless teachers who are in a position to create by their presence an atmosphere of joy in working, of security and friendliness. Whoever is acquainted with such teachers can have only the greatest respect for their work. However, to what extent can these social qualities be made fruitful for the work in the school, if the instruction itself—the most important opportunity for deeper human contact—is no longer present, and if the teacher is unavoidably driven into the role of a mere "supervisor"? There are, however, other aspects of the "industrialised" school system of which account must be taken.

Unrest among Young People

There is something puzzling about the ferment which has entered the younger generation in the past few years, and which broke out in full force in various parts of the world in the revolts of 1968.

This unrest in the world of youth cannot be explained away by saying it is the usual defiance of the younger generation against the older. The opposition does not direct itself against our shortcomings and weaknesses, but rather against that which many have considered the strong side of our present civilisation, such as the emphasis on the material pleasures of life, the pursuit of greater economic growth, higher salaries and a higher standard of living. People thought that this pursuit would go on interminably, that there would always be bold new material goals for us to strive towards. But now youth comes along and throws a spanner in the wheels of production. They no longer wish to remain part of this drive. They are looking for quite different goals. They dress in patched jeans and clogs, they abandon their studies, they refuse to bother about a career, and spend their time in protest meetings and demonstrations. The appearance of many of them is reminiscent of an Indian Sadhu with a mild, vacant gaze behind round glasses, framed in an abundance of hair and beard, and in all its strangeness can be viewed as an important cultural symptom. The interest for Yoga, Zen-Buddhism, and primitive religions seems to be constantly growing and bears witness to spiritual needs which cannot be satisfied within the generally recognised pattern of living in the West.

The Student Revolt

What was the student revolt actually about? Was it an indication of the increasing "move to the left", of the growing influence of Marx Marcuse and Che Guevara, of the social denial of traditional capitalism, of the increasing participation in all that is going on in the outside world, of the enormous "generation-gap" ("trust no man over thirty"), of the protest against vulgar Western materialism? Certainly it contained elements of all this. Future historians will probably have difficulty when they try to grasp the intricately fluctuating threads of idealistic motives and locally conditioned problems. There is, however, one basic fact which already stands out clearly and which cannot be overlooked; the world-wide upheaval began almost everywhere as a protest against the institutionalised type of instruction in the universities.

A Swedish university instructor has presented some important and comprehensive views about the history of the origin and rise of the revolts. He says "One can say with considerable certainty what the student revolt was *not* against. It was not a revolt against the professors or lecturers themselves, except inasmuch as they represented, associated with, or defended "the establishment". It was not in his capacity as an academic instructor that Roche, the President of the University of Paris, was for a while the most unpopular man in the city, but rather because of his position as a high government official and as the president appointed by the state. On the other hand, the anti-bureaucratic tendency of the revolt was quite obvious, something of which not only Roche was made aware. It was not the instructors at Columbia or Berkeley University that the students wanted to dispose of, but the board of directors, the administration, which consisted not of scholars but primarily of businessmen and prominent members of society" (Gunnar Brandell, 'Skolreform och universitetskrisis' / School Reform and University Crisis).

That the student revolt assumed such a radical form in France is undoubtedly due to the traditionally centralised tendency of the school-system there. "The French university administration is an administration in a literal sense. The arrangement of examinations, teaching schedules, the appointment of academic lecturers and Vice-Chancellors. even all the personnel of the university down to the kitchen staff is decided on an official state level and under the direct aegis of the Minister of Education" (Hans Magnus Enzenberger, Kursbuch 13). In 1963 the French Minister of Education, Fouchet, proposed a plan which openly amounted to "industrialising" the universities and the students. "The most important features of the Fouchet reform, the two-class studies, the early specialisation, lessening the period of study, proliferation of examinations and tests, direct influence of the industrial associations, accentuate even more the official regimentation of the educational institution which has had strong roots since the time of Napoleon" (H. M. Enzenberger).

To a lesser or greater extent, this same motive has been underlying in nearly all student revolts. The intense resistance to the subordination of university curricula to the requirements of industry has seldom found such a precise formulation as when a number of students on the Berkeley campus, during a revolt, accused the educational establishment of trying to make the students into IBM-cards.

There are two features that characterise the "industrialization" of the schools and the universities. Firstly, the requirements which ensure a rapid and continuous rise in production must be the determining factor in planning the curriculum and arranging study projects. Secondly, it is the computer that decides whether or not the individual measures up to these requirements. The constant stress on the need for efficiency cannot conceal the fact that the application of these two basic principles is fundamentally inhuman.

Origin and Cause of Revolt

From his special point of departure, the concept of the human individuality as an inviolable spiritual reality, Rudolf Steiner made a prediction more than fifty years ago which today appears even more relevant. It was then said only with regard to the schools, but it is equally applicable to all levels of instruction. Rudolf Steiner said: "... the spirit however will not let itself be suppressed. Institutions which try to regulate education merely from the point of view of the economic life would be an attempt towards such a suppression. This would cause the free spirit of man to be in a constant state of revolt, welling up from its very depths. Constant disruption in the social structure would be the unavoidable consequence of an arrangement which tried to organise the school system on the same basis as the processes of production." (From the essay 'Freie Schule und Dreigliederung' / The Free School and the Three-fold Social Order'.) It is no accident that an increasing number of students in all types of colleges throughout the world are setting their hopes on the founding of free universities, and that the officials in many lands, not only in France, are looking for ways to implement these demands.

It should be obvious that a school system freed from the requirements of the state and of industry is an absolute necessity if one wishes to avoid a continual student revolt, which would in turn lead to constant disturbances even among the children still at school.

THE INDEPENDENT SCHOOL

Not only the student revolts, but other phenomena of the times as well, reveal how relevant and vital is the question of an educational system that is independent of both political and economic demands.

In the industrialised countries of the world there are within the framework of the school system three groups of people who actually belong together, but who have been forced apart by the way society functions today.

A good many parents tend to feel that their children are slipping away from them. Leisure activities and standards of behaviour which are foreign to their parents have assumed an increasingly greater significance in the lives of the younger generation. Nor is there a real contact with the school. There are it is true invitations to parents' evenings, and perhaps a teacher will 'phone a parent on occasions when something is not in order, but within the framework of the school there is strictly speaking no type of problem which cannot be solved without the help of the parents.

Most likely many teachers as well suffer from insufficient contact with their pupils. The demands of the curriculum, the methods of teaching, as well as deeply-rooted prejudices, build barriers which are not easily surmounted. The fact that teachers and pupils are forced into assuming roles of opposition to one another only serves to show how far the school has departed from its educational task. There are no doubt many pupils who consciously or unconsciously long for more human contact, not only with their parents but also with their teachers. However they suffer from the unwritten law that one must stand apart from the world of adults.

The Social Significance of the Waldorf School

Something is needed to bring these three groups together. There is one kind of institution which can indeed fulfil this objective and that is an independent school, of which a Waldorf school is an outstanding example. Parents who take part in founding a Waldorf school take on a great burden. When funds are scarce—and that is almost always the case —then the parents must be ready to make sacrifices. At least during the first year and possibly later, they must be ready to help out by doing carpentry and painting, if such is necessary. Bazaars and school festivals need to be arranged. On parents' evenings, through lectures and courses, they gain insight into the actual work of the school, as well as into the anthroposophical foundations upon which the special teaching methods are based. By sharing in the experiences of the school the parents are able to find the strength to help to carry the burdens. A close contact with teachers arises. In many cases even true friendships develop. The needs and viewpoints of the parents are to a large extent taken into consideration in the life of the school and in the common concern for the children. Parents are also represented on the administrative body. In the battle for the rights of the independent school the parents also confront the public school board and state officials.—The children feel that their parents are working for *their* school in a concrete and visible manner.

The teachers take an enormous amount of work upon themselves, lengthy teachers' meetings, discussions with parents and pupils, general meetings, as well as meetings for parents of a particular class, late evenings preparing lessons and marking books, financial worries, negotiations with education authorities, lectures and discussions for the general public. Life is not made easier by founding a Waldorf school but it becomes much more interesting.

The pupils may indeed meet certain difficulties, for instance if they have to move to another school, or when they leave school and join the ordinary working community, because they are accustomed to a more spiritually-orientated environment. They encounter too the same phenomena of contemporary civilisation as do other youngsters. Their manner of responding to them, however, is strikingly individualistic, and they often have really wide interests. Above all, their particular kind of education has helped them to develop a quality which in our time is of inestimable value, and that is the capacity to have trust in their fellow human-beings. As an adult one can easily enter into a conversation with them. School plays a real role in their lives. A a rule they love their school. Many feel as secure at school as they do at home.

We are here talking about a social function of the greatest significance. In the environment of the thoroughly organised industrialised society, the independent, non-industrialised school, which cultivates the purely human aspects of life, forms an indispensable element. Among those working in the official educational sphere there are idealists who believe in all seriousness that by establishing cafés in the schools, through educational democracy, friendship-campaigns, and similar measures, they will be able to provide the necessary counter-balance to the impersonal and joyless atmosphere which is the unavoidable consequence of the industrialised school.

One can feel the greatest sympathy and respect for many of these efforts towards reform. But whoever has played a part and shouldered the burdens in building a lasting and truly deep feeling of community between children, parents and teachers, will consider such measures insufficient. Such a lasting relationship can only develop slowly through the experience of both pain and joy, perhaps under financial difficulties, superhuman burdens of work and irritating human conflicts —but never through theoretically-conceived arrangements. The reward of this solidarity can be summed up in one word. It is a word which is used here not because it sounds attractive but rather because it bespeaks a reality which is just as difficult to bear as it is inspiring to live with—freedom.

Waldorf Pedagogy in State Schools?

The question is often asked whether there are any features of Waldorf pedagogy which can be incorporated into the state school system. In spite of a certain amount of interest, education authorities on the whole are still rather sceptical about such a possibility. This attitude probably stems from the opinion that the way a Waldorf school is run is incompatible with the state-school curriculum and examination requirements.

If the industrialisation of the school were to be fully implemented then there would be two different pedagogical currents, which in fact would be irreconcilable. On the other hand there is a reasonable hope that the concept of the independent school with its own particular leaving certificate which is yet generally accepted on its own merits can, in the long run, gain ground in ever more countries. The association of parents and teachers will play a decisive role in these organisations.

The Problem of Examinations

Experiences in a number of countries seem to show, however, that Waldorf pupils who follow the necessary course of study can do well in the traditional examination system. Through its many years of practice and its wide experience the Waldorf school movement in Germany, for instance, can show well-established results. They demonstrate the possibility of combining in the Waldorf school concern for the individual with a systematic discipline of learning. A circular letter from the Association of Waldorf Schools, dated March 10, 1969, makes this clear: "Taking the total number of pupils into account, our results since the war in comparison to the state school have been good. It is not easy to establish a valid comparison because the state school, of course, constantly separates out the less able pupils from the fifth class on. It is interesting that the pupils in our examination classes on the average are a good year younger, so that not repeating a class has its effect. Bearing in mind the limited value of statistics in assessing situations in real life, it is nevertheless clear that we take a higher percentage of pupils through to their school-leaving examination than the state schools. They 'weed out' many late-developers who, in our case, later on achieve good results." Other countries have had similar experiences.

The problem of making the experiences of the Waldorf schools of value for the state schools lies in essentials on a different level from that of curriculum demands and examination results.

A number of features which distinguish the Waldorf schools as well as some other independent schools, for instance block study periods, a strong artistic element, early instruction in foreign languages, have been taken up by some state schools; other experiments along similar lines have had good results.

Anthroposophy and Waldorf Education

If by "Waldorf education", however, one means the art of education which was founded by Rudolf Steiner, then it is not merely a question of a sum-total of pedagogical methods, but rather a way of viewing the whole of life. That which gives the Waldorf schools their unique quality and special value is the fact that the group of teachers responsible for the school have the same spiritual aims. To be aware of these aims is not an obligation, but rather an inspiration. Teachers cannot really fulfil their tasks without continually deepening their knowledge of Rudolf Steiner's conception of child development and following the anthroposophical path of inner self-education.

Does this mean the Waldorf school movement can only unfold its activity within very limited circles? No! Neither anthroposophy nor Waldorf pedagogy is, by its nature, exclusive. Both answer deep inner needs of our time, needs that cannot be disregarded, and which become more pressing with each passing decade.

It is conceivable that far-sighted education authorities in various countries might encourage and finance the founding of national or regional Waldorf schools and yet leave them

sufficient educational freedom. The state-schools in the canton of Bern (Switzerland) in which the Waldorf teaching methods are used, about a hundred in number, are an interesting example along these lines. Large-scale experiments of this kind could be fruitful in other places too.

At the same time, however, it must be realised that the true spirit of Waldorf education can only come to full expression within an independent and free school for which parents and teachers carry joint responsibility.

Factors Involved in Establishing Independent Schools

In many countries the laws and legal practices put obstacles in the way of the founding of such schools.

An interesting and important task for official and individual groups whose representatives have realised the unique social significance of the Waldorf school must be the attempt to remove such obstacles. One of the difficulties of founding a free Waldorf school is that parents who wish to send their children to such a school contribute to the life of this school through school fees and other fund-raising efforts. At the same time, however, they have to finance the official state schools through a part of their taxes.

The following may be read in the Supplementary Record of 11. 1. 1953, to the proceedings of 4. 1. 1950, of the Council of Europe on the Protection of Human Rights and Basic Freedoms: "No one shall be refused the right to be educated. In carrying out any activity which the state may take upon itself with respect to education and instruction, the state should respect the right of the parents to ensure for their children education and instruction which are in keeping with the religious and philosophical convictions of the parents." In those countries in which independent schools still receive no public subsidies for their activity, there exists the danger that the above-mentioned rights, to which all parents are entitled, may in practice be available only to those financially well-off. This situation is contrary to the social aims and origin of the Waldorf school, and is certainly considered deeply unsatisfactory by many people. But so far it has not yet come to the formation of a unified international opinion which might call for a new solution of these matters. Once a comprehensive idea of a new social order has been established according to the real demands of our time, as they were presented at the beginning of this book with the idea of the threefold social order, then the foundation will be laid for the unfolding of an independent life of the spirit. A constructive reformation of society can only take place on such a basis. Independent Waldorf schools in which parents, teachers and pupils work together are in this sense centres where the most important pioneering project of the present and near future can be initiated.

A WORLD-WIDE SCHOOL MOVEMENT

The death of Rudolf Steiner on March 30, 1925, did not interrupt the pedagogical work which he had started. It was carried on by his students and began to spread. His lecture tours in various countries were fruitful in that a whole series of independent Waldorf schools were established; Hamburg-Wandsbek (1922), The Hague (1923), London (1925—this school later moved to Forest Row, Sussex); Basel (1926), Hannover (1926), Berlin (1928), Dresden, New York City, and Bergen in Norway (1929), Breslau and Kassel (1930), Hamburg-Altona (1931). After the second World War a new growth of Waldorf schools began, and now there are altogether over 220. A survey is given here of the development of the Waldorf school movement in those countries in which it has gained a firm footing:

Germany:

A large part of Rudolf Steiner's activity took place in Germany. Thus it was only natural that in this country the Waldorf school movement unfolded and flourished most vigorously. Visitors were frequent at school functions, and the pedagogical lectures given by the teachers were well attended. In 1935 the National-Socialist Government forbade the German Waldorf schools to accept new pupils and in 1938 forced most of these schools to close down. This blow struck the Waldorf school movement at a stage of thriving development. In 1945 the work was able to start anew.

Shortly after the downfall of the Third Reich a number of former pupils and teachers gathered in Stuttgart. They cleared away the debris of the bombed central building of the first Waldorf school. "Wherever a Waldorf school teacher landed, be it as a result of the war or as a political refugee, parents came to him. And so various Waldorf schools arose immediately after the collapse." So Ernst Weissert wrote in 'Wo stehen wir heute' / 'Where do we stand today?' in 'Erziehungskunst', 2/3/4/1961. Today in Germany there are 120 Waldorf schools with approximately 50 000 pupils. In almost all schools there is a Class Thirteen for those pupils who are willing and able to take the state school-leaving examination. Many of them incorporate a kindergarten.

A remarkable attempt to realise anew the concept advocated by Rudolf Steiner of a "comprehensive" school, and this time including vocational training, was undertaken by the Hibernia School in Wanne-Eickel in the Ruhr district. Once again a school was founded as a result of collaboration with a factory, which quickly became independent. Not only does this school provide a general education for all pupils, artistic activites up to the Twelfth Class and in one special department preparation for university entrance, but during the last school-years it offers trainings too in specialised professions such as kindergarten teacher, laboratory assistant, gardener, cabinetmaker, machinist, tool-worker, mechanic, or electrician. Similar arrangements for helping pupils to make the transition to a profession while still at school were established in Nürnberg, Kassel and Bochum.

Switzerland

In this country too Rudolf Steiner's educational impulse has found a good response and the work was able to go on even during the Second World War. Besides the schools in the larger towns such as Basel, Zürich, Bern, Biel and St. Gallen (altogether 19) and three boarding schools, there are in the canton of Bern about a hundred state schools in towns and villages where, through individual teachers, instruction is given according to the methods of the Waldorf school.

Holland

The Dutch Waldorf school movement, just as in Germany and Norway, was interrupted by the Second World War. In the end nevertheless this misfortune worked out positively. When the Free School ("Vrije School") was closed in the Hague in 1941 at the command of the occupation officials, about three hundred pupils had to attend other schools. Things went so well when they entered and passed through these schools that the methods of Waldorf education won respect and the proponents of Waldorf education came into close contact with the representatives of other school systems. Today Waldorf education is well recognised in Holland, and among other effects this had practical consequences for the structure of the state schools. Today there are Free Schools in 81 Dutch towns.

Great Britain

All the British Waldorf schools were able to carry on their work throughout the war with only minor disturbances. As a rule they have kept to the English tradition of the boarding school, to which belong a country atmosphere, participation in sports, a smaller number of day pupils, and so on. Through relatively modest fees and through the structure of the school organism an attempt has been made to avoid the socially and intellectually exclusive character of the ordinary English public school. The fact that both pupils and teachers live at or near the school contributes to deepening the good contact between them, and this appears to be one of the distinctive features of the English Waldorf school.

North America

The Waldorf school movement has had to fight hard for its expansion here. The usual orientation in America towards an obviously "purposeful" and utilitarian education, for instance for future technicians or businessmen, became even more pronounced in 1957 as a result of the successful Sputnik experiment by the Russians. It is not easy for a pedagogy which aims at an all-round, non-specialised human development, and which moreover is of non-American origin, to gain a footing. Despite this there are now 61 schools which appear to be making good progress,

A Faculty for training Waldorf teachers was established at Detroit University in 1967 and in 1968 the first Canadian Rudolf Steiner school was foundet in Toronto (today there are 8 schools).

The Scandinavian Countries

In Denmark the liberal educational policy of the country has been favourable to the founding of Waldorf schools. All independent schools, including the ten Waldorf schools, receive generous subsidies from the state. In Norway a number of individuals who had made a name for themselves in the general cultural life became active in the Waldorf school movement. This helped considerably to create general interest in the schools in Oslo, Bergen and Baerum. A new law that is favourable to independent schools has recently been approved by parliament. In Sweden and Finland the attitude of the public and the educational authorities has been decidedly positive and open, so that knowledge of the educational ideas of Rudolf Steiner has penetrated relatively wide circles. There are nine schools in Sweden, and three in Finland.

In addition to the above-named countries there are at present Waldorf schools in Europe (Belgium, Austria, France, Italy); in South America (Argentina, Brazil, Ecuador, Chile, Uruguay); also in Australia, New Zealand and South Africa. Each Waldorf school is however an organism in its own right, a "school individuality". This makes it even more difficult to give an all-embracing view of the variety of problems and possibilities which the Waldorf school movement confronts in the different parts of the world. Here only a few questions will be considered.

Bilingual Schools

In several countries, for instance in Brazil, Argentina, South Africa, Belgium, Finland, a school which wishes to be open to all sectors of the population and also to stand as a representative of general human tenets must instruct in two languages. This leads to complicated questions, for instance, which of the two languages is the more important? How is the educational work to be financed if a linguistic minority wishes to have separate small classes? In some countries it is only the Waldorf school which unites under one roof two languages which are in competition with each other on a national scale.

Tests and Examinations

In many countries there are strict examination regulations with officially determined tests. In England, for example, these begin in the primary schools. The Waldorf schools stand firmly against examinations which through the principle of selection disturb the course of education and the development of the child. Because of this all tests are avoided in the lower classes of the Waldorf school. On the other hand the examination regulations must be taken into account in the higher classes to ensure the transition to professional education. Yet one must guard against curtailing for this purpose those subjects which are an essential part of an all-round human culture. If one increases the period of schooling by a year, that need not necessarily mean such a long delay for further education because the "lost" time can be regained, completely or partially, through a more concentrated period of study and the benefit of a greater maturity. In fact in some countries the student has to fill in time for a year after passing his entrance examinations before he is old enough to be accepted at a university. Nevertheless, there are parents who worry about this, and it is not always easy to satisfy them.

The Cost of Freedom

Behind all these questions there is the necessity of arranging the education according to the requirements of a free spiritual life and of freeing it from political and economic compulsion.

The financial and social problems which are connected with the support of a free school can, according to the prevailing circumstances in each country, manifest themselves in quite different ways and accordingly must be differently solved. There are countries which give no state support for the running of such schools, nor for expenditure on new buildings, countries in which schools are not even permitted to receive larger sums from private donors. Wherever subsidies are received, whether on a national or regional basis, the tax burden becomes very noticeable. However, if great financial burdens are imposed upon the parents, how is one to avoid the danger that the Waldorf schools, contrary to their original purpose, become schools for the children of the rich? In many schools a circle of private benefactors have made it possible for needy children to attend the school, as happens also in Switzerland where basically no official financial assistance is given. Even if this problem is solved, other questions may arise. Even if a reduction in fees or full bursaries are granted for many of the children, where does one draw the line?

To what extent should financial considerations be a deciding factor in this matter? Should parent representatives determine pupil admission on the basis of social structure or should they at least belong to the decision-making panel? To what extent may, and to what extent can, the teachers be burdened with financial and administrative tasks? The co-operation of a conscientious body of parents is of great si nificance in all these special side-issues connected with the life of the school and the struggle for freedom in cultural life.

Of course the problem of teachers' salaries plays an important role in this context. Since Waldorf schools usually suffer from financial difficulties, the teachers' salaries, with a few notable exceptions, are often relatively low. They are almost always below the official norm.

If a school is to fulfil the demands made by Waldorf education, then the teachers must enter into their tasks with their whole heart and soul. A circle of people who in this way have pledged themselves with complete devotion to a common task cannot accept that certain formal criteria, such as examination results or qualifications in special subjects, would entitle them to a higher level of pay. On the other hand, there are quite different viewpoints according to which the salaries are still differentiated, consideration for family conditions, the number of children, additional social obligations, the length of the teacher's journey to school, unpaid loans he still owes from his time as a student etc. Thus the problem of salaries is settled according to individual needs in most Waldorf schools. What matters is to achieve a method of fair apportionment on this basis. There are certain Waldorf schools in which each teacher declares how large a salary he "needs". The monetary requests are totalled accordingly and it is usually surprising to see that in many cases the required sum agrees with the amount allotted in the budget. The questions put forward here are not hypothetical but are taken from real life. People who wish to start an independent school have no choice but to come to terms with these questions.

Teacher Training

An encouraging sign for the future is the fact that more and more young people want to train to become Waldorf schoolteachers. Such training centres are found at the Goetheanum in Dornach, Switzerland, at the Lehrerseminar in Stuttgart, Mannheim and Witten-Annen, Germany, at Emerson College in Forest Row, England, at the Rudolf Steiner Seminar in Järna, Sweden, and at the Waldorf School in Detroit. The training at these colleges includes a study of human development and a study of the way of teaching, which forms the basis of the work at a Rudolf Steiner school, as well as participation in a variety of artistic courses. Practical teaching periods at a Waldorf school are part of the course. Rudolf Steiner had actually hoped that a full teacher-training course would last three years. The present courses last from one to two years according to the student's previous knowledge of anthroposophy an other general preconditions. It should be emphasised that a teacher-training course of this kind cannot be thought of as replacing special studies in particular subjects which the teacher needs for his work. The course of instruction is arranged to develop basic educational capacities in the individual and these will be of use in teaching at any level.

EDUCATION TOWARDS FREEDOM

The word "freedom" has occurred often in this book. The meaning of this word should in each case be taken in relation to its context. It is more fully considered in the section "Concerning the Idea of Freedom". Nevertheless it may be appropriate at the conclusion of this book yet again to emphasise what is actually meant here by "freedom".

Freedom is nothing absolute. It always depends on the inner activity of the individual himself. The richer and the more manifold the potentialities of expression which are at one's disposal through the physical organism and the inner soul-life, and the more consciously the ego of man can use these resources in coming to well-considered decisions, then the greater is one's inner freedom. When as a mature adult a person can take upon himself the responsibility for his own further development, then the capabilities and resources at his disposal are largely dependent upon the efforts made throughout his childhood years by his parents and teachers. A form of education which strives to remove as far as possible the physical and spiritual obstacles which can place themselves in the way of the conscious mastery of the ego, or self, in adult years, can be called an "education towards freedom". It is hoped that the illustrations and text of this book will reveal the vast richness of productive possibilities which can be called forth in children through an education which works in this manner. The goal of the artistic activity within a Waldorf school is not—and once again this must be expressly emphasised—to produce artists, but rather to develop human beings who can be creative in all walks of life.

The task of helping to unfold the latent inner capabilities of the growing human being can only be undertaken by educators who have learned to know him thoroughly and who have grown accustomed to the educational demands which arise anew in the daily life at school. The future of mankind depends on the extent to which parents and teachers are successful in this joint activity.

The representatives of political and business life should refrain from interference with this sensitive and decisively important process through unsuitable methods of teaching curricula and examination demands. On the other hand, for those teachers and parents who are able and willing to take on their task with full pedagogical responsibility, and who develop independent initiative in this direction, the state and industry, as far as education is concerned, would have to concentrate on the tasks which lie within their own sphere, namely to provide an atmosphere of freedom and the financial assistance necessary for the realisation of this independent initiative.

The contribution which can be made to the development of mankind by a truly free form of education, was summarised by Steiner in a few words which may serve as the motto of this book: "One should not ask: 'What does a person need to know and to be able to do for the existing social order?' but rather: 'What gifts does a person possess and how may these be developed in him?' Then it will be possible to bring to the social order ever new forces from each succeeding generation. Then this social order will always be alive with that which each fully developed individual brings with him into life, rather than that each succeeding generation is made to conform to the existing social organisation." (From the essay 'Freie Schule und Dreigliederung' / 'The Free School and the Threefold Social Order', in 'Aufsätze über die Dreigliederung des sozialen Organismus und zur Zeitlage', 1915-1921, Dornach, 1961).

LITERATURE ON WALDORF EDUCATION

This is a selection of relevant publications in the English language. The year cited in each case is the date of the most recent edition.

Further information on Waldorf education and other books available can be obtained from the following Anthroposophical centres:

Great Britain
The Secretary, Rudolf Steiner House, 35 Park Road, London NW1.
U.S.A.
The Secretary, The Anthroposophical Society, 211 Madison Avenue, New York City 16.
Canada
The Secretary, The Anthroposophical Society, 81 Lawton Boulevard, Toronto, Ontario, M4V 126.
South Africa
The Secretary, The Anthroposophical Society, 2 Osborne Road, Mowbray 7700.
Australia
The Secretary, The Anthroposophical Society, 234 Boundary Street, Roseville, N.S.W. 2069.
New Zealand
The Secretary, The Anthroposophical Society, 222 Taupehi Road, Turangi.
A complete list of Waldorf Schools throughout the world can be obtained from: Bund der Freien Waldorfschulen, 7 Stuttgart, Heidehofstraße 32, Germany.

Educational Works by Rudolf Steiner

The Education of the Child in the Light of Anthroposophy (Essay, 1909).
1st edition in English, 1927. 2nd edition (1965) 3rd impression, 1975.
Study of Man. General Education Course (14 lectures, Stuttgart, Aug. 21–Sept. 5, 1919).
1st edition in English, 1947. 2nd edition (1966) 2nd impression, 1975.
Deeper Insights into Education
The Waldorf Approach. Three lectures out of Vol. 302a.

Discussions with Teachers (discussions held in Stuttgart, Aug. 21–Sept. 26, 1919 at the foundation of the Free Waldorf School).
Education as a Social Problem (6 lectures. Dornach, Aug. 9–17, 1919).
1st edition in English, 1969.
A Modern Art of Education (14 lectures, Ilkley, Aug. 5–17, 1923).
1st edition in English, 1928 with title "The New Art of Education". 3rd edition, 1954 with title "Education and Modern Spiritual Life". 2nd impression of 3rd edition with new title, 1972.
The Kingdom of Childhood (7 lectures and answers to questions, Torquay, Aug. 12–20, 1924).
1st edition in English, 1964. 2nd impression, 1975.
Human Values in Education (9 lectures, Arnhem, July 17–24, 1924).
1st edition in English, 1971.
Education and Art. Education and the Moral Life (2 articles, May, 1923).
1st edition in English, 1923.
The Steiner Schools Fellowship, Emerson College, Forest Row, Sussex, England may be able to supply translations of other works by Steiner.

Some Books by Other Authors

General:
A. C. Harwood –
The Recovery of Man in Childhood. Hodder & Stoughton, 1975.
The Way of a Child. 1974.
Francis Edmunds –
Rudolf Steiner's Gift to Education – the Waldorf Schools. 1975.
W. zur Linden –
A Child is Born. Pregnancy, Birth and First Childhood. 1973.
Educating as an Art
Essays on the Rudolf Steiner Method – Waldorf Education. Edited by Ekkehard Piening and Nick Lyons, with an introduction by Henry Barnes.
Parenting
A Path through Childhood by Dotty Turner Coplem.
The Waldorfschool Approach to History by Werner Glas.
N. Glas –
Conception, Birth und Early Childhood. 1972.
E. M. Grunelius –
Early Childhood Education and the Waldorf School Plan.
K. König –
The First Three Years of the Child. 1969.
E. Frommer –
Voyage through Childhood.
A. Howard –

What about a Steiner School?
C. v. Heydèbrand –
Curriculum of the First Waldorf School. 1972.
Childhood: The Study of the Growing Soul.
E. A. K. Stockmeyer –
Rudolf Steiner's Curriculum for the Waldorf Schools.
1969.
Steiner Schools Fellowship –
Child and Man Extracts. 1975.

Books on Special Subjects

H. von Baravalle –
Astronomy: An Introduction. 1st edition, 1974.
Geometric Drawing and the Waldorf School Plan. 1st
edition, 1959. 2nd enlarged edition, 1967.
Introduction to Physics in the Waldorf Schools.
The Balance Between Art and Science.
1st edition, 1959. 2nd enlarged edition, 1967.
Perspective Drawing. 1st edition, 1968.
Rudolf Steiner as Educator. 1st edition, 1952.
2nd revised edition, 1960.
The Teaching of Arithmetic and the Waldorf School
Plan, 1st edition, 1967.
J. Bothmer –
Gymnastic Education.
G. Grohmann –
The Plant. 1974.
H. Hauck –
Handwork: Indications by Rudolf Steiner.
E. Lebret –
Pentatonic Songs for Nursery and Kindergarten.
P. S. Moffat –
Twenty-One Plays for Children.
W. Pelikan –
The Secrets of Metals. 1973.
H. Poppelbaum –
A New Zoology. 1961.
G. Wachsmuth –
The Evolution of Mankind. 1961.
O. Whicher –
Projective Geometry. Creative Polarities in Space and
Time. 1971.
R. Wilkinson –
A series of pamphlets on the teaching of specific
subjects.

Educational Periodicals from Many Lands

Erziehungskunst. Monatsschrift zur Pädagogik Ru-
dolf Steiners. Herausgegeben vom Bund der Freien
Waldorfschulen. Stuttgart: Verlag Freies Geistes-
leben.
Der Elternbrief: Ratschläge und Hilfe für die Erzie-
hungspraxis. Schaffhausen, Switzerland: Novalis
Verlag.
Child and Man. Journal for Waldorf (Rudolf Steiner)
Education. Published by the Steiner Schools Fellow-
ship, London.

Triades-Education. (Supplement to the Journal "Tria-
des") Editions Triades, Paris.
Vrije Opvoedkunst. Social paedagogisch tijdschrift.
Redactie: L. Beuger, A. H. ten Böhmer, Mw. Mr. J.
J. Gerretsen-Emmen Riedel (hoofden eindredactie),
Mr. A. C. Henny, C. A. Henny, M. Mastenbroek,
mw. Drs. B. Udo de Haes, Mr. P. C. Veltman, W. F.
Veltman.
På Väg mot en ny pedagogik. Tidskrift för Rudolf
Steinerpedagogik. Redaktion: Bertil Frid, Karin
Neuschütz, Gunilla Tovatt. Bromma / Schweden.